Book Supplement Series to the
Journal of Chinese Philosophy
Editor-in-Chief: Chung-ying Cheng

EUROPEAN AND CHINESE PHILOSOPHY:
ORIGINS AND INTERSECTIONS

Edited by
Chung-ying Cheng,
Eric Nelson and Linyu Gu

This edition first published 2013
© 2013 Journal of Chinese Philosophy

Registered Office
John Wiley & Sons Ltd, The Atrium, Southern Gate, Chichester, West Sussex, PO19 8SQ, United Kingdom

Editorial Offices
350 Main Street, Malden, MA 02148-5020, USA
9600 Garsington Road, Oxford, OX4 2DQ, UK
The Atrium, Southern Gate, Chichester, West Sussex, PO19 8SQ, UK

For details of our global editorial offices, for customer services, and for information about how to apply for permission to reuse the copyright material in this book please see our website at www.wiley.com/wiley-blackwell.

The right of Chung-ying Cheng to be identified as the author of the editorial material in this work has been asserted in accordance with the Copyright, Designs and Patents Act 1988.

All rights reserved. No part of this publication may be reproduced, stored in a retrieval system, or transmitted, in any form or by any means, electronic, mechanical, photocopying, recording or otherwise, except as permitted by the UK Copyright, Designs and Patents Act 1988, without the prior permission of the publisher.

Wiley also publishes its books in a variety of electronic formats. Some content that appears in print may not be available in electronic books.

Designations used by companies to distinguish their products are often claimed as trademarks. All brand names and product names used in this book are trade names, service marks, trademarks or registered trademarks of their respective owners. The publisher is not associated with any product or vendor mentioned in this book. This publication is designed to provide accurate and authoritative information in regard to the subject matter covered. It is sold on the understanding that the publisher is not engaged in rendering professional services. If professional advice or other expert assistance is required, the services of a competent professional should be sought.

Library of Congress Cataloging-in-Publication Data has been applied for.

Set in 11.25 on 13.25pt Times Ten by Toppan Best-set Premedia Limited
Printed in Singapore by Ho Printing Singapore Pte Ltd.

01—2013

Book Supplement Series to the

Journal of Chinese Philosophy

Editor-in-Chief: Chung-ying Cheng

EUROPEAN AND CHINESE PHILOSOPHY:
ORIGINS AND INTERSECTIONS

Edited by
Chung-ying Cheng, Eric Nelson and Linyu Gu

Special Theme

CHUNG-YING CHENG / Preface: Origins and Relations of Philosophy: European and Chinese	1
ERIC S. NELSON / Introduction: Intersections between Chinese and Western Philosophies	5
ERIC S. NELSON / Heidegger, Misch, and the Origins of Philosophy	10
CHUNG-YING CHENG / Deconstruction and *Différance*: Onto-Return and Emergence in a Daoist Interpretation of Derrida	31
WILLIAM DAY / *Zhenzhi* and Acknowledgment in Wang Yangming and Stanley Cavell	51
TAO JIANG / Isaiah Berlin's Challenge to the Zhuangzian Freedom	69
STEPHEN R. PALMQUIST / Mapping Kant's Architectonic onto the *Yijing via* the Geometry of Logic	93
GRAHAM PARKES / Lao-Zhuang and Heidegger on Nature and Technology	112
MARTIN SCHÖNFELD / World Philosophy and Climate Change: A Sino-German Way to Civil Evolution	134

LIN MA / Levinas and the *Daodejing* on the Feminine: 152
    Intercultural Reflections

LINYU GU / "Waiting for Godot"? Contemporaneity, 171
    Feminism, and Creativity

CHUNG-YING CHENG

PREFACE:
ORIGINS AND RELATIONS OF PHILOSOPHY: EUROPEAN AND CHINESE

Heidegger has held that philosophy originated in Greece, and there was no other place that philosophy had originated. Even though he has learned or absorbed meditative thinking from Laozi 老子 and Zhuangzi 莊子, he only recognizes ontological difference in the Greek philosophy, that is, it is the Greek that discovers the Being in beings. Unfortunately, this represents one grave philosophical prejudice of European philosophers both before him and after him against Eastern philosophy, including Chinese philosophy. In the Greek awakening to nature or Being (*phusis*) as this awakening is primarily considered as a matter of shining out and emerging and presencing (as conveyed in the verb form of *phusis*, namely *phuein*). It is based on this understanding that Heidegger sees the beginning of philosophy that makes philosophy a discovery or disclosure (*aletheia*) of Being in all things. On the other hand, approximately at the same time or even earlier than either Parmenides or Heraclitus in the sixth century BCE, there has been both *Yijing* 《易經》 and *Daodejing* 《道德經》 in which we see vision and experience of the *dao* coming of its own, which gives a meaning to our experience of change *yi* 易 (namely, *jianyi* 簡易) and natural spontaneity (*ziran* 自然).

For Confucius the ultimate vision of reality of *dao* in *tian* 天 should lead to the awakening of *ren* 仁 in man that defines the being of humanity and as such acts as root and source of all virtues that hold humanity together. For Confucius *dao* 道, *de* 德, and *ren* are together to disclose the freedom and creativity of the humanity. Later the *Zhongyong* 《中庸》, the *Mencius* 《孟子》, and the *Xunzi* 《荀子》 address to humanity as human nature *xing* 性 and see it as embodying the form of goodness (*shan* 善), which must obtain *via* different routes for Mencius and Xunzi. If this understanding of reality and humanity is not philosophical, what is it? What is philosophy anyway? Why do we as human beings need philosophy as a quest at all? If philosophy does not originate from such experience and vision of reality and moral truth, where does it originate from?

Since there are many philosophical traditions in the world in which we find similar experiences and visions of Being and truth, there is no reason therefore to see philosophy as originating from the Greek tradition alone and not in other great philosophical traditions. However, there is a major difference between the Greek perception of Being and the Chinese perception of Being: the former is ontological, whereas the latter is both ontological and onto-generative, which lead to many forms and concepts as manifested in an open, pervasive, and holistic networking of all philosophical ideas in a time that Jaspers designates as "axial age."[1] This implies that for the Greek there is more exclusiveness, whereas in the Chinese, there is more inclusiveness in philosophical practice.

In the Chinese tradition, how to realize the *dao* and actualize the goodness of humanity is a deep concern inherited throughout Chinese philosophy. As Dai Zhen 戴震,[2] a mid-eighteenth-century Confucian text-criticism scholar, declared, the purpose of studying a text is to be awakened by the *dao* as the power of producing, sustaining, and ordering life. Dai Zhen even went so far as to write a three parts treatise on the origin of goodness, which is a matter of ontological and onto-generative understanding of cosmic life and humanity. Short of this understanding, one would not see real significance of any scholarly pursuit nor could one make any sense of criticizing wrongs of the society. Of course, to witness the occurrence and presencing of *dao* is one thing, to articulate the *dao* in one's language so that one could communicate with others is another. In light of these, we see the origin of philosophy in Chinese tradition as a matter of truth and goodness coming to manifest itself clearly in Dai Zhen's work on inquiry into origin of goodness (*Yuanshan* 《原善》).

If we contrast Heidegger's description of the origin of philosophy in the concept of Greek *phusis* (with verb *phuein*) with the creative formation of concepts of *dao*, *yi* 義, *ren*, *li* 禮, *qi* 氣, etc. in Chinese philosophy, it is worthwhile to note that the Greek work *phusis*, whether denoting nature or emergence of nature in the eyes of the Greeks, is not too far in meaning or significance from the Chinese philosophical idea of *sheng* 生 as creative act of generation or as life-giving natural formation of things that makes our disclosive concepts of *yi*, *dao*, *yin-yang* 陰陽, and *ren* existentially possible in the *Yijing* tradition. In fact, it is not only *sheng*, but also *sheng-sheng*, which conveys the idea of continuous emergence and manifestation of nature and life, which I have described as incessant creativity or onto-generativity (*shengsheng buxi* 生生不息) of *benti* 本體 (root-body) in my philosophy of the *Yi* and onto-hermeneutics.

By the same token, in a quest for explaining existence of things in the world, concepts of *li* and *qi* are identified and become extremely important in Chinese philosophy by the time of twelfth century in Song period. Again *li* and *qi* are no doubt philosophical concepts that arrive to disclose structure and activity of Being or Becoming. As one must see, it is these concepts, together with the concepts of *ren* and *dao*, that have made impact on the Enlightenment philosophy of Leibniz, Voltaire, and Kant in Europe. It is not simply a matter of discovery of Being but a matter of discovery of Reason. This means that there is no unique origin of philosophy in the Greek tradition nor unique time in which philosophy is to be discovered.

Philosophy originates where there is concern and vision for reality, for wholeness, for knowledge, for harmony, and for goodness, which could happen to us in our everyday experience of reality now and then. All these can be said to define what philosophy is about and what philosophy is for. The way philosophy is understood now and the way it is articulated now in whatever language, it can be made clear in a language of logic or may be let to remain obscure in words of poetry. But it must always make appeal to life because it is needed by life for improving life and for solving problems of life as well as for self-understanding of life within oneself or within a community.

In this fundamental sense of philosophy, we must see philosophy as taking place in many different tongues and in many different cultural contexts which, in principle, must be capable of relating to *phusis* of the Greek and the *dao or ren* of the Chinese or even the reason of the European. It is in this light that the *Journal of Chinese Philosophy* initiates this volume on the origins of philosophy and their relations in philosophical languages, be it Chinese or Greek or European as not merely derived from the Greek.

In light of this understanding, we see how a philosophical issue could be discussed significantly from both the European–Western position and the Chinese perspective. Each position and perspective embodies a different historicity and viewpoint as experienced in the vision and pursuit of reality and humanity. As human being is basically a philosophical animal, it can be seen that human mind could encounter philosophical issues from different points of view. The contrast between the European and Chinese traditions of philosophy is impressive and yet mutually stimulating as shown in the works of Heidegger and post-Heideggerian authors.

Eric Nelson's article is extremely meaningful as he was one of the few who could bring some unfamiliar and yet insightful and important views of German philosophy into the scene for understanding an issue or a methodology. His discussion on Dilthey and Misch is most valuable as he opens the issue of origination of philosophy and shows clearly how Dilthey and Misch should be recognized to correct the prejudiced and dogmatic view of Heidegger and others. Other papers in this issue are equally invaluable, and they illustrate how the European–Western and Chinese approaches could be complementary and yet together could be philosophically insight-productive. I am grateful to Eric Nelson who has organized and reviewed the papers for this volume together with me, and Linyu Gu, who had done extensive work on further organizing, commenting, and editing. My heartfelt thanks also go to all of our authors in this stimulating volume.

UNIVERSITY OF HAWAII AT MANOA
Honolulu, Hawaii

Endnotes

1. See Karl Jaspers, *The Origin and Goal of History*, trans. Michael Bullock (New Haven: Yale University Press, 1953).
2. See Dai Zhen, *Yuanshan*《原善》 (For English version, see Chung-ying Cheng, trans., *Tai Chen's Inquiry into Goodness* [Honolulu: East-West Center Press, 1969]).

ERIC S. NELSON

INTRODUCTION: INTERSECTIONS BETWEEN CHINESE AND WESTERN PHILOSOPHIES

I. A Question of Interpretation

The articles gathered in this supplementary issue of the *Journal of Chinese Philosophy* provide an opportunity for exploring several interpretive intersections, encounters, and divergences between Western, primarily modern European, and classical Chinese philosophies. This collection brings together five newly written articles and four articles, some of which have been revised, from past issues of the journal. These contributions taken as a whole directly and indirectly raise anew questions of whether there is such a thing as "Chinese philosophy," a possibility that is denied by prevalent trends in Western philosophy from the Enlightenment and romanticism to contemporary ahistorical universalisms and postmodern occidental particularisms, and whether philosophy should be understood as one unified monistic form of thought or as a more diverse and inclusive plurality of philosophies.

To speak of philosophies, instead of philosophy, might risk sounding peculiar to ears trained and habituated to thinking of philosophy as either one universal theoretical truth or as one particular historical and fateful transmission from the Greeks to their self-declared modern occidental inheritors. Yet if, as the hermeneutical life-philosopher Georg Misch argued in the 1920s, the unity of philosophy does not consist in the identity of one theoretical vision or one historical tradition, then its universality need not entail the negation of the particularities through which it occurs and is enacted.[1] Philosophy only has its living actuality in the concrete moments in which, according to Misch, there is an existential encounter, crisis, or breakthrough (*durchbruch*) that leads to critical reflection on life and its conditions and to personal and social transformation. These concrete moments of disorientation and reorientation—of breakthrough, reflection, and transformation—occurred in diverse forms in China, India, Israel, Persia, and so on, as well as in ancient Greece and the modern Enlightenment that have a unique historical significance for Western civilization.

Philosophy and its overcoming in meditative mindfulness (*Besinnung*) only happens for the few and the rare for a thinker such as Heidegger.[2] But an earlier hermeneutical conception of reflective mindfulness (*Besinnung*), one articulated in the writings of Misch and his teacher and father-in-law Wilhelm Dilthey, suggests that critical reflection is a constant possibility of the social and individual self-reflexivity of everyday human life.[3] Philosophy is not an impersonal event of being; it is a deeply personal encounter with the internal and external conditions of one's life.

As such, philosophizing can happen anew each time such a moment occurs. This encounter is indicated in the Chinese expression "I understand" (*wo zhi* 我执). Like another thinker influenced by Dilthey, Martin Buber, Misch was particularly taken by the figure of Zhuangzi 莊子. Misch's first example of such a disorienting breakthrough and reorienting life-reflection is the great river's shock and surprise when it encountered the sea. In "Autumn Floods" (*Qiushui* 〈秋水〉) in the *Zhuangzi* 《莊子》, the river egotistically delighted in its own power and greatness, which absorbed all the streams and channels that flowed into it, until it was exposed to the limitless expanse of the northern ocean.[4] The "breakthrough" of the world in the self does not occur through any particular content; it is noticeable in the Buddha's reorienting exposure to the suffering of others or in the dialogical endeavors of Mengzi 孟子 to awaken King Hui of Liang (Liang Hui Wang 梁惠王) to his responsibility. The occurrence of breakthrough, reflection, and potential transformation occurs in the midst of the context of biological-historical life. It need not presuppose one universal philosophical doctrine, a hidden metaphysical reality beyond the conditions of the nexus of life, or the myth of one coherent and continuous metaphysical tradition stemming from Hellas and culminating in Western modernity.

In contrast to the frequent exclusion of Kongzi 孔子 from the philosophical canon by Western thinkers, Misch remarked that Socrates could not be considered a philosopher either if the same criteria were consistently applied; for example, dialogical and indirect teaching instead of an explicit systematic theoretical discourse, reflecting on ethical life rather than speculation about nature or the supernatural, and the immanent hermeneutical enlightening of historical life to itself in conjunction with individual self-cultivation (*Bildung*) in contrast with the impersonal and neutral external or transcendent point of view favored by modern Western philosophy.[5]

Given Misch's pluralizing and individuating hermeneutical understanding of philosophies as a singular plural point of departure, works discussed in the essays collected here—such as the *Yijing* 《易經》, the *Daodejing* 《道德經》, and the *Zhuangzi*—can emerge as philosophically worthwhile texts that can be considered in their own right without requiring that they conform to restrictive conceptions of what counts as philosophy and non-philosophy. Once textual sources are explored and explicated responsively from out of themselves in their own terms, then genuine interpretive encounters and intersections can take place and be articulated between texts of diverse provenance without assuming either a common identity or their incommensurability. Such a pluralistic hermeneutics leaves open and undecided the difficult questions of philosophy about nature, religion, and morality that have been posed, answered, and posed anew.

II. Andenken

In this context of engaging in intercultural and comparative philosophy, it is fitting to recall the life of a scholar and teacher whose works concerned German hermeneutics and life-philosophy, intercultural East-West philosophy, Japanese and global feminism, and a critical encounter with and reflection on the conditions of life of women in modern Japan and Asia. I am thankful that she encouraged me—as a graduate student writing a dissertation about history in Dilthey and Heidegger in the late 1990s—to expand my philosophical horizon beyond Europe. I wish to devote this moment to remembering a dedicated scholar, encouraging mentor, and a generous friend, Sakiko Kitagawa 北川 東子 (1952–2011). Because of her role in facilitating the encounter and dialogue between East Asian and European philosophy, she had been invited to contribute to this issue. After years of fighting against her illness, she passed away too early, and will be sorely missed by myself, her family, friends, and colleagues, and as a contributor to this special collection.

III. Interpretive Intersections

A number of essays engage the divide and intersection between Chinese and Western philosophies by focusing on the classic Daoist texts of the *Daodejing* and the *Zhuangzi* in relation to twentieth-century Western thought. Chung-ying Cheng discusses in his article the affinities and differences between deconstruction and *différance* staged in the writings of Jacques Derrida and the movement of the *dao* 道 through reversal, return, and emergence in the *Daodejing* in order to offer a Daoist onto-hermeneutical reinterpretation of and critical response to Derrida. Tao Jiang reexamines in his essay Zhuangzi's soteriological project of personal liberation in light of Isaiah Berlin's distinction between positive and negative freedom. The liberal notion of negative freedom limiting state power correlates with and corrects the deeply personal yet apolitical meditation on freedom exhibited in the *Zhuangzi*. Lin Ma considers why the feminine articulated in Levinas's early work loses its importance in his later thought from an intercultural perspective. She reassesses Levinas's at times problematic thinking of the feminine with respect to the feminine, for example, the water metaphor and *ci* 雌, expressed in the *Daodejing*.

Three essays redeploy Chinese and Western philosophies and their dialogical intersections to address tenacious problems of present-day life. By drawing on the idea of "creativity" in Whiteheadian process feminism and Chinese *Yijing* philosophy, Linyu Gu articulates the notion of "mutual connectivity" to assess the contemporary problematic of gender. In particular, she examines the realities of being a gendered intellectual through experiences of contemporaneity, deferral, separation, and waiting for a tomorrow that does not come and a promise that is not fulfilled. Her approach, informed by process philosophy and the thought of the *Yijing*, anticipates and unfolds the potential for creative balance in gender studies today. While philosophy disturbingly remains one of the least gender diverse fields in academia, our environment continues to be degraded at an alarming rate. Graham Parkes explores the ongoing devastation of the natural world from the comparative philosophical context of Laozi, Zhuangzi, and Heidegger. Parkes argues for articulating a critical stance toward technology from the resonance between these thinkers and calls for a reflective use of less damaging technologies. Martin Schonfeld's paper is likewise focused on the current ecological crisis. He examines possibilities for a civil evolution that would more adequately answer our environmental plight. Schonfeld concludes that such a step beyond the present impasse emerges from a progressive Eurasian dialogue between German "worldly wisdom" (*Weltweisheit*) and classical Chinese wisdom (*zhi* 智).

The three remaining articles illustrate additional aspects of the intersections and tensions between Chinese and Western philosophies. William Day contrasts "real knowing" (*zhenzhi* 真知) in Wang Yangming 王陽明 with "acknowledgment" in Stanley Cavell. Wang's unity of knowing and acting is then interpreted through Cavell's argument that knowing another's pain demands its acknowledgment. Stephen R. Palmquist investigates in his essay how Kant's critical philosophy and the *Yijing* can be analyzed as architectonic structures that encompass four perspectival "levels," each of which has an increasingly complex systematic structure. He demonstrates how each level illuminates the others and reality. Finally, I look at the question of the origins of philosophy by contrasting the unitary ontological understanding of philosophy and history in Heidegger's works with their pluralistic life-philosophical conception developed in Misch's work on the multiple origins of philosophy in China, Greece, and India.

UNIVERSITY OF MASSACHUSETTS LOWELL
Lowell, Massachusetts

ENDNOTES

I would like to express my gratitude to Professor Chung-ying Cheng for warmly inviting me to organize and co-edit this supplement issue, which was originally inspired by an ISCP panel at the Pacific APA in Seattle 2012. I am also thankful to Alice Frye, Dan Lusthaus, Robin Wang, Tao Jiang, and Liu Yang for their encouragement, and in particular Linyu Gu for her substantial suggestions and editorial work that guided this supplemental issue into publication.

1. Georg Misch, *Der Weg in die Philosophie* (Leipzig: Teubner, 1926). This work was translated in a substantially altered and revised form as *The Dawn of Philosophy: A Philosophical Primer* (Cambridge: Harvard University Press, 1951).
2. Martin Heidegger, *Beiträge zur Philosophie (Vom Ereignis)*, ed. Friedrich-Wilhelm von Herrmann (Frankfurt am Main: Vittorio Klostermann, 1989), 11.
3. On the affinities and divergences between Heidegger and Dilthey, see my essay "Heidegger and Dilthey: A Difference in Interpretation," in François Raffoul and Eric S. Nelson, eds., *The Bloomsbury Companion to Heidegger* (London: Bloomsbury Publishing, 2013), 129–134.
4. Misch, *Der Weg in die Philosophie*, 14; *The Dawn of Philosophy*, 16.
5. Misch, *The Dawn of Philosophy*, 44, 172.

ERIC S. NELSON

HEIDEGGER, MISCH, AND THE ORIGINS OF PHILOSOPHY

Abstract

I explore how Heidegger and his successors interpret philosophy as an Occidental enterprise based on a particular understanding of history. In contrast to the dominant monistic paradigm, I return to the plural thinking of Dilthey and Misch, who interpret philosophy as a European and a global phenomenon. This reflects Dilthey's pluralistic understanding of historical life. Misch developed Dilthey's insight by demonstrating the multiple origins of philosophy as critical life-reflection in its Greek context and in the historical matrices of ancient India and China. Misch's approach to Confucius and Zhuangzi reveals a historically informed, interculturally sensitive, and critically oriented life-philosophy.

I. Questionable Beginnings

Conceptions of what should and should not count as philosophy can be interpreted as temporally constituted phenomena, differing according to the social-historical circumstances of philosophical discourses. Such historically oriented contextualizing approaches to philosophy appear to risk becoming "just so" historical retellings of arbitrary opinions or sociological theories of subjective worldviews and relative social systems of knowledge that remain external to the internally motivating questions of the validity and truth of the thought, which are independent of the thinker and the idea's transitory historical conditions. This suspicion was raised by Martin Heidegger, in a comment that might seem prescient, when he stated in a 1924 lecture course on Aristotle that it is sufficient biographical information about the philosopher to state that he lived and thought: "Regarding the personality of a philosopher, our only interest is that he was born at a certain time, that he worked, and that he died"[1] The author's biography and the empirical historical conditions of the

---

ERIC S. NELSON, Associate Professor, Department of Philosophy, University of Massachusetts Lowell. Specialties: Chinese philosophy, European philosophy. E-mail: eric_nelson@uml.edu

author's life do not illuminate but obscure and displace the more originary historicity of philosophical questioning in which it is thinking that thinks the thinker and language that speaks the speaker.

Heidegger, and his pupil Hans-Georg Gadamer, continue to be at the center of standard accounts of the character, tasks, and scope of hermeneutics as a philosophical instead of a philological enterprise. It is underappreciated how deeply Heidegger in the 1920s and Gadamer in *Truth and Method* are motivated to critically redefine and rethink hermeneutics against its earlier nineteenth-century incarnations. In particular, the internal moment of philosophical truth as the disclosure of world and language is intended to overcome the social-scientific, context- and biographical-oriented study of philosophy associated with Wilhelm Dilthey (1833–1911) and his learned studies in modern European intellectual and cultural history and biography.

Dilthey and his student and son-in-law Georg Misch (1878–1965), who composed a pioneering *History of Autobiography* that included Arabic, Chinese, and other "non-Western" sources, emphasized the unique personal adaptation to and configuration of natural and social-historical forces in the living and cultivation (*Bildung*) of a concrete individual life. In this immanent and personalistic species of life-philosophy (*Lebensphilosophie*), the conception of life encompasses more than the general physical, organic, and historical features of life shared by each and all; it is more fundamentally an indication of *a* life. It is here in the conditional and contingent circumstances of a life—forming a singular life-context or nexus (*Lebenszusammenhang*)—that reflection and philosophy begin and unfold in contrast to originating in a primordial experience of being or truth abstracted from that individual life.

Hermeneutics cannot be detached from the interpersonal relation in Dilthey and Misch, as it is defined as the art of interpersonal understanding that proceeds to others through their behaviors, expressions, objectifications, and monuments. The interpretive art has been cultivated in multiple ways in various cultural situations, this cultivation of hermeneutics outside the West includes in particular—Misch notes—the Confucian literati in China.[2] The disagreement between a contextualizing person-oriented and an ontological hermeneutics has a number of implications for the question: what is philosophy? In both interpretations of hermeneutics, the response to the question of what is and is not to be considered philosophy is articulated in relation to an understanding of the philosophy of history. Philosophy as the history of truth interpreted as unconcealment and disclosure, as the metaphysical concealment and displacement of its first Greek beginning, can uniquely originate in archaic Greece in Heidegger's narrative of the history of being. Philosophy as the fateful destining of being culminates in the current impoverishment and plight of being, in the homelessness and disenchantment of modern technological Western civilization. The East and the South only derivatively participate in Heidegger's history of being to the extent that they are increasingly assimilated through the planetary advance of the technological world-picture—and its reduction of beings to instrumental calculation—which originates in the Greek experience of nature as *physis* (φύσις).[3]

II. Heidegger, History, and the Question of Origin

In the context of post-Kantian German philosophy, the question of whether there can be a Chinese, Indian, or African philosophy is determined by the interpretation of philosophy's history as more than a fortuitous contingent process or collection of facts. In his early thought of the 1920s, Heidegger unfolded a distinction developed in the correspondence and writings of Dilthey and Count Yorck von Wartenburg. History as the facts and explanations of historiography (*Historie*) is contrasted with history as occurrence and event (*Geschichte*).[4] Whereas *Historie* concerns the external reconstruction of contingently related phenomena, *Geschichte* points toward the temporal and historical occurrence of human existence as "being here" (*Dasein*). Dilthey described *Geschichte* as the living experience (*Erlebnis*), expression (*Ausdruck*), and interpretive understanding (*Verstehen*) comprising the first-person participant perspective of individuals. *Geschichte* becomes the ontological event of being in Heidegger, who confronted the conventional everyday and historiographical understandings of history with the facticity of history as an enactment (*Vollzug*) and as event (*Ereignis*) of being.

The living sense of one's own historicity must be interpreted ontologically rather than biographically and psychologically. This experience of being is presupposed yet not directly understood in the first-person perspective. It requires a critical destructive confrontation (*Auseinandersetzung*) with the sedimentations of ordinary life and the metaphysical tradition to be encountered and properly thought as a question.

It is the destructuring, deconstructive dimension of Heidegger's project that binds philosophy to its Greek origin. The dismantling, which is called *Destruktion* ("destruction") in German in *Being and Time*, of the history of metaphysics motivates Heidegger's readings of the philosophers that pushes the inquirer back into the question of the origin. It is in the wonder of the origin that the thinker rediscovers more than the conditional and transient ontic beginnings of philosophy. In this situation of dismantling the historical transmission in order to confront its originary source (*Ursprung*) anew, and thus reawaken the radicalness of the origin, any empirical ontic starting point (*Beginn*) of thought—which can happen anywhere and anytime—is distinguished from philosophy's primordial ontological origin and destiny.

III. HEIDEGGER AND THE OCCIDENTAL ESSENCE OF PHILOSOPHY

Heidegger has been a widely used and yet abused inspiration and source for comparative philosophy. A recent work by Lin Ma has deftly exposed the mythology surrounding the subject of Heidegger and the East.[5]

Still, unlike most twentieth-century philosophers, Heidegger had a continuing interest in Asian forms of thinking since the 1920s when he read aloud from the *Zhuangzi* 《莊子》 at social gatherings. Heidegger repeatedly incorporated images and phrases from translations of Daoist and, less frequently, Zen Buddhist texts. He is particularly concerned in these instances with the Daoist discourse of emptiness and the word "*dao* 道" itself as the fundamental concept and guiding word of Chinese thinking. Heidegger found an affinity between Zhuangzi's free and easy wandering (*xiaoyaoyou* 逍遙遊) in the *dao* and his thinking that he described as a way (*Weg*) and a "being underway" (*Unterwegssein*) without a predetermined goal or destination. Heidegger is often described as enthusiastically discussing Asian poetry and thinking with Asian students and visitors, even attempting to co-translate the *Daodejing* 《道德經》 with Xiao Shiyi 蕭師毅 in the mid-1940s. Heidegger's actual dialogues with Chinese and Japanese students and visitors are taken up in a number of his writings.[6]

Despite Heidegger's lively interest and the vast literature in the West and the East deploying Heidegger's concepts and strategies to interpret Asian texts and figures, this attention should not be conflated with an endorsement of Asian thinking as philosophical. On the contrary, Heidegger himself consistently and explicitly opposed the possibility of a Chinese or other forms of non-Western—that is to say a non-Greek—philosophy. In a typical utterance, Heidegger claimed that: "The style of all Western-European philosophy—and there is no other, neither a Chinese nor an Indian philosophy—is determined by this duality 'beings—in being.' "[7] For Heidegger, insisting on the Greek origin and exclusively European essence (*Wesen*) of philosophy, "the West and Europe, and only these, are, in the innermost course of their history, originally 'philosophical.' "[8] Heidegger argues that the peoples of "ancient India, China, and Japan" are not "thought-less" though this thought cannot be thinking "as such."[9] The thoughts of the East are not determined by the Greek conception of *logos* (λόγος) and its fate that characterizes what Heidegger calls "thinking 'as such'" and "our Western thinking."[10] Heidegger's destructuring confrontation with the *logos*-orientation of Occidental philosophy remains bound up with its historical conceptualization as essentially and necessarily Western, as do the later critiques of logocentrism developed by Jacques Derrida and Richard Rorty.[11]

In Heidegger's worst and more sinister moments in the 1930s, the original Greek origin of philosophy and the evening land (*Abendland*) and its repetition is identified with what he describes as a "decision against the Asiatic" in 1934.[12] Decision, as expressed in the German word *Entscheidung*, means a crucial transformative cutting apart and separation of the Greek vis-à-vis the Asiatic world. The image of a Greek confrontation with and overcoming of Asiatic hordes reoccurs throughout his lecture courses and writings on early Greek philosophy and the German poet Hölderlin, who—according to Heidegger in 1934/35—creatively surpassed "the Asiatic representation of destiny" as the Greeks originally and singularly overcame "Asiatic fate."[13] Prefiguring Germany's task, Heidegger's envisions the "Greeks" as only becoming a people (*Volk*) by creatively confronting and differentiating themselves from what was "most foreign and most difficult to them—the Asiatic."[14] In 1936, Heidegger likewise spoke of the need for the "preservation of the European peoples from the Asian," playing the geopolitical philosophical game of an alien Asiatic threat menacing and overwhelming the European world and thereby justifying National Socialist politics.[15] We should note that Heidegger's former teacher Edmund Husserl can be said to celebrate the unique achievements of Occidental civilization in his writings on history and science during this period; yet his situation is fundamentally different, since Husserl interprets the basic tendencies of Western culture to be ethical and rational and directs them against the irrationalism and fascism characteristic of the geopolitical situation in the 1930s.

Heidegger's provocative and fearful language concerning the menacing and uncanny presence of the Asiatic is primarily applied to Soviet communism in the 1930s. However, Heidegger still opposes the "Asiatic," as the primary antagonist of the Greek, in the 1960s, contrasting its threatening darkness with the Greeks ability to reorder it through the imposition of order, measure, and light upon it: "The Asiatic element once brought to the Greeks a dark fire, a flame that their [i.e., Greek] poetry and thought reorder with light and measure."[16] Although this could be construed as the generous gift of heavenly flame, the fire of heaven of the Greeks inspiring the native poet of which Hölderlin speaks, the statement is problematic given

Heidegger's association of the Asiatic with the irrational and the emphasis here on reordering and illuminating rather than guarding this "dark fire."[17]

Despite the totalizing character of the technological modernity of the West, Heidegger warned in the 1966 *Spiegel* interview "Only a God can save us" of "any takeover (*Übernahme*) of Zen Buddhism or any other Eastern experiences of the world (*Welterfahrungen*)." Whatever affinities Heidegger noted between his conception of way and a non-coercive "letting releasement" (*Gelassenheit*) with Chinese *wuwei* 無為 and Daoist and Zen Buddhist expressions of letting and responsiveness, Heidegger reasserted in this interview that the question of philosophy and of Europe is necessarily an internal one: the needed shift in thinking (*Umdenken*) is only possible through a new appropriation of the European tradition.[18] The crisis of European philosophy and culture that characterizes modernity can be countered only through a return to and emancipating confrontation with the Greek origin that determines it.

The question of philosophy is consequently and persistently a question of the German (in the 1930s and early 1940s) and, after the end of World War II, of the European and Western confrontation with the history of metaphysics from its initial Greek origins to its unfolding in the modern technological world-picture. In Heidegger's account, globalization, and the emergence of phenomena such as "world philosophy," is a further realization of the enframed and reified world of Western modernity.

IV. On the Prejudices of the Philosophers

The historical account of the developmental unity of European philosophy from the Greeks to the moderns is a common dominant trope of much European philosophy. From Herder and Hegel through Heidegger to Derrida and Rorty, only that which stands in an internal historical relation to philosophy's Greek origins is considered philosophy in contrast with other forms of thought and reflection. It is notable that this Hegelian narrative continues to shape the approaches of those thinkers claiming to explicitly oppose the totalizing nature of Hegel's philosophy of history as the developmental unfolding of spirit toward the absolute.

Heidegger not only problematized the modernity that is the culmination of Hegel's narrative, he also questions the height of classical Greek civilization for the sake of what it purportedly conceals: the experience of being as *physis*, as upsurge and holding sway into the openness of being. The "other beginning" (*der andere Anfang*) that

Heidegger began to articulate in the 1930s does not occur through imitating the first Greek beginning (*der erste Anfang*), but rather by confronting it, exposing all that is questionable and uncanny (*unheimlich*) in it.

Heidegger's division of the philosophy of the evening land (*Abendland*) of the West and the non-philosophical thinking of the morning land (*Morgenland*) of the East presupposes his destructuring of metaphysical thinking underway to its origin. The other beginning is suggestive in that it might be taken as a beginning outside of Greece.[19] Nonetheless, non-Western thought cannot constitute another beginning for Heidegger insofar as it is not a differentiating confrontation (*Auseinandersetzung*) with the first Greek beginning.

The Eurocentric paradigm defining the present scope of philosophy depends on a particular conception of history and consequently can sound odd to non-philosophers while remaining academic philosophy's dominant paradigm. This Eurocentric strategy, challenged by Misch, has had significant implications for contemporary thought as it operates as the basis of claims of Derrida and Rorty that there is no philosophy outside of the West.[20] Heidegger's strategy is revised and radicalized in Derrida's and Rorty's deconstructive unweaving of the tradition of Western metaphysics that indirectly and in the last analysis preserve the primacy and privilege of the Western essence of philosophy. In contrast to the "dialogue of peoples" articulated by thinkers such as Georg Misch, Helmuth Plessner, and Martin Buber, even the discourse of the competition between Athens and Jerusalem—as representing Greek philosophy and its Jewish other—in Leo Strauss, Levinas, and the later Derrida remains too restrictive insofar as it is closed to Qufu 曲阜 or what is exterior to the dynamic of this dyad.[21]

V. Another "Another Beginning"?

I would like to propose here that there is another "another beginning" in thinking about the origin of philosophy. In the hermeneutical life-philosophy of Dilthey and Misch, philosophy does not have one unique starting point. It has multiple temporal beginnings as do all sciences, life-attitudes, and worldviews. There is no one origin insofar as they are born of various provenances and inevitably mediated by personal and social life. In the multiplicity and singularity of human life, in its strivings and conflicts, typical patterns emerge that can serve as heuristic models to begin to approach and interpret individuals and peoples across diverse historical cultures.

The nineteenth-century German historical school or historicism had taught the relativity of all forms of life such that one needs to perceive and interpret a perspective from the inside in order to understand it. Dilthey, however, checked historicism's radical perspectivalism and relativism by developing notions of structure and pattern as well as the anthropological dimension of human existence. The dynamic social, psychological, and anthropological structures of human life are relational and positional rather than defined by an underlying essence or constant identity. These common formations are investigated in the human sciences as well as how they are individuated in myriad ways in the lives of individuals and peoples. Such structured formations limit and place a check on the incommensurability of forms of life and language games. It also challenges, as evident in the critical responses of Misch and Plessner to Heidegger and Carl Schmitt, the possibility of a pure historicity and existential decisionism that denies all natural and anthropological determinations and limits.[22]

This alternative conception is one that Heidegger explicitly rejected. Heidegger critiqued Dilthey's thesis of the plural ontic origins of philosophy in the name of the unity of the question of being, which can fundamentally only be the one question of philosophy, in his winter semester 1928–29 lecture-course *Introduction into Philosophy*.[23] In his 1928–29 lecture-course, Heidegger presented his last sustained reflection on Dilthey's thought and indirectly Misch's interpretation and extension of it. Misch's role has been little noticed in scholarship about Heidegger despite the fact that, in an interesting footnote in *Being and Time*, Heidegger mentioned his reliance on Misch's interpretation of Dilthey.[24] In the lecture-courses of the late 1920s and early 1930s, Heidegger takes up and responds to a number of topics from Misch, including Misch's work *Life-philosophy and Phenomenology* (*Lebensphilosophie und Phänomenologie*) that developed one of the earliest extended critiques of *Being and Time*.[25]

Heidegger claimed in *Introduction into Philosophy* that Dilthey's worldview thinking is absorbed and lost in the ontic starting points of thought and reflection, as if there were any other points of departure but those of ontic life, without recognizing the dignity and unity of the ontological origin. This origin consists in the ontological difference between beings as separate entities (*Seiende*) and being (*Sein*) itself. Heidegger concluded that Dilthey leaves us adrift in an endless sea of ontic multiplicity and human scientific investigations without a proper relation to the ontological origin.[26]

Despite the insights Heidegger acknowledged gaining from Dilthey in the 1920s, Dilthey cannot be counted a philosopher. It is the human scientist and historiographer who investigates the plurality of contingent conditions of ideas and worldviews.[27] The philosopher in Heidegger's estimation must rise or return to a higher vocation in the movement from history as a science to history as the event of being.

Whatever the other merits or faults of Heidegger's understanding of history and philosophy, and its impact on contemporary thought through Derrida and Rorty, it presents the idea of philosophy primarily in a monistic manner. This manner can be interpreted as an existential a priori that binds the questioner and as a method of discovering the ontological in the ontic. Heidegger described this as a hermeneutical anticipation or formal indication that abstracts from the particularity of one perspective in order to allow the multiplicity of concrete particulars to be encountered. The unity of the ontological difference would consequently permit the plurality of concrete forms of existence and ontic ways of being to be disclosed and recognized.

I want to propose here that Heidegger's method of formalization is not formal enough.[28] It remains committed to a particular kind of experience and bound to an ontological prejudice that marginalizes the ontic empirical particularities that are the plural points of departure for self-reflection (*Selbstbesinnung*) in the context of *a* life. In the context of the hermeneutical life-philosophy of Dilthey and Misch, and in classical Chinese philosophy as evidenced in Chung-ying Cheng's onto-generative hermeneutics of the *Yijing* 《易經》, the point of departure for reflection is life itself instead of an abstract conceptuality. Such life is a changing and dynamic holistic nexus rather than the static identity of one determinate origin or a determinate systematic totality that subordinates all elements.[29]

Heidegger might well break with the prejudices of abstract theorizing and mathematical vision that limited Husserl's phenomenology. The ontological prejudice prevents Heidegger, in spite of himself to the extent that he wishes to prepare for a dialogue with Eastern thought, from recognizing philosophy in different settings that do not stem from the Greek origin and do not prioritize the question of being. As Misch and Plessner both suggested in the politically charged atmosphere of 1931, Heidegger's idea of philosophy is intrinsically Eurocentric.[30] It addresses the "being-there" of the Indian, the Etruscan, or the Egyptian only insofar as they can adopt themselves to a classical-Christian tradition.[31] Heidegger's vision of philosophy is transfixed by and beholden to an "ethnocentric a priori" that still structures contemporary Western philosophical discourses and institutional practices, even if in the guise of Rortyan "ethnocentric relativism." Philosophy has been enthnocentric to the extent that its very idea is restrained to a particular—whether racially or culturally conceived—ethnically based historical tradition.

It is remarkable that modern and contemporary Western philosophy continues to conceive of itself as a closed universe. Medieval and early Modern European thinkers were aware of and in discussion with Jewish, Arabic, and eventually Indian and Chinese sources.

Whereas Leibniz and Malebranche assessed elements of Chinese philosophy positively or negatively in relation to Christianity, philosophers since Herder and Hegel have excluded Chinese thought as incommensurable with Western philosophy. Even after the end of explicit developmental teleological philosophies of history that conclude with the triumphant culmination of Greek *logos* in modern Western thought, this ethnocentric a priori remains operative in its critics.

VI. Georg Misch and the Multiplicity of Origins

One hermeneutical tendency understands interpretation as proceeding from the self to the other as it extends itself into the world, expanding the circles of its horizons, and eventually returning to itself in self-understanding. Another tendency finds the self confronted with misunderstandings, obstacles, and resistances that cannot be overcome and integrated into the presence and mastery of the self. Such experiences of alterity and difference lead the interpreter to recognize the irrevocable multiplicity, particularity, and perspectivality of things. For Misch, as for Dilthey, intercultural interpretation follows the model of all interpretation as an oscillation between the typical and the unique, the general and the singular: what appears alien and other is initially approached through the typical at the same time as the typical needs to be reformulated through the experience of, reflection on, and responsiveness to the individual.[32]

This alternative conception of the philosophy of history allowed Georg Misch to recognize the multiple beginnings of philosophy across different cultures and epochs. The beginning of philosophy, according to Georg Misch in his 1926 work *Der Weg in die Philosophie* (*The Way into Philosophy*) is not the self-certainty or self-presence of the origin to itself.[33] Philosophy did not only begin once in Greece; it occurs as a unitary phenomenon in the ruptures of ordinary experience that provoke a reflective questioning and reconsideration of that experience.[34] Philosophy is an internal break with immediacy and entrance into self-reflection, which has no necessary or one culturally specific origin (*Ursprung*). Philosophy, according to Misch, is not bound to one particular form or one given question; in the breakthrough or cutting through (*durchbruch*), "it strikes us like a message from another world."[35] This assumption is both born within the European philosophical tradition, the horizon of Misch's point of departure, and looks beyond the boundaries of this horizon.[36]

The very first illustration Misch provided for such a beginning of philosophy, the transition from one particular horizon to another horizon that characterizes the philosophical break-through, is the story of "Autumn Floods" (*Qiushui* 〈秋水〉) in the *Zhuangzi*.[37] The great river believes itself to be greater than all the small tributaries and channels that lead into it until it encounters the great sea. In this encounter, the ordinary self-conception is placed in question as a one-sided, partial, and limited perspective. In Misch's portrayal of this Zhuangzian narrative, the limited and partial is confronted with the expansive. There is a break-through out of the ordinary natural attitude of everyday life to reflection on that life that proceeds through the "categories of life" or what his Göttingen colleague Plessner called "the material a priori."[38]

The narrative from the *Zhuangzi* permits Misch to challenge the ordinary one-sided and limited conception of life and the relation of philosophy to it. The shifting multi-perspectivalism of Misch's hermeneutical life-philosophy allows the play of perspectives in the *Zhuangzi* to come forth not only as another alien form of thought but as a specific form of philosophical reflection in response to a question that in its structural affinity addresses the human condition.

In Misch's second chapter on "breaking through," the other beginnings of philosophy are located across divergent points: in the Buddha's experience of the fundamental reality of suffering, in Spinoza's articulation of ethical decision and moral personality from the reality of the whole, and in Plato's Socrates proceeding from the limited and qualified to the good as such in the allegory of the cave.

As if preemptively answering Heidegger, Misch maintained that all four examples are: "not the primordial utterances of philosophy; they were rather revivals and recollections of an original knowledge which is anterior to them both logically and historically. And the echo they awoke in us may just be something that the natural course of human life awakes in every human, quite spontaneously, at one time or another."[39]

Philosophy begins in "metaphysical need" and in the cultivation and expression of a feeling of life: this need is echoed in manifest ways that hearken to this origin of self-reflection in the midst of life.

Exemplary moments such as autumn floods indicate and repeat in their own manner the reflective break with the natural unreflective attitude. Misch identifies this with the genuine beginning and the way of philosophy. This multiplicity of ontic beginnings cannot count as the origin of philosophy for Heidegger who remains beholden to the ethnocentric a priori as much as Hegel. Hegel claimed that "we" modern educated interpreters of world history can only begin to feel at home in history with Greece, since only here do we arrive at the origins of spirit.[40] While Hegel—unlike many of his successors—did in fact use the word philosophy in non-Western contexts, he also explicitly stated that "genuine philosophy" arose only in the Occident with its "freedom" of "individual self-awareness" that he considered to be in principle contrary to the "Oriental spirit."[41]

Misch refused to identify the unity and necessity of philosophy with one unique and necessary historical experience of individual freedom in classical Greece (Hegel) or with an originary experience of being in the early Pre-Socratic philosophers of archaic Greece (Heidegger):

> The assumption that Greek-born philosophy was the "natural" one, that the European way of philosophizing was the logically necessary way, betrayed that sort of self-confidence which comes from narrowness of vision. The assumption falls to the ground directly [when] you look beyond the confines of Europe. The Chinese beginning of philosophy, connected with the name of Confucius, was primarily concerned with those very matters which according to the traditional European formula were only included in philosophy as a result of the reorientation effected by Socrates, namely, life within the human, social, and historical world. The task of the early Confucians was to achieve a rational foundation for morality which should assure humans their dignity and provide an ethical attitude in politics.[42]

In an earlier essay published in 1911, after his return from a journey to India and China, Misch remarked that "the rational gestalt of personality," which is encountered in and through history, is as much Chinese as it is Greek. Rational moral personality is a good discovered in the ancient Chinese Enlightenment-movement of Confucianism as well as in the modern European Enlightenment and an ethically oriented life-philosophy.[43] This is further supported by the influence of Confucian moral-political thought on the European Enlightenment, notably in Leibniz, Wolff, and Voltaire.[44] Integrating rationality and the historical sensibility of concrete ethical life, ideal norms and practical affairs, reverence for humanity and particular local affective bonds, early Confucianism is a primary exemplar of an enlightened "philosophy of life." Misch describes it as "the supreme example of a movement of thought grounded in life itself."[45]

Confucius emerges in Misch's writings as a figure evoking the immanent ethical and historical enlightenment (*Aufklärung*) and moral cultivation (*Bildung*) of life—which is the vocation of philosophy in Misch's estimation—in contrast to the powers of myth, mysticism, and nature; or, of being. The Confucian form of rationality disenchants and demystifies, yet it is not therefore purely atheistic for Misch. The passages concerning heaven (*tian* 天) in the *Analects* (*Lunyu* 《論語》) reveal background metaphysical and cosmological inspirations and an ethical and philosophical form of monotheism, which Misch discusses in relation to the priority of the ethical moment in the Hebrew prophets.[46]

Misch reformulated the point made in the above quoted passage in his 1931 work *Life-philosophy and Phenomenology*: the Chinese origins of philosophy do not begin in the enchantment of the question of being. Its beginnings arise from ethical self-reflection, questions of proper governance and the appropriate way to live, and the anxious care for right action such that Heidegger's reductive identification of philosophy with the thinking of being restricts and distorts philosophy itself.[47]

The Greek origin has a necessity through the concrete moment of reflection (*Besinnung*) of life concerning itself. It is as inadvertent and provisional as other origins of self-reflective thinking from the unreflective natural attitudes of ordinary life. Its significance, unity, and necessity arise through the moment of interpretive self-reflection (*Selbstbesinnung*) in relation to one's own life-experiences (*Lebenserfahrungen*). This movement of life understanding and interpreting itself from out of its multiple ontic conditions is what allows the plurality of thought with all of its varied contents of diverse provenance to come into view as a whole:

> Despite this diversity, however, we can speak of the beginning of philosophy, using both words in the singular. Thus we approach the historical facts on the assumption that philosophy is a unity. This assumption comes from our European tradition; and with our modern view of history, which has learnt to look beyond the bounds of the European horizon, it might seem a mere prejudice. For we meet with a plurality of beginnings and first efforts regarding which one may well enquire whether the one name philosophy should be applied at all. The historical positivism of our time, which everywhere breaks down the universal into the particular, naturally seeks to do the same in respect of philosophy by resolving its ideal unity into a multiplicity of philosophies. And it is true that we do encounter such a multiplicity at the very outset. Nevertheless the historical facts, once their significance is properly understood, reinforce our conviction that philosophy is a unity.[48]

Ontic multiplicity is not the negation of the essence and dignity of philosophy, if it is the arena in which philosophy takes place as an event and enactment not of impersonal being and neutral Dasein—a formal neutrality that is derived "after the fact" of the partiality and perspectivality of historical life—but, following Dilthey's interpretive individualism, of individual and personal life.[49] Misch extended Dilthey's immanent and pluralistic personalism, challenging the conceptualization of the person as universally human and yet at the same time oddly particular (exclusively Occidental) that led European thinkers to denigrate non-Western cultures. This view is expressed in Hegel's contention in his philosophy of history that: "World history travels from East to West, for Europe is absolutely the end of world history, Asia the beginning."⁵⁰ The end of history, as the dynamic realization of free individual consciousness and spirit (*Geist*) as what guarantees the common life of such subjects, is an ultimately modern Western achievement prefigured in classical Greek culture.⁵¹

The multifaceted concern with interpreting and cultivating an individual life is not solely a Western one, as Misch persuasively illustrated in his *History of Autobiography*, since autobiographical and biographical literature from direct narrative to deeply personal self-reflection is found throughout the world.⁵² Misch does not deny that Western modernity has produced a particular way of experiencing and conceptualizing the person nor does he posit an unchanging underlying "person" independent of the self's contextual formation (*Bildung*). The individual person emerges immanently through the formative interpretive practices that address life as *a* life in the context of the contingency of historical conditions and a multiplicity of intersecting roles and diverging and conflicting perspectives.

The universality of philosophy does not appear directly then in the form of a concept, intuition, or originary experience of being. Universalization is achieved indirectly through processes of mediation as ideals, norms, and values are formed from the contents of concrete empirical existence. The center emerges out of flux and creative formative individuality from Hume's "bundle of instincts and feelings."⁵³ The universal emerges from a metaphysical need and urge—born within the immanence of life—that motivates the struggle for the clarification, enlightenment, and self-understanding of life in the midst of the particularities of specific linguistic, historical, and environmental circumstances.⁵⁴

Philosophy occurs in the interruption of the ordinary experiencing and thinking of the "natural attitude" and in the distancing from one's everyday absorption in oneself and one's situation that allows life as a whole to be experienced as a question. Philosophy was once born in Greek wonder about *physis* and cosmos (κόσμος); yet it was not born here alone and consequently cannot be defined as one determinate fated destiny. Philosophy is reborn repeatedly anew from a metaphysical need for transcendence that follows the routes of self-questioning and reflection rather than the routes of religious mystical experience or of religious authority, devotion, and faith.

One basic tendency of philosophy is born from the metaphysical need and urge for transcendence. This urge toward the beyond is countered and mediated in its conflict with the tendency toward self-clarification and enlightenment that is philosophy's other fundamental dimension. There is not solely the Greek origin of philosophy in wonder that prioritizes the experience of nature as *physis* and cosmos, which Misch also identifies as a singular experience of nature that prepares the way for the natural sciences. There is the Indian origin that turns the self inward upon itself to examine the subjectivity and interiority of that self. There is a Chinese origin of philosophy from out of the practical lived-experience (*Erlebnis*) of the concrete bonds of social life and in self-reflection (*Selbstbesinnung*) on the possibilities of cultivating moral personality within this life-context. Misch thus indicates in a life-philosophical way the *xing* 行 character of classical Chinese thought in which knowledge is bound to practice and action.

None of the origins of philosophy persist within themselves as a destiny with a determined outcome or "cultural mind-set." Developing Dilthey's conception of peoples, a people cannot be characterized through an unchanging essence or the collective identity of a substantial "soul of a people" (*Volkseele*). A people are generationally and historically constituted through the tensions and affinities of individuals; that is, from the differentiating responses of individuals, and the associations and institutions that they form, to shared questions and tasks and through the irresolvable conflict of worldviews and interpretations.

Accordingly, in Misch's reading of Greek philosophy, there is no one defining essential Greek experience of being as *physis*. Even in ancient Greece there are multiple divergent and incompatible experiences and conceptualizations of philosophy, some of which became more dominant than others during different generations. To speak schematically: while the Pre-Socratics focused their gaze on the natural world, Socrates marked a turn toward the ethical question of the self, the Socratic schools focused on issues of moral personality and the good life, and later Neo-Platonism and early Christianity shifted Greek thought toward the experience of the subjective interiority of the self.

In Misch's multi-vocal narrative, multiplicity does not only apply between distinct cultures, as if each one had one fixed and constant identity, but within cultures as formational historical realities. Chinese philosophy did not only find its expression in the Confucian cultivation of moral personality and concern for the health and vitality of ethical life. It is also expressed Daoist sensibilities about the natural world and subjective self as well as legalist conceptions of power, order, and stability. Ancient Chinese philosophy, according to Misch, ought to be interpreted not so much as a reified monolithic unity, which led European thinkers to one-sidedly praise or condemn a reified image of "China," but through the affinities, tensions, and disputes between interconnected yet competing and differentiated forms of life and reflection within a given hermeneutical situation. Misch adjusted Dilthey's thinking of the interpretive encounter and agonistic confrontation between worldviews for the sake of an intercultural art of philosophizing: the intercultural interpreter reflectively and responsively interprets an historical nexus from the typical to the particular in order to articulate its shared structures and the dynamics of their differentiation and conflict.

Misch's thinking of the tension between the typical and the unique is still salutary given contemporary discourses that continue to reduce the specificity of a form of lived-experience and reflection to a generic formula whether it is mysticism, skepticism, the perennial philosophy, or the question of being. Because of specific features in its social-historical milieu, texts such as the *Daodejing* and the *Zhuangzi* cannot be reduced to the abstract formula of mysticism.[55] Misch argues that early Daoism differs from Greek and Indian philosophies of the subject or self. Daoism did not achieve the same results, as a formulaic definition of mysticism might suggest, since it cannot break with its own contexts and conditions such as the broader formative concern in early China for ethics and politics. Misch is particularly concerned with the tensions between—to employ his vocabulary—the realistic power politics of the "realists" (legalists), the focus on a moral ideal of humanity and social integrity in Confucianism, the idealistic reformism of Moism, and the multi-perspectivalism, the emancipatory power of symbolic expression, and free sensibility of life evoked in the *Zhuangzi*.[56] The tensions form a pattern indicating the early Chinese concern for an immanent worldly understanding of life—whether understood more naturally or culturally—and how to comport oneself and the community within this space between heaven and earth. The counter tendencies in such cultural matrices, for instance of Buddhist non-self (*anātman*) vis-à-vis Hindu self (*ātman*), reveal the power of a dominant model in a given culture.[57]

The plurality of feelings of life, perspectives, and arguments constitute a shared pattern constituted through its tensions and in distinct responses to common questions that form focal points of this pattern. To this extent, each classical philosophical culture had its prevailing and countervailing tendencies toward understanding and articulating life. Life is a structuring-structured nexus with myriad perspectives and possibilities for differentiation and integration, individuation and connectedness, in the hermeneutical *Lebensphilosophie* of Dilthey and Misch. Life can accordingly be experienced through nature in the sense of *physis* and cosmos in Greek thought, through the interiority of the subject in classical Indian philosophy, and through social and ethical community in early Chinese philosophy.

Notwithstanding Misch's critical appreciation of Confucius, Zhuangzi has the first and last hermeneutical life-philosophical word for Misch. The "poet-thinker" Zhuangzi challenges, expands, and switches our horizons by liberating us from our conditional limited perspectives through relativizing them and by immanently locating and articulating life from and in life itself: hiding the world in the world so as not to lose it.[58]

VII. Conclusion

Heidegger's poetic anti-modernistic thinking of being has frequently been taken as a resource for intercultural philosophy even if his openness to the possibility of a Chinese or other varieties of non-Western philosophy is limited, and has been highly exaggerated, as Lin Ma has shown.[59] It is correct that Heidegger engaged at times with elements of Asian thought and culture and adopted them for his own purposes. Still, Heidegger consistently denied that any thinking that does not stem from the Greek origin and shared in the fateful destiny of Occidental metaphysics culminating in modernity should be called philosophy. Heidegger's argumentation has been decisive for thinkers such as Levinas, Derrida, and Rorty. They contest, reverse, and pluralize Heidegger's history of being and yet fail to overcome the disavowal of non-Western philosophizing.

The understanding of philosophy as proceeding from Greece has been associated with historical thinking, as it is articulated in historically oriented thinkers, particularly Hegel and Heidegger. Does then a commitment to the historicity and specificity of philosophy commit one to it being a Western endeavor? In another group of German historical thinkers we find that this is not the case. Plessner argued that Dilthey, who in numerous ways is an intermediate between Hegel and Heidegger, unlocked new possibilities for thinking and "a new responsibility" by relativizing "the reactive absolutizing of European value systems."[60] The art of interpretively understanding the other described by Dilthey has an ethical and political dimension insofar as it requires releasing the other by abandoning or challenging power over the other.[61]

Dilthey and Misch identified multiple origins and lineages of philosophy that emerge and unfold in relation to the feeling, expression, and interpretation of life. Heidegger described philosophy as the primordial possibility of Dasein, of human existence as "thrown" in the world; and yet there is only in the end Occidental philosophy. Philosophy is born of a fundamental mood and attunement (*Stimmung*) in Dilthey, an insight adopted by Heidegger in the 1920s. But Dilthey analyzed a broader array of existential moods and dispositions than Heidegger's focus on anxiety in *Being and Time* or extreme boredom in "What is Metaphysics?" In Dilthey's approach, the "feeling of life" and life's dispositional mood can be altered as it is expressed—and intensified or deflected—in wonder or doubt, reverence or anxiety, enthusiasm or boredom. This feeling of life finds its expression not only in classically conceived Greek discourses concerning ontology and metaphysics but in religion, poetry, ethics, politics, and other forms of self-reflective historical life.

Misch explicitly extended this point further by demonstrating the multiple origins of philosophy within the Greek context, which have religious, poetic, and ethical dimensions as well as ontological ones, as well as in other cultural matrices such as those of ancient India and China. In contrast to thinkers such as Heidegger and his successors, who take history to entail an exclusive dynamic and potential that now afflicts the entire globe while remaining a primarily Occidental question, Misch interpreted philosophy historically as both a local—through the exemplary cases of ancient Greece, India, and China—and as a global and existentially human phenomenon. The hermeneutical attentiveness to the object in Dilthey and Misch encourages the articulation of the historical fabric of life as intrinsically heterogeneous and irreducible in its unfathomability to one—no matter how dynamically conceived—perspective or model.

UNIVERSITY OF MASSACHUSETTS LOWELL
Lowell, Massachusetts

Endnotes

This article was originally presented at a panel of the International Society for Chinese Philosophy organized for the 2012 meeting of the Pacific Division of the American Philosophical Association in Seattle. I also presented a version of it at Peking University in December 2012. I would like to express my appreciation to all those who commented on this article and, in particular, Chung-ying Cheng, Linyu Gu, Dan Chen Ding, and Robin Wang. This article has not appeared in print elsewhere and its errors are the author's responsibility.

1. Martin Heidegger, *Gesamtausgabe*, hereafter cited as GA plus volume number, GA 18: *Grundbegriffe der aristotelischen Philosophie* (Frankfurt: Klostermann, 2002), 4. Trans. *Basic Concepts of Aristotelian Philosophy* (Bloomington: Indiana University Press, 2009).
2. Georg Misch, *Der Aufbau der Logik auf dem Boden der Philosophie des Lebens: Göttinger Vorlesungen über Logik und Einleitung in die Theorie des Wissens* (Freiburg: Alber, 1994), 566.
3. On the European character of modernization and globalization, compare Martin Heidegger, GA 79: *Bremer und Freiburger Vorträge* (Frankfurt am Main: Klostermann, 2005), 65. Trans. *Bremen and Freiburg Lectures: Insight into That Which Is and Basic Principles of Thinking* (Bloomington: Indiana University Press, 2012); and Martin Heidegger, *Sojourns: The Journey to Greece* (Albany: State University of New York Press, 2005), 25–26.
4. On the different conceptions of history and philosophy in Dilthey and Heidegger, see my essays: Eric S. Nelson, "History as Decision and Event in Heidegger," *Arhe* 4, no.

8 (2007): 97–115; Eric S. Nelson, "Interpreting Practice: Epistemology, Hermeneutics, and Historical Life in Dilthey," *Idealistic Studies* 38, no. 1–2 (2008): 105–22; and Eric S. Nelson, "Heidegger and Dilthey: A Difference in Interpretation," in François Raffoul and Eric S. Nelson, eds., *The Bloomsbury Companion to Heidegger* (London: Bloomsbury Publishing, 2013), 129–134.
5. Lin Ma, *Heidegger on East-West Dialogue: Anticipating the Event* (New York: Routledge, 2008). Note that this significant study provides further context to some of the arguments that are developed in this article.
6. Such as, for instance, "A Dialogue on Language between a Japanese and an Inquirer" (1958); published in Martin Heidegger, *On the Way to Language* (New York: Harper and Row, 1971), 1–56.
7. Martin Heidegger, *What Is Called Thinking?* (New York: Harper & Row, 1968), 224.
8. Martin Heidegger, *What Is Philosophy?* Trans. William Kluback and Jean T. Wilde (Lanham: Rowman & Littlefield, 1956), 31.
9. Heidegger, *Bremen and Freiburg Lectures*, 137.
10. Ibid.
11. On the reverse or negative Eurocentrism of the deconstruction of the history of Western metaphysics as logocentrism, see Eric S. Nelson, "The *Yijing* and Philosophy: From Leibniz to Derrida," *Journal of Chinese Philosophy* 38, no. 3 (2011): 382–85, 388–89. For an alternative onto-generative conception of hermeneutical philosophy in critical response to Heidegger's ontological thinking, see Chung-ying Cheng, "Confucius, Heidegger, and the Philosophy of the *I Ching*: A Comparative Inquiry into the Truth of Human Being," *Philosophy East and West* 37, No. 1 (1987): 51–70.
12. Martin Heidegger, GA 16: *Veröffentlichte Schriften 1910–1976, Reden und andere Zeugnisse eines Lebensweges: 1910–1976* (Frankfurt am Main: Klostermann, 2000), 333.
13. Martin Heidegger, GA 39: *Hölderlins Hymnen "Germanien" und "Der Rhein"* (Frankfurt am Main: Klostermann, 1999), 173.
14. Martin Heidegger, GA 13: *Aus der Erfahrung des Denkens 1910–1976* (Frankfurt am Main: Klostermann, 2002), 21.
15. Martin Heidegger, "Europa und die deutsche Philosophie," in *Europa und die Philosophie*, ed. Hans-Helmut Gander (Frankfurt am Main: Vittorio Klostermann, 1993), 31.
16. Heidegger, *Sojourns: The Journey to Greece*, 27.
17. Compare Ma's discussion of this passage in *Heidegger on East-West Dialogue*, 118.
18. Richard Wolin, *The Heidegger Controversy: A Critical Reader* (Cambridge: MIT Press, 1993), 113.
19. I developed this point in relation to early Chinese thinking in "Responding to Heaven and Earth: Daoism, Heidegger and Ecology," *Environmental Philosophy* 1, no. 2 (2004): 65–74.
20. Nelson, "The *Yijing* and Philosophy," 388–89.
21. One of the most questionable expressions of this dyad is evident in Levinas's remark: "I always say—but under my breath—that the Bible and the Greeks present the only serious issues in human life; everything else is dancing." Emmanuel Levinas and Jill Robbins, *Is It Righteous to Be?: Interviews with Emmanuel Levinas* (Stanford: Stanford University Press, 2001), 149. I discuss the case of Levinas and China, the misunderstandings and possibilities for communication, in Eric S. Nelson, "Levinas and Early Confucian Ethics: Religion, Rituality, and the Sources of Morality," *Levinas Studies* 4 (2009): 77–207. The Eurocentrisms of Levinas and Derrida are respectively updated in Philippe Nemo, *What Is the West?* (Pittsburgh: Duquesne University Press, 2006) and Rodolphe Gasché, *Europe, or the Infinite Task: A Study of a Philosophical Concept* (Stanford: Stanford University Press, 2009).
22. Particularly Georg Misch, *Lebensphilosophie und Phänomenologie* (Leipzig: Teubner, 1931); Helmuth Plessner, *Macht und menschliche Natur* (1931) republished in *Gesammelte Schriften 5: Macht und menschliche Natur* (Frankfurt am Main: Suhrkamp, 1981).
23. Martin Heidegger, GA 27: *Einleitung in die Philosophie* (Frankfurt: Vittorio Klostermann, 2001).

24. Martin Heidegger, SZ 527, fn 14: "This is not necessary since we have G. Misch to thank for a concrete presentation of Dilthey that aims at the central tendencies that is essential to any discussion of his work." Compare Charles B. Guignon, *Heidegger and the Problem of Knowledge* (Indianapolis: Hackett, 1983), 49.
25. Georg Misch, *Lebensphilosophie und Phänomenologie* (Leipzig: Teubner, 1931).
26. Compare, however, Cheng, "Confucius, Heidegger, and the Philosophy of the *I Ching*," 51–70. The *Yijing*'s logic of the multiplicity and temporal transience of origins can well be said to offer further support for Misch's argumentation in contrast with Heidegger's more monistic depiction of origins.
27. Heidegger criticizes Dilthey's ontic pluralism in GA 27: 347–350. I examine the difference between Dilthey and Heidegger concerning worldviews and ontic multiplicity in Eric S. Nelson, "The World Picture and Its Conflict in Dilthey and Heidegger," *Humana.Mente: Journal of Philosophical Studies* 18 (2011): 19–38.
28. Despite the limitations of Heidegger's approach in relation to non-Western philosophy and the multiple origins of philosophy, Heidegger's practice of formalization and emptying remains significant in a comparative philosophical context. I developed this point in Eric S. Nelson, "Language and Emptiness in Chan Buddhism and the Early Heidegger," *Journal of Chinese Philosophy* 37, no. 3 (2010): 472–92. On formal indication, see Eric S. Nelson, "Questioning Practice: Heidegger, Historicity and the Hermeneutics of Facticity," *Philosophy Today* 44 (2001): 150–59; Eric S. Nelson, "Heidegger and the Ethics of Facticity." *Rethinking Facticity*, eds. François Raffoul and Eric S. Nelson (Albany: State University of New York Press, 2008), 129–47.
29. On the logic of transformational multiplicity and unity in the *Yijing*, see Cheng, "Confucius, Heidegger, and the Philosophy of the *I Ching*," 51–70.
30. Misch, *Lebensphilosophie und Phänomenologie*, 14; Plessner, *Macht und menschliche Natur*, 157.
31. Plessner, *Macht und menschliche Natur*, 157.
32. Georg Misch, "Von den Gestaltungen der Persönlichkeit," in Wilhelm Dilthey, ed., *Weltanschauung Philosophie und Religion in Darstellungen* (Berlin: Reichl & Co, 1911), 82.
33. Georg Misch, *Der Weg in die Philosophie* (Leipzig: Teubner, 1926); which was published in a substantially altered and revised English translation as *The Dawn of Philosophy: A Philosophical Primer* (Cambridge: Harvard University Press, 1951).
34. Misch, *Der Weg in die Philosophie*, 29; *The Dawn of Philosophy*, 39.
35. Misch, *Der Weg in die Philosophie*, 13; *The Dawn of Philosophy*, 1, 12.
36. Misch, *The Dawn of Philosophy*, 39.
37. Misch, *Der Weg in die Philosophie*, 14; *The Dawn of Philosophy*, 16.
38. Misch, *The Dawn of Philosophy*, 25.
39. Ibid., 25.
40. Georg Wilhelm Friedrich Hegel, *Lectures on the History of Philosophy: The Lectures of 1825–1826* (Berkeley: University of California Press, 1990), 9–10.
41. Georg Wilhelm Friedrich Hegel, *Lectures on the Philosophy of World History: Introduction, Reason in History* (Cambridge: Cambridge University Press, 1975), 97.
42. Misch, *The Dawn of Philosophy*, 44.
43. "Die Vernunftgestalt der Persönlichkeit ist sowohl chinesisches als griechisches und modern-europäisches Aufklärungsgut." Misch, "Von den Gestaltungen der Persönlichkeit," 95.
44. On hermeneutical Enlightenment, and the relation between Chinese and European Enlightenments, see Eric S. Nelson, "Leibniz and China: Religion, Hermeneutics, and Enlightenment," *Religion in the Age of Enlightenment* 1 (2009): 277–300.
45. Misch, *The Dawn of Philosophy*, 172.
46. Ibid., 184–87.
47. Misch, *Lebensphilosophie und Phänomenologie*, 14.
48. Misch, *The Dawn of Philosophy*, 39.
49. Misch, *Lebensphilosophie und Phänomenologie*, 47.
50. Hegel, *Lectures on the Philosophy of World History*, 97.
51. Ibid., 54.

52. For instance, on the significance of Arabic biography, see Georg Misch, *Geschichte de Autobiographie* (Bern and Frankfurt: A. Francke und Gerhard Schultke-Bulmke, 1949–69), III, 2, 980.
53. Misch, *The Dawn of Philosophy*, 7.
54. Compare Misch, *Lebensphilosophie und Phänomenologie*, 317.
55. On the problematic reduction of the *Zhuangzi* to unitary positions such as mysticism and skepticism, see Eric S. Nelson, "Questioning Dao: Skepticism, Mysticism, and Ethics in the *Zhuangzi*," *International Journal of the Asian Philosophical Association* 1, no. 1 (2008): 5–19.
56. Compare Misch, *Der Weg in die Philosophie*, 221, 229; Misch, *The Dawn of Philosophy*, 202.
57. Misch, *Der Weg in die Philosophie*, 221.
58. Misch, *Lebensphilosophie und Phänomenologie*, 89–90.
59. Ma, *Heidegger on East-West Dialogue*.
60. Plessner, *Macht und menschliche Natur*, 162–63.
61. Ibid., 164, 185.

CHUNG-YING CHENG

DECONSTRUCTION AND *DIFFÉRANCE*: ONTO-RETURN AND EMERGENCE IN A DAOIST INTERPRETATION OF DERRIDA

Abstract

In inquiring into the nature of deconstruction in Derrida we see that it hides an opposite aspect of onto-generative emergence as stated in the wording of the *Yijing*. What is hidden is the movement of difference-making and generalizing repetition by way of certain presupposed reality. In examining Derrida's notion "*différance*" (difference), his contrast between an ontology of presence and a philosophy of absence, in explaining the origin of meaning à la de Saussure, has transformed into the polaristic structure of all differences, whether it be in language or in things. The Saussurian distinction between the signifier and the signified no doubt reflects this polarity but not reveals an underlying transcendent-immanent principle called "*différance*," or, the *dao* 道 in Chinese philosophy. This "difference" in language leads to ramification of meanings which could be self-deconstructive such as the extended use of the word "spirit" demonstrates.

I. The Question of "Spirit"

In Derrida's book *Of Spirit*, Derrida demonstrated how Heidegger extended the German word *Geist* (usually translated as "spirit") beyond the established meanings of the Greek word *plasma* and the Latin word *spiritus*.[1] According to Derrida, Heidegger's use of the German word *Geist* and its adjective forms (*geistlich*, as distinct from *geistig*), encompasses a field of meanings that includes ghost, flame, and ashes.[2] This usage occurred during the twenty-five-year period after Heidegger's work *Being and Time*, first published in 1927, where he stated that terms such as *Geist* need to be avoided and used it suspiciously only within quotation marks. This means that Heidegger intentionally and explicitly avoided the word "Geist" because of its

---

CHUNG-YING CHENG, Professor, Department of Philosophy, University of Hawaii at Manoa; Visiting Zhiyuan Chair Professor, College of Humanities and Arts, Shanghai Jiaotong University. Specialties: Confucianism and Neo-Confucianism, hermeneutics/onto-hermeneutics, philosophy of language. E-mail: ccheng@hawaii.edu

Journal of Chinese Philosophy, Supplement to Volume 39 (2012) 31–50
© 2013 Journal of Chinese Philosophy

abstractness and remoteness from *Dasein*. But then, only a few years later, in association with the rise to power of National Socialism, he reintroduced it (and its adjectival forms) as a term for speaking about abstract concepts such as historicity, world and people (*Volk*) in the context of practical political affairs and even university legislation.

As a matter of fact, Heidegger came to speak of a "spiritual world" in culture and civilization during his time as rector of the University of Freiburg. In his 1933 "Rectorial Address," he even speaks of sprit as the essence of Being (*Sein*), which is of course the guiding word and question of his thinking: "spirit is the full power given to the potencies of entities as such and in totality."[3] Even after the Second World War, evoking his own language in the 1930's, Heidegger spoke of "spirit" in 1953[4] in the context of fire, flame, burning and conflagration. This illustrates how Heidegger's *Sein* came to overcome and vanquish his earlier conception of *Dasein*.

"Spirit" is not inevitably a bad word. It has an affirmative meaning in classical German religious, philosophical, and poetic discourses and can even have a critical significance. Nonetheless, the German word "Geist" became associated with fire, burning, and ash in the twentieth century. It became identified with the heinous crimes of annihilation and Holocaust committed by National Socialist Germany.[5]

Derrida is engaged in a repletion and differentiation of the work of deconstruction in *Of Spirit*, confronting the word-concept of spirit as it is employed by Heidegger as well as by Hitler and the wider discourse of National Socialism.[6] A reader can appreciate how Derrida's thinking wanders and moves in this text from small and infinitesimal differences to their more extensive implications and resonances. Accordingly, in this work, to deconstruct is in fact to reveal the true face and range of meanings of the original term and concept in order to show how its uses could be considered to be unjustified and even inconsistent through the very repetition of the word. Instead of presupposing the constant identity of meaning, Derrida articulates a kind of difference in repetition. This deconstructive strategy shows how the word is at its core unstable and consequently it reveals how language is indeterminate and non-determinable.

II. Deconstruction and *Jingshen* 精神

One may well pose the question of why deconstruction—the formulation of which is related to the task of "destruction" or "dismantling" (*Destruktion*) developed in Heidegger's *Being and Time*—is needed or necessary. The answer might be that deconstruction is employed to reconsider and restore the use and significance of a term in and through its repetition and differentiation. The relentless repetition of a word leads to its multiplication and inflation as it becomes pregnant with inconsistency, self-contradiction, and performative incoherence in practice.

Derrida's strategy, related to Heidegger's hermeneutics of thinking what is *unthought* in a thinker, is to explicate the implicit and articulate the significance that remains hidden in a word. Derrida came to see the promise and the questionable aporia of repetition, as the use and inscription of a concept is bound up with a wider range of contexts and social situations. Thus, it is by deconstruction that we re-encounter the word and its meanings, which in its simplicity and freshness cannot even be defined as Heidegger's *unthought.* Our question is accordingly how repetition operates through digression and how this involves the difficulties and the potential impossibility of understanding.

Any discussion of deconstruction cannot ignore how concepts are both differing and deferring. There are no words or no concepts without difference and this is what Derrida describes as *différance*, which means that differing is deferring.[7] Given this Derridian model of analysis of a discourse or text, we can come to see how difference cannot become another form of identity. It must be itself deconstructable as deferred and differing from itself.

In this context, I wish to offer a new reflection on the repetition spoken of by Derrida by examining the metaphorical extension of a term in its referential and semantic dimensions as we use it in contexts other than those where we have used it before. We may not necessarily harbor the purposes of deconstruction or want to hypothesize that it must be forthcoming; much less insist that deconstruction must always be at work and thus a matter of repetition.

In the first place, we can analyze a word that is similar to the German word *Geist* in a Chinese context with the intention of showing how a linguistic-semantic extension can suggest an alternative process of the formation of concepts that would challenge and resist the movement of deconstruction.

There is a Chinese expression *jingshen* 精神 that roughly corresponds to the German word *Geist*. It is generally used to translate the German word and is thus translated as "*Geist.*" In writing, *jingshen* is composed of two words: *jing* 精 and *shen* 神. These two refer respectively to the "quintessence of life" and "spirit of creative change" that is seen as the essence of the life force in a grain of rice or in the whole cosmos. As such, they are also seen in the seeds of the human person (ova or semen) and by extension in the spiritual or divine powers that make the vital seeds of life possible. In fact, we may say that *jing* is the visible part of the whole unity that is called *jingshen*, whereas *shen* is the invisible part of the whole unity that makes life possible. Each separate word carries its own respective meaning and reference; yet together they refer to a unity of life that encompasses both a visible part and an invisible part that supports the visible parts. This doubling is what makes life possible and sustainable, and it distinguishes living from non-living material beings. The latter beings are substantial objects that have no power or spirit that would allow them to actively become and creatively thrive.

When the word "*jingshen*" was first used in the *Lieyukou* 〈列御寇〉 chapter of the *Zhuangzi* 《莊子》, it says, "That ultimate man (*zhiren* 至人), his spirit (*jingshen*) returns to the 'No Beginning' and rests silently in the land of nowhere" (*Bi zhiren zhe, gui jingshen hu wushi er gan ming hu wuheyou zhi xiang.* 彼至人者，归精神乎无始而甘冥乎无何有之乡。). "Sprit" in this context has a definitive connotation based on the unification of the life-elements *jing* and *shen*, one of which is *yin* 陰 and the other *yang* 陽. However, we have to be aware that this unification of the life elements is based on an implicit concept that is conveyed by the word "*qi* 气." *Qi* is the principle of vitality that makes the motion, formation, and transformation of all things possible. It is the principle of change from the visible to the invisible and from the invisible to the visible. *Qi* is thus considered the principle of the continuum of life activities that is the root and source of the material form that embodies both *jing* and *shen*. Thus the *Yizhuan* 《易传》 speaks of *jingqi* 精气, and we may also further speak of *shenqi* 神气. Articulated together as a theory, we can speak of *jing qi shen* 精气神. This understanding of *qi* is necessary for medical purposes and perhaps could be said to give rise to a biomedical understanding of human life as we find in the *Huangdi Neijing* 《皇帝内经》. This understanding of *qi* also implies a cosmic picture that gives rise to Chinese medicine and harkens back to the onto-cosmology of the *Yijing* 《易經》 that I have described in other writings.[8]

By tracing of the term *jingshen* we can see the combined meaning of *jing* and *shen* which reflects an invisible life as well as the purpose of life in an individual, a community, a people, a nation, a world, and even the cosmos. Indeed, *qi* can be employed to indirectly clarify the senses of *plasma* in Greek and *spiritus* in Latin. Of course, we cannot immediately identify "*qi*" with "*plasma*" or "*spiritus*." But we can understand that the latter two concepts can be interpreted in the context of *qi* as referring to the natural phenomenon of *plasma* or *spiritus*. We can extend and accordingly retrace a model of transformation from *qi* to *jingqi* 精气, from *qing* 精 to *shengqi* 神气 and to *shen* 神. We can see how the word *jingshen* in Chinese can be applied to concrete terms of larger and broader scope such as those of community, state, world, and cosmos. It can also be applied to abstract qualities and disciplines such as ethics and political philosophy so that we can appropriately speak of the" spirit" of ethics or the "spirit" of *ren* 仁 and *yi* 義. This amounts to making *ren* and *yi* a part of the *qi* located in a person or a people.

At this point we can perceive two opposite directions in which the human mind moves: (i) the direction which would lead to the emergence of a new scope of the use of terms by means of linguistic conjunction and conceptual generalization, as conceived by Peirce; and (ii) the direction in which the mind reflects on its originating actions that are strained by being overextended, and which are not empirically or perceptually established, or which result in a hidden or manifest inconsistency and incoherence, or the lack of self-criticism, logical blindness or being ensnared in logical paradoxes. It should be noted that the direction of overreaching can lead to such logical paradoxes or contradictions that could be logically discoverable or discovered as a result of textual explication or deliberate annotation on the basis of some linguistic trace. The first case is the Aristotelian construction of concepts lies in contrast with the Humean reduction to impressions; whereas the last case is where Derridean deconstruction lies in contrast with the Russell's analysis of Fregean class logic. As we can see, it is not necessary that the mind must take the second route in the direction of deconstruction and onto-return or return to an ontological root insofar as it can find a range and scope of experiences that offer insights into one's intellectual vitality, strength, and potentiality. Of course, this is not to say that we cannot restrict *jingshen* to merely the present healthy state revealed in the face of a human person; instead we may see its likeness in the devotion and pursuit of the solidarity of people toward a worthwhile goal. It is in this sense that we can speak of the Christian spirit of *agape*, the Moist spirit of *jianai* 兼爱, the Daoist spirit of following *ziran* 自然 (naturalness and spontaneity), or the Confucian spirit of *renyi* 仁义 (benevolence and righteousness).

It is necessary to practice deconstruction in response to false idolatry, misused faith, or empty knowledge. We no doubt need a destructive or deconstructive critique in Heidegger's sense in *Being and Time* in order to go back to the originating sources of our experience; yet this cannot exclude experience or the need for reconstruction and reinvention. In this regard, I believe that Derrida is insightful and correct in his critique of Heidegger's generalization of the term and concept *Geist* and its problematic social-political connotations.

In the Chinese language, *jingshen*, as a combination of two words, may suggest that the condition for the extension of *jing* and *shen* is best accomplished by realizing the reality in which the conjunction of the two words is fully justified. This is no doubt a conceptual insight that is prompted by an insight into a reality that emerges from within an originating situation. We must experience the force and function of Daoism, Moism, and Confucianism—and, for that matter, Christianity—before we can speak of spirit or *jingshen*. We must therefore recognize a creative reality that is regenerative and also onto-generative in such a way that the new formation of unities and wholes is always possible and can be practically experienced. The onto-generativity of the emergence of novelty from the creative changes of reality becomes or should be regarded as the very nature of the things that we confront and encounter in the world.

III. Four Questions

At this juncture it is only fair to consider several questions arising from Derrida's deconstructive strategy:

1. Derrida is typically understood as an anti-metaphysical thinker and my approach in this article appears to oppose this by taking his thought in a more metaphysical direction. Is my reading then reproducing the logo-centrism and metaphysical thinking that deconstruction is an attempt to contest?

My answer to this question is explicit: Derrida is bound by his limited sense or conception of metaphysics as either the first principle of being of beings which he shared with Heidegger. They both strongly reject overly abstract essentialist notions of beings, Being, or the being of beings. They do not recognize that the metaphysical is what generates the non-metaphysical or the onto-generative basis of both metaphysics and non-metaphysics that I explain and illuminate as *benti* 本体. It is in this sense that I wrote my article entitled "Metaphysics of No Metaphysics."[9] The point is that the metaphysical is not separable from the non-metaphysical, the originating from the non-originating, the invisible from the visible, the present from the non-present, the *you* 有 from the *wu* 無, the *yang* from the *yin*, the transparent from the opaque. For this reason, the *dao* or *dao*–symbol in Daoism has three basic meanings that require both vision and feeling to be understood; namely the visible, the invisible, and their intertwining. It is never simply one or two but one and many together. It is thus best described as the change (*yi* 易) that is ever changing or productive of different things and admits no identity without difference and for that matter no identity of identity.

2. Perhaps *dao*-centrism is another form of or analogous to logo-centrism?

From the above we see how *dao* should be conceived. It is to be conceived for what it is and at the same time for what it is not. Hence, you do not have something called *dao*-centrism. A better image is *dao*-dispersion. But then this should make our logo-centric thinking relatively meaningful and important: we have to identify things and we have to know and we have to act and practice by using our scheme of strategies of things and thus distinguish among difference things. What is wrong about logo-centrism is that it only sees logo-centrism without seeing it from a non-logo-centric point of view. If we really understand what Laozi says about "*Dao fa ziran* 道法自然" (the *dao* follows what comes out of its own) and what Zhuangzi says about "*Dao tongyuyi* 道通于一" (the *dao* penetrates oneness), one can see why one must not be bound by one's schema of language or ideas and yet still use them to achieve freedom of mind and spirit at the same time.

3. Derrida argues that there is no origin to which to return and that we are in the endless circulation of the text, of differing and deferring. How then do I address this question of the lack of pure origins in Derrida; that possibility is based only in impossibility, and the present in a past that never was?

We are indeed in an endless circulation of the text that results from differing and deferring. But we may also see something deeper or higher that emerges from the circulation which does not need to end anywhere teleological or become complete. This is what the hermeneutical circle suggests to us. I take one step further than Heidegger and Gadamer by regarding this circle as onto-generative and thus speak of the "onto-generative hermeneutic circle" (*benti chuanshi xunhuan* 本体诠释循环). Besides we have to admit we need to make our own decisions as we are in the middle of indecision of the *dao*. We have our life to live and our action to act and adventure to venture. Nothing forbids us to creatively raise our questions and then answer our questions because what we do to explicate a text is to go beyond it and realize the *dao*. This is the idea of Dai Zhen 戴震:"*Shizi, ranhou zhidao.* 识字, 然后知道。"[10] Although there is no one real origin to return to in a text, we could speak of an origin which is not an origin precisely because it is no origin. This origin of no origin cannot be identified or described, as the opening lines of the *Daodejing* 《道德經》 state, but it is what gives us the discourse or communication as well as their disruptions and breakdowns. I refer to this origin/non-origin as the creative void or simply creativity which is the *dao* in a different guise. To move or step back to it is to have an onto-return or a return to what is yet to be formed and just forming or just un-forming or transforming. We may otherwise call it "indeterminate return."

We might also observe that we may have to appeal to some original experience or facticity to search for new perspective or new approach for correcting, improving, or changing our earlier perspective or approach in describing or presenting a position or model. Or simply see this: we could naturally wander into new perspectives and cannot get the original perspective back. We may wish to draw a better circle and yet we may end in drawing a worse one. As a matter of experiencing time, we could be carried away by time so that we cannot find any position to return much less to the "original position." For anyone who knows the painting style of the modern French artist Henri Matisse, many of his impressionist paintings often have versions in doubles or triplets which cannot be seen as equal identities, but they are rather similes with differences arising from different perspectives or different degrees of abstraction of an initial model or pose. One cannot but feel that the difference/*différance* of Derrida finds its most vivid illustration in the drawings of Matisse.

4. Another Derridean moment that I touch on briefly in this article is the theme of generosity. How then do I see the roles of generosity and hospitality in Derrida, which are crucial to his later ethical writings, often with reference to the works of Levinas?

I see Derrida as following three unannounced traditions that need not be deconstructed but rather are to be constructed in order to have a better understanding of Derrida's works. The first tradition is the Cartesian tradition of making clear distinctions whenever necessary and these distinctions must lead to difference by way of deferring. The second tradition is the Levinasian tradition that stressed the impossibility of understanding the other as the other should be. In fact, the essence of difference is otherness, and this presupposes my point about onto-generativity: to be generative is to generate differences and substantively other things. If we do not understand them, even if we know them, there is no way for us to relate to them. Hence, there is the third tradition for Derrida to rely upon; namely the tradition of loving your people or others through hospitality and generosity, trust, and responsibility. This is a great principle for both religion and ethics, and this is a principle that will bring no harm. I believe that Derrida eventually came to take this third principle as the final principle of his philosophy in his later ethical writings.

IV. "Spirit" and *Benti*

In the above spirit of clarification we arrive at another term used in Chinese philosophy. It likewise manifests onto-generativity and its emergent openness in our experiences of reality when we come to experience and use the term as a combination of two fundamental experiences of changing reality; namely the experience of *ben* 本 and the experience of *ti* 体. As each word discloses, *benti* 本體 has its originating experiences (i) in our encounter with how a plant grows from the soil (*ben*) and (ii) how we experience our own body and how our body embodies and perhaps "bodies forth" our life activities (*ti*). With these two words, we come to the wise combination and irreducible union of the word *benti*.[11] *Benti* would refer to an originating constitution of a thing or human being from a source and origin that incorporates all the relevant functions of an originated worldly body such as the human body. It can feel, it can sense, and it can think and perform actions. It is so conceived therefore as the dynamic living substance of a person or anything that can be portrayed as a basic coherent organism of living functioning parts. By the same token, we can speak of the *benti* of any developing *reality* that can be perceived to have interconnecting parts and that consequently forms a whole organism of life and spirit which can be said to be traced to a soil and root that is its originating source or beginning of such a life-reality. Hence, we can speak of cosmos as a cosmic or cosmological *yuzhou benti* 宇宙本体, or of the pervasive life across all things sharing life, as *shengming benti* 生命本体.

It should be noted that when Chinese philosophers come to speak of the *benti* operative in all levels of being, they are not just referring to being as such or being in itself. They are in effect referring to being as forming a body from an embodying origin. This means that we must not ignore the process from which the originating origin would develop or grow into the body and the way of this development journeys on a way of creative transformation and consolidation. The way of development is no doubt most important; since it is responsible for the origin to be developed and constituted and even sustained with continuing support and provisions. Here we speak of the *dao* 道 as a way of development from an originating beginning in the formation of the concrete and coherent systematic wholeness of a body. This means the coming into existence of things by way of their internal organization and external interaction with other originating bodies.

Of course, we can speak of *dao* as the *dao* of this or that activity with this or that goal. But when we speak of the *dao*, we are actually speaking of the world or cosmos as a whole body that is open to further transformations. It is composed of interconnected parts or constituents that have had their individual experiences of being and non-being. In this sense, when we speak of ontology against the background of Chinese *benti*, we do not mean the ontology of being (*Sein*) but the ontology of *benti*, which presupposes the formation of things by the *dao* and in which *dao* is regarded as the universal and ultimate source of change and transformation. We also must bear in mind here that *dao* is itself an extension of the way which we walk toward a destination or the way in which any other living bodies enjoy a living state. The word *dao* is metaphorical and symbolic in nature. Insofar as it does not contain a definitive reference, it is not a name of a thing.

Based on what we have said above, the world can be seen as composed of things originating from a creative source and forming realities by way of the sustaining *dao*. In this sense, *dao* is both the source and the body, albeit an indefinite one. The substances given rise to the *dao* can be said to be the functioning (*yong* 用) of the *dao* insofar as it is generative and productive of things. Therefore, we have a reality that is to be described as *benti*, which is made possible by the *dao* and has a power of creativity leading to the emergence of the human being as an entity of onto-generativity and understanding.

V. Dao and *Différance*

Apart from the very idea of deconstruction, there is no doubt that "difference" is the most important notion in Derrida's critique of the semiology of language and his challenge to traditional European metaphysical thinking. However, when we speak of "*différance*," we may easily misrepresent or misconstrue Derrida's intended meaning of the term. Derrida insists after all on many occasions that "difference" is neither a concept nor a word. For example, he remarked in his essay on "difference" that "*Différance* is neither a *word* nor a *concept*." Then he explains what "difference" signifies:

> In it, however, we shall see the juncture—rather than the summation —of what has been most decisively inscribed in the thought of what is conveniently called our "epoch": the difference of forces in Nietzsche, Saussure's principle of semiological difference, differing as the possibility of (neurone) facilitation, impression and delayed effect in Freud, difference as the irreducibility of the trace of the other in Levinas, and the ontic-ontological difference in Heidegger.[12]

From this it is clear that "*différance*" is a cluster of encounters and ideas that are manifested in various philosophical systems, but it is not dominated by any one single definition or principle. Derrida himself considered "*différance*" a "*strategic* note or connection."[13] It cannot be captured in any conceptual scheme. This immediately reminds one of Laozi's beginning statement in the *Daodejing*: "The *dao* that can be spoken is not the constant *dao*; the name which can be named is not the constant name." As we shall see, "difference" perhaps enjoys the same status as the *dao*. One speaks of it for the purpose of understanding its non-speakability; one names it for the purpose of understanding its unnameability. This leads us to Derrida's own observation that "difference" is a word which does not exist in ordinary language. It had to be invented by him for the purpose of indicating the non-wordness of the word "*différance.*"

Derrida gives his own reasons for inventing the word, or the non-word, "difference." He points out the Latin verb *differre* and the French verb *differer* (hence the English verb, "to differ") has two meanings: (i) it can mean making a difference; (ii) it also can mean the action of postponing, which leads to the meaning of "deferring" and "delaying." One may therefore say that "differ" means to make a difference in space as well as to make a difference in time. Derrida thematized this temporal difference-making as temporalizing. He claims:

> "To differ" in this sense is to temporalize, to resort, consciously or unconsciously, to the temporal and temporalizing mediation of a detour that suspends the accomplishment or fulfillment of "desire" or "will," or carries desire or will out in a way that annuls or tempers their effect.[14]

Derrida interprets temporalization as distancing and differing in time in analogy with the distancing and differing in space. Derrida suggests for that reason that what is involved is "space becoming temporal and time becoming spatial."[15] "To differ," therefore, is the very basic action of the primordial constitution of space and time. Since there is no single word in present usage to suggest the combined meanings of the Latin *differre*, and since both the English and French words for "difference" only reflect the abstract quality of differentiation or non-identity without any suggestion of either spatial or temporal distancing and delaying, Derrida coined the word *différance* (with an "a" substituting for the "e" in "difference") in order to indicate the original meaning of *differre*. In fact, he coins the word "difference" to suggest a delay of the action of differing together with the promised difference deferring produces: that is, to suggest a deference in difference and a difference in deference. In this way he would neutralize the action of differing and yet, at the same time, encompass the result of effected difference. Derrida would thereby produce a complex system of both the presence and non-presence of meaning and non-meaning, of being and nothingness. He thus concludes:

> Within a conceptual system and in terms of classical requirements, *différance* could be said to designate the productive and primordial constituting causality, the process of scission and division whose differing and differences would be the constituted products or effects. But while bringing us closer to the infinitive and active core of differing, "*différance*" with an *a* neutralizes what the infinitive denotes as simply active, in the same way that "parlance" does not

signify the simple fact of speaking, of speaking to or being spoken to. Nor is resonance the act of resonating.[16]

It is clear that in this intended sense Derrida writes "difference" as indicative of an indeterminate state of neutrality between activity and passivity. Yet it does not exclude but, in fact, encompasses and comprehends both passivity and activity. Derrida suggests that "difference" in this sense works in language formation, meaning formation, world formation, as well as in thought formation. Derrida regards "difference" as "an operation which is not an operation"; and hence, it is a passion which is not a passion, an action which is not an action, a word which is not a word, a notion which is not a notion. One may indeed ask how this non-word and non-notion, "difference," stands ontologically or metaphysically. With regard to this question no single metaphysical statement can be made, because any single metaphysical statement delimits and inappropriately limits the "notion" of "*différance*." Again, this is very similar to the situation of understanding the *dao* in the *Daodejing*: no single metaphysical statement can capture *dao*. *Dao* is the ever deferring and difference-making activity that defies, escapes, and challenges description and systematization. In light of this, we may suggest that "difference" is itself a result of the play of "*différance*," of presence and non-presence.

With all this said, we may raise the following question: how do we adequately understand "*différance*' as a philosophical 'notion'"? Could we reconstruct or interpret this "notion" in such a way so that it can be deconstructed or de-interpreted? Methodologically speaking, if we have an important and suggestive intuition emerging in our thinking, how do we truly grasp it until we are able to both interpret and de-interpret it, to both construct and deconstruct it?[17]

Derrida both interprets, as he himself admits, and de-interprets "difference." It can refer to "the whole complex of meanings at once," as "difference" is "immediately and irreducibly multivalent."[18] Therefore, it seems necessary to ask what complex of meanings and what multivalent structures "difference" represents. The need for construction and interpretation, even for the purpose of deconstruction and de-interpretation, becomes evident and necessary. Since there is no place where Derrida gives a systematic interpretation of "difference,"[19] and since his "notion" of "difference" intuitively suggests a similarity to the Daoistic notion of the *dao*, we are justified in developing a Daoistic interpretation or reconstruction of "difference" in light of the Daoist philosophy of the *dao*. In the following, we will unfold our interpretation on two levels: (i) the metaphysical level and (ii) the linguistic level. We will also explore the interface and the interrelation between these two levels. Although the *dao* that can be said is not the constant *dao*,

dao nevertheless is saying or speaking. So there always remains the important question of how the *dao* (language) that can be said comes into being from the *dao* (non-language) that cannot be said.

As "difference" is a complex "notion," we must start our Daoistic interpretation by pointing out at least three aspects of "difference" in light of three aspects of the *dao*. The first aspect of the *dao* is what Laozi refers to as *wu*. *Wu* ("nothingness" or "void") is said to give rise to *you*, "being" or "reality."

It is said that the ten thousand things in the world are generated from reality, and reality is generated from the void (*wu*). Therefore it can be seen that *wu* is full of generative power. It implies a process of creative movement. Indeed, *wu* is the same as the *dao* because it is the *dao* which gives rise to oneness, and one gives rise to two, two to three, and three to the ten thousand things.[20] In this sense, we should interpret it not simply as "void," but as the "creative void." *Wu* is not simply the origin of *you*, but it coexists in *you* and becomes the dynamic and functional aspect of *you*. That is why Laozi said that vehicles, utensils, and rooms are *useful* simply because they contain *wu*. To be useful in this sense is to be able to function in relation to other things, and to become significantly involved and valued with other things. In this sense, *wu* defines the real identity of a thing in the world in reference to other things.[21]

As the creative void, *wu* is inexhaustible and constantly productive, leading to a manifold of things not dominated by any single power or controlled by any single purpose. This is the virtue referred to as the "profound virtue" of "giving birth without procession," "doing things without domineering," and "growing things without controlling."[22] In so far as all things have their own inner identity and yet are harmoniously related, there is creative voidness of the *dao*. It is also appropriate to note in this connection that to say the *dao* does not do anything and yet everything becomes done.[23] That is to say, *dao* is the creative void which creates things by not asserting, and hence voiding, itself.[24] It is a statement simply saying that the *dao* does not act in the same way that things act. Hence, the *dao* makes the generation of things possible. This reflects the status of a creative unity of transcendence and immanence in the *dao*.

The transcendent aspect of *wu* is the, the immanent aspect is the *you*; the creative unity is the constant arising of *you* from the *wu*. In this sense, of course, not only does *dao* do nothing, it is revealed in any state of being which involves *wu*. For example, it is shapeless, soundless, tasteless, orderless.[25] In the case of human beings, *dao* is also revealed in any state of "*wu*-" understood as *lessness*, such as speechlessness (*wuyan* 無言), desirelessness (*wuyu* 無欲) in Laozi; and mindlessness (*wuxin* 無心) and selflessness (*wuji* 無己) in Zhuangzi. This shows how creative voidness is concretely revealed in individual things, and therefore how it forms the essential quality of things insofar as things are seen in their generativity. From this understanding of the *dao* as the creative void, we see that the Derridian "difference" in at least one of its modalities can be categorized as the creative void of the *dao*. This is because "difference" makes differences in time and space possible, and yet it is not itself one of the differences. Consequently, it cannot be categorized in terms of things which embody differences. If things can be known as or in their presence (being or ousia), then "*différance*" can only be known as the voiding of presence, as absence (*wu*). Its production of differences is like the production of reality from *wu*. Thus, it plays the role of the creative voiding of the *dao*. It also shares with the dao its transcendence–immanence characteristic insofar as it cannot but produce differences in time and space by deferring identify itself as a difference. In this sense, Derrida speaks of "difference" as not being a sign representing a presence as determined by a presence or constituted by a system of signs such as language. That is to say, as the creative void, "difference" is not "difference," in the same spirit that the constant *dao* as *wu* is not a thing or anything.

The following statement particularly illustrates the Derridian understanding of "difference" as the dao insofar as the *wu* aspect of the *dao* is concerned:

> In this way we question the authority of presence or its simple symmetrical contrary, absence or lack. We thus interrogate the limit that has always constrained us, that always constrains us—We who inhabit a language and a system of being in general as presence or absence, in the categories of being or beingness (*ousia*).[26]

We can see clearly in this passage a Daoist insight into the non-categorizable and language-transcendent nature of the *dao*. But we must also note that for both Derrida and Laozi, this non-categorizable and language-transcendent nature of the *dao* does not prevent the *dao* from being constantly creative of things, and for that matter, generative of language as well. That is how our system of language and thought, which is based upon distinctions of categories and differences of concepts, comes into being.

In Laozi, there is a statement to the effect that "being" (*you*) and "nothing" (*wu*) mutually generate each other.[27] Frequently the question arises how one can reconcile this statement with the statement on the generation of *you* from *wu* quoted earlier. Without going into greater detail here, it can be simply said that, as the creative void, *wu* is the *dao* and therefore always generates *you*. But when *wu* is seen in a relation of polarity with *you*, then *you* and *wu* can function together as opposite complements to each other. Namely, *you* is the *wu* of *wu*, and *wu* is the *you* of *wu* or *wu* of *you*. By the principle of creative voiding, *you* and *wu* accordingly generate each other. This can be further explained in terms of the Derridian notions of differing and deferring. *You* and *wu* mutually differ and defer to each other; hence, these two give rise to a system of differences. On the other hand, deferring and differing are one in "*différance*," just as *you* and *wu* are one in being creative in the *dao*. Derrida's notion of "difference" is suggestive of the inclusion of two dimensions of the *dao*: the differing *you* and the deferring *wu*. Hence, apart from being illuminated by the notion of *dao*, it respectively illuminates the *dao*.

A second important aspect of the *dao* is its self-transformation (*zihua* 自化). Laozi mentions that the ten thousand things will transform by themselves.[28] In the *Zhuangzi*, the notion of self-transformation is explained in terms of a spontaneous succession of things in nature without any domination from any inside or outside forces. He says:

> Day and night succeed each other; no one knows how it began. It is naturally so. As to how it started, one may say that without others there is no I; without myself nothing can be understood. Yet no one knows what makes it so. If there are any two controlling forces, it can never be seen.[29]

The important point about self-transformation of the *dao* is that no one should force one's concepts, or so called knowledge, into an explanation of the happenings of nature. Instead, one should recognize the movement of things is naturally inherent in things and acknowledge them with a creative receptiveness and broad-mindedness. In this manner, one can be said to have a true understanding by illumination (*yiming* 以明). Actually, self-transformation can be further understood in terms of the *Zhuangzi*'s statement:

> One moment there is birth, another moment there is death; one moment there is death, another moment there is birth. One moment some-thing is permissable, another moment it is not permissable; one moment something is not permissable, another moment it is permissable. Because there is right, there is wrong; because there is wrong, there is right.[30]

In this passage, it can be seen that self-transformation is the transformation of one thing in the context of the transformation of all things. It is relating one perspective to another. This relating is inevitable because it is the nature of the *dao* that all things are related in permutation and contrast in order to be things. On this basis, we can also see that the things are not defined simply by their simple presence, but instead by the contrast of presence with absence, which is not simply present. In more precise terms, things are defined by their transformational relationship in terms of presence and absence and their interdependent contrast.

This play of presence and absence naturally leads to Derrida's criticism of the so-called "metaphysics of presence" or ontology of beings. Not only are things not solely defined by the presence of being or beingness, but in language symbols are not given by reference to the presence of things alone. Both things and language symbols must acquire their identity—whether in being or in meaning—by implicit reference to absence or non-present relational transformations. But this very idea of self-transformation belongs deeply to the "notion" of "*différance.*" "*Différance*" has to produce a system of differences. One should not ignore that this involves an acknowledgement of transitional processes or a natural movement of the differing/deferring activities of "*différance.*"

Derrida does not want to see "difference" in the sense of an ontological being, such as God, which gives rise to an order of things by dicta. The concept of causality has no place in his understanding of "difference" as temporalization or as spacing. It must be understood as a self-transformative movement that both preserves its own identity and gives rise to something different from itself. In one place, Derrida did suggest that this process of difference-giving is a process of "scission and division"; even in this case, however, we cannot forget that "difference" does not lose its own transcendent albeit immanent status; namely, its own identity as "*différance,*" the creative void. Perhaps this is why he introduced the Freudian concept of "trace" to indicate this self-transformational aspect of "*différance.*" The "trace" is always the deployment of the presence of the absence, namely "*différance,*" in a system of presences. One passage from Derrida speaks very well about the idea of self-transformation that intersects with the dao in the *Zhuangzi*:

> What differs? Who differs? What is *différance*? If we answer these questions even before examining them as questions, even before going back over them and questioning their form (even what seems to be most natural and necessary about them), we would fall below the level we have now reached. For if we accepted the form of the question in its own sense and syntax (What? What is? Who is?), we would have to admit that *différance* is derived, supervenient, controlled, and ordered from the starting point of a being-present, one capable of being something, a force, a state or power in the world, to which we could give all kinds of names: a what, or being-present as a subject, a who. In the latter case, notably, we would implicitly admit that the being-present (for example, as a self-present being or consciousness) would eventually result in differing: in delaying or in

diverting the fulfillment of a 'need' or 'desire,' or in differing from it–self. But in none of these cases would such a being-present be 'constituted' by this *différance*.[31]

"*Différance*," like *dao*, is neither subject nor object. It transforms by not-transforming and does not transform in its transforming; this is self-transformation. This leads to the third aspect of the *dao*: namely, the *dao* is capable of producing a system of different things which are internally related and which are mutually transforming. This is included in the concept of self-transformation.

Laozi has clearly stated that all different things come from the *dao*. In fact, different things are unlimited in their numbers, as reflected in the rich content and potentiality of the *dao*'s creativity. He also indicates that there is an underlying unity and harmony among all things if all things are seen as rooted in the *dao*. For Laozi, conflict and evil arise from losing sight of this underlying unity and harmony of things in the *dao*. Therefore, he advocates a going back to the *dao* as the origin.[32] For Zhuangzi, the multitude of things as produced from the *dao* is not to be lamented, but to be appreciated and enjoyed. In fact, from Zhuangzi's point of view, the world is a place in which one can wander and enjoy one's wandering because each thing has its own self-importance and self-identity; and yet they are in perpetual transformation from being to non-being and non-being to being. Every moment, therefore, is a creative occasion for making a difference, as well as a moment for relating and identifying. *Dao* cannot be separated from the world of things. It is inherent in every single part of the world.

One needs to point out an important feature of the things produced by the *dao*. They form a system of polarities: namely, a system of opposite complements, such as reflected in the concepts of yin and yang. Both Laozi and Zhuangzi have elaborated this polaristic aspect of things generated by the *dao*. Laozi has referred to being and non-being, difficult and easy, long and short, high and low, tone and a sound. In fact, all things are things because there are opposite things complementing them. The same principle applies to the *dao* itself: *dao* is opposite and yet complements all things. Similarly, things need *dao* to become a true totality of reality. Without understanding the polaristic structure of things and the process of the transformation of things, one will not understand a thing in itself. Zhuangzi also made this point in speaking of this and that, life and death, right and wrong, good and bad, agony and beauty, etc. Of course, he also pointed out that the *dao* of all things is united in oneness. The whole essay of *Qiwulun* is intended to elaborate the relativity of polarity among things and their consequent unity and equality in the self-transforming process of the *dao*.

VI. Conclusion

In inquiring into the nature of deconstruction in Derrida we see that it hides an aspect or a reveals an opposite aspect of onto-generative emergence in the wording of the *Yijing*. What is hidden is the movement of difference-making and generalizing repetition by way of some presupposed reality. In examining Derrida's notion of "*différance*," one cannot help but feel that his contrast between an ontology of presence and a philosophy of absence in explaining the origin of meaning à la de Saussure has transformed this insight into the polaristic structure of all differences, whether it be in language or in things. The Saussurian distinction between the signifier and the signified no doubt reflects this polarity. Unfortunately, de Saussure did not realize that this distinction revealed an underlying unity and an underlying process of a transcendent-immanent principle called "*différance*" or *dao*. "*Différance*," as the onto-generative force for a system of differences, which is found necessarily to give rise to a language that is always polaristic.

Although Derrida himself did not give sufficient attention to this polaristic structure of language that is a system of polaristic substructures, he does recognize the mutual interdependence of speech and language, speaking and writing, which are a necessary consequence of his understanding of "*différance*."[33] Hence, we can justifiably suggest that "difference" for Derrida also contains the dimension of polaristic interdependence among all other things generated from "*différance*."

With our discussion of the three aspects of the *dao* in Laozi and Zhuangzi, we can come to conclude that the *dao* presents the self-transformation of the creative void into a manifold of polarities of things. Similarly, with our discussion of relevant points of Derrida's "notion" of "*différance*," we may also suggest that "*différance*" can be interpreted as presenting the self-transformation of the creative void into a manifold of polarities, and therefore, as the *dao* understood in the Daoistic sense. This interpretation will not only establish a philosophical affinity between Daoist philosophy and Derridian thinking; it will also enable us to explain Derrida in a more systematic and perhaps even in a sense more metaphysical fashion. But to say this is not necessarily to ignore that each systematic and metaphysical formulation is one-sided and biased against the true understanding of the *dao*, or "*différance*," and therefore to be deconstructed to reveal a more appropriate insight into reality. It is clear that Daoist philosophy provides both constructive and deconstructive modalities for such insight-preserving and reality-disclosing thinking. This will be particularly true when we apply this understanding of "*différance*" in the context of this interpretation to the reconstruction and deconstruction of a language system or language as a phenomenon.

How language arises from our understanding of reality and comes to obstruct and obscure it, and how language should be deconstructed, transcended, and finally merged with the *dao* for restoring and refreshing our understanding of reality forms one of the most important topics for Laozi, Zhuangzi, and Derrida. Although I intended to deal with this vital side of Daoistic/Derridian philosophy, I have to *defer* this for another occasion to do so because of the shortage of time.

UNIVERSITY OF HAWAII AT MANOA
Honolulu, Hawaii

Endnotes

This is a substantially revised and expanded version of my earlier publication in Chung-ying Cheng, "A Taoist Interpretation of 'Difference' in Derrida," *Journal of Chinese Philosophy* 17, no. 1 (1990): 19–30. Professor Eric Nelson reviewed and thoroughly copyedited this new version, and Dr. Linyu Gu proofread and made further corrections. I thank their help and I am responsible for the possible errors remained.

1. Jacques Derrida, *Of Spirit: Heidegger and the Question* (Chicago: University of Chicago Press, 1987); originally published as *De l'esprit: Heidegger et la question* (Paris: Galilée, 1987).
2. Derrida, *Of Spirit*, ix.
3. Ibid., 67.
4. See Heidegger's work *Introduction to Metaphysics*, German original published in 1953, translation appeared in 1959.
5. Edith Wyschogrod has powerfully depicted this in *Spirit in Ashes: Hegel, Heidegger, and Man-Made Mass Death* (New Haven: Yale University Press, 1985).
6. Adolf Hitler, on February 1, 1933, addressing the German nation as Chancellor for the first time, *Volkischer Beobachter*, August 5, 1935, spoke of his government's "first and foremost duty to restore the unity of spirit and purpose of our *Volk*." This citation is from Richard Steigmann-Gall, *The Holy Reich: Nazi Conceptions of Christianity, 1919–1945* (Cambridge: Cambridge University Press, 2003), 115.
7. One may add the word "detach" to suggest a spatial image of separation that could result from deferring in time and even deferring in respective distance.
8. See my articles on the *Yijing* and onto-cosmology in Chung-ying Cheng "Philosophy of the *Yijing*: Insights into *Taiji* and *Dao* as Wisdom of Life," *Journal of Chinese Philosophy* 33, no. 3 (2006): 323–33; "Onto-Hermeneutical Vision and Analytic Discourse: Interpretation and Reconstruction in Chinese Philosophy" in *Two Roads to Wisdom? Chinese and Analytic Philosophical Traditions*, ed. Bo Mou (Chicago: Open Court, 2001), 87–129; "Inquiring into the Primary Model: *Yi-Jing* and Chinese Ontological Hermeneutics," in *Comparative Approaches to Chinese Philosophy*, ed. Bo Mou (Aldershot: Ashgate, 2003), 33–59.
9. See my article on the nature of Chinese metaphysics, "Chinese Metaphysics as Non-metaphysics: Confucian and Daoist Insights into the Nature of Reality," in *Understanding the Chinese Mind*, ed. Robert E. Allinson (Oxford University Press, 1989), 167–208.
10. Dai Zhen, Dai Zhen Quanshu 《戴震全书六》, 275–276.
11. This combination is first used by the Han Dynasty scholar Xun Shuang 荀爽 in his commentaries on the *Zhouyi* 《周易》. He used the term "*benti*" to describe the state

of re-assertion of vitality in connection with the fifth line of the 12th Hexagram "*Pi* 否" in the *Yijing* 《易經》. See *Sikuquanshu* 《四库全书: 周易郑康成注》.

12. Jacques Derrida's *Speech and Phenomena and Other Essays: On Husserl's Theory of Signs*, trans. David B. Allison (Evanston: Northwest University Press, 1973), 130. Also compare his approach to this question in *Positions*, trans. Alan Bass (Chicago, University of Chicago Press, 1981).
13. Derrida, *Speech and Phenomena*, 131.
14. Ibid., 136.
15. Ibid., 136.
16. Ibid., 137.
17. Ibid., 130.
18. Ibid., 137.
19. Although Derrida wrote much of "*différance*," making it the central "notion" of his philosophy, and even invented many new terms explaining "*différance*," the net result is that there is so much to be integrated into a whole unity in terms of metaphysical theory and/or a language theory. My interest in his "notion" of "*difference*" is to work out "*difference*" as a metaphysical strategy as well as a linguistic strategy, which to this extent is a means of understanding through indirect illumination even for the purpose of deconstruction itself.
20. Chapter 42.
21. Chapter 11.
22. Chapter 10.
23. Chapter 37.
24. The silk manuscripts of the Mawangdui 馬王堆 *De Dao Jing* texts provide the alternative statement that the Dao does not do everything and does not do anything for any purpose: *Dao chang wuwei er wuyiwei.* 道常無為而無以為。This still can be seen to give rise to the same result of having everything done because *wuwei.* ("doing nothing") always implies the movement of creative void which is the condition for the arising of all things.
25. Chapter 14.
26. Derrida, *Speech and Phenomena*, 139.
27. Chapter 2.
28. Chapter 37.
29. *Qiwulun* 〈齊物論〉.
30. *Qiwulun*.
31. Derrida, *Speech and Phenomena*, 140.
32. Chapter 16.
33. Derrida, *Speech and Phenomena*, 160.

WILLIAM DAY

ZHENZHI AND ACKNOWLEDGMENT IN WANG YANGMING AND STANLEY CAVELL[1]

Abstract

This article highlights sympathies between Wang Yangming's notion of *zhenzhi* (real knowing) and Stanley Cavell's concept of acknowledgment. I begin by noting a problem in interpreting Wang on the unity of knowing and acting, which leads to considering how our suffering pain figures in our "real knowing" of another's pain. I then turn to Cavell's description of a related problem in modern skepticism, where Cavell argues that knowing another's pain requires acknowledging it. Cavell's concept of acknowledgment answers to Wang's insistence that knowing and acting are one, and corrects Antonio Cua's very different appropriation of "acknowledgment" to explain Wang's doctrine.

I. Introduction

The distinction between *zhenzhi* (real knowing) and *changzhi* (ordinary knowing) in the thought of the Neo-Confucian philosopher Wang Yangming (1472–1529 CE) is central to his well-known teaching of the unity of knowing and acting. In the *Chuanxilu* and elsewhere, ordinary knowing is delineated most often not by its object of knowledge or the context of knowing but by what it fails at or falls short of—a necessary, affective responsiveness, something that either immediately yields to action or itself counts as action. But this active responsiveness is not to be understood as an ingredient that, added to ordinary knowing, yields real knowing; in other words, real knowing is not ordinary knowing *plus* something else. As Wang says, "Those who are supposed to know but do not act simply do not yet know";[2] real knowing is a wholly distinct accomplishment.

While much interest in Wang Yangming revolves around his descriptions of how one comes to embody real knowing—through recovery of the original unity of knowing and acting by, specifically, a

WILLIAM DAY, Associate Professor, Department of Philosophy, Le Moyne College. Specialties: aesthetics, American philosophy, theory of knowledge. E-mail: daywb@lemoyne.edu

constant effort at eliminating the darkening influence of one's selfish desires, however we are to characterize that effort—I want to focus on Wang's suggestion (emphasized in Philip J. Ivanhoe's reading) that what stands in the way of real knowing is oneself, so that ordinary knowing is less a positive form of knowing than a form of self-deception, and its giving way to real knowing requires a kind of therapy on the self.[3]

This, as it happens, is language prevalent in American philosopher Stanley Cavell's discussion of the form of knowing appropriate to our engaged life with others—what he calls "acknowledging." Cavell's concept of acknowledgment, as distinct from propositional knowing, likewise is internally related to the notion of (affective) responsiveness, or expressiveness, toward others. It is not propositional knowing *plus* affective response, a view that can make our life with others appear to be mere "behavior" added onto "cognition." Instead, acknowledgment marks the recognition of a difference in one's attitude to the world and to others. As with Wang's notion of ordinary knowing, the *failure* of acknowledgment is not a product of ignorance but a form of self-deception, a kind of willed blindness. There is, however, a difference between these two pairs of knowing-distinctions, one which may nonetheless point to an affinity: whereas in Wang's thought the obscuring of our *liangzhi* ("good knowing" or innate knowledge of the good) can be caused by a too theoretical or intellectualist approach to self-cultivation, for Cavell the failure of acknowledgment is not the effect of a theoretical exuberance but more like the condition for the possibility of that exuberance we call philosophical skepticism. That is, for Cavell, skepticism about whether we can know with certainty the existence of the world or of other minds is merely one reflection of the general human failure to accept the world and to acknowledge others.

The present article is meant to observe and deepen these sympathies between Wang's and Cavell's pairs of knowing-distinctions. I begin by noting a problem in interpreting the central passage in Wang's conversations with his pupil Xu Ai on the unity of knowing and acting. This will lead to considering how our having or suffering pain figures in our "real knowing" of another's pain. To clarify that relation, I turn to Cavell's description of an imaginary scenario offered to address a related problem in modern skepticism, a scenario that would seem to satisfy the Skeptic's craving for certainty about what another person is feeling. That discussion culminates in Cavell's suggestion that what we want in knowing another's pain is captured not by the concept of certainty but by the concept of acknowledgment. I end by arguing that Cavell's concept of acknowledgment answers to Wang's insistence that knowing and acting are one, as well as corrects Antonio Cua's very different appropriation of the concept of acknowledgment to explain Wang's doctrine.

II. WANG YANGMING AND *ZHENZHI*

What does Wang Yangming's doctrine of *zhi xing he yi*, the unity of knowing and acting, mean? Among English-speaking commentators of the past thirty years there is disagreement over whether Wang's doctrine is meant to pertain only to moral knowing, as Antonio Cua[4] claims, or to knowing in all its manifestations, as Warren Frisina[5] argues. There is also disagreement over to what extent Wang's distinction between real knowing and ordinary knowing should be identified with Gilbert Ryle's distinction, offered in the middle of the last century, between "knowing how" and "knowing that" (as discussed by Cua, Philip Ivanhoe,[6] and Yang Xiaomei[7]). Behind both of these questions is the more pointed worry whether "the unity of knowing and acting" can really, when all is said and done, plausibly be maintained.

It is this last question that I wish to address here, with the modest goal of clarifying what is required to understand Wang's claim. My guiding thought in interpreting the claim is that Wang understood the doctrine of *zhi xing he yi*, first and foremost, pedagogically. That is not to say that the claim "knowing and acting are one" is not in some sense true, even literally true. But that a claim is true is not, by itself, reason enough to say it. Wang makes clear that his motive for stating what he understands as the truth is not to promote a doctrine but to aid in his disciples' moral cultivation. As he says at the end of the section of the *Chuanxilu* that we will examine shortly,

> This is serious and practical business. What is the objective of desperately insisting on knowledge and action being two different things? And what is the objective of my insisting that they are one? What is the use of insisting on their being one or two unless one knows the basic purpose of the doctrine?[8]

Wang writes toward the end of his life, in a letter to Ku Tung-Chiao, "*Only because* later scholars have broken their task into two sections and have lost sight of the original substance of knowledge and action have I advocated the idea of their unity and simultaneous advance."[9] To consider the meaning of Wang's doctrine "the unity of knowing and acting" is above all to consider how discovering its meaning—and that means overcoming the tendency (in Wang's time and ours) to misread it, that is, to read it doctrinally—can be a form of moral therapy, and can itself contribute to the reform of one's knowing/acting.

Here it is important to note that what Wang's doctrine claims the unity of is not our mistaken notions of "knowing" and "acting." This much seems clear from Wang's first words to Xu Ai early on in the *Chuanxilu*, in response to Xu's inquiries about the doctrine. Xu had offered a straightforward counterexample to the claim of the unity of knowing and acting—namely that people can fully know what they should do (that they should exhibit filial piety, for example) and still fail to act accordingly. Wang responds, "The knowledge and action you refer to are already separated by selfish desires and are no longer knowledge and action in their original substance."[10] If we believe (falsely) that someone can have knowledge without completing that knowledge in action, we are already operating with mistaken notions of "knowing" and of "acting." Thus part of the pedagogical task of Wang's doctrine, and so part of the work of helping his students unite knowing and acting in their lives, is (odd as it sounds) to show what "knowing" (*zhi*) and "acting" (*xing*) mean. We are already some distance from their proper meaning when we speak of them as separate.

A second problem with Xu Ai's counterexample, as revealed by Wang's response, is that it assumes a false idea of how knowing *might* exist in unity with acting. Wang explains:

> Suppose we say that so-and-so knows filial piety and so-and-so knows brotherly respect. They must have actually practiced filial piety and brotherly respect before they can be said to know them. It will not do to say that they know filial piety and brotherly respect simply because they show them in words.[11]

This would seem to go some way toward defeating a thought implied in Xu Ai's counterexample, that someone who declares "Parents should be served with filial piety" is, as it were, halfway to Wang's teaching, and need only put this "knowledge" into practice to "unite" knowing and acting in his life. Instead, Wang makes clear, the knowing that is to be identified with acting is not (as we now say) propositional; it is the false sense that one *knows* something in declaring "Parents should be served with filial piety" that can stand in the way of progress toward uniting knowing and acting. Wang's remark can give the mistaken impression, on the other hand, that he is advocating a kind of moral empiricism—specifically, that a prerequisite to my knowing some good X is that I first experience, i.e., do or perform, that good X—an interpretation that would cause problems for Wang's later emphasis on and transformation of Mengzi's notion of innate knowing of the good (*liangzhi*). But what the passage (as translated) says is not that *my* knowing of filial piety and brotherly love depends on my earlier practice of filial piety, but that *your saying that* I know filial piety (your bearing witness to my character, we might say) depends on my having practiced filial piety. Only if I show filial piety is your claim that I know filial piety proper, not saying more than you know.

And yet Wang's next words seem to raise a difficulty for this interpretation as well as more broadly. He says, "Or take one's knowledge of pain. Only after one has experienced pain can one know pain. The same is true of cold or hunger. How can knowledge and action be separated?"[12] Here Wang's claim is not merely that the veracity of your saying that I know pain depends on my experience of pain, but that *I* know pain only after I have experienced it. What's more, he says not simply that I know *my* pain once I have experienced it, but that I know *pain*, know what pain is. Scholars have expressed various degrees of disappointment with this example, most often in noting that pain is an affection or reflexive response and not an action.[13] But what these scholars overlook—perhaps because the obvious is easily overlooked—is that what we call pain, including the pain of cold and the pain of hunger, belongs not accidentally but essentially to the natural history of humans. My having experienced pain in no way distinguishes me from others, as my having practiced filial piety would. Pain—as Wang knows we must, in some sense, see—is universal to the human condition. If Wang's intent in this passage continues to be to "restore" "knowledge and action in their original substance,"[14] then his purpose in stating the necessary commonplace that I know pain only after (or because) I have experienced it ("How can knowledge and action be separated?") must be in order to correct something false in my understanding of my relation to pain. What might that false understanding be? The most likely candidate, indeed the obvious candidate that is nevertheless easily overlooked, is my imagining that I can separate my experience of pain from my knowing what pain is. And how might I and others, caught up in our selfish desires, do that? I would suggest: by denying in our actions toward others the universality of pain; or, put more simply: by denying another's pain. The point of the example of pain, then, would be not that my experiencing pain shows the unity of knowing and acting, but that my responding to another's pain (real, imagined, or imminent) shows this. Only in my response do I show, or fail to show, what I know from my own (unexceptional) experience. And in either case—that is, whether I show what I know or fail to show it—I am, we might say, *implicated* by the other's pain.

III. STANLEY CAVELL AND ACKNOWLEDGMENT

It is at this point, in thinking about what my response to pain has to teach me about the unity of knowing and acting, that I want to shed light on Wang's doctrine by turning to the thought of Stanley Cavell.

I must begin with a striking contrast, however, in Cavell's starting point. For Cavell, whose philosophical lineage is tied to the later writings of Wittgenstein, problems of knowledge are cast as problems of, or in response to, the philosophical skepticism that began a century after Wang Yangming and half a world away, in the skeptical procedures of Descartes. In particular, and as one version of the so-called Problem of Other Minds that will be the focus of this discussion, the Skeptic says that another person—say, the next person you meet—could be in pain at that moment but not show it; in such a case, the Skeptic argues, that person knows, based on her feeling pain at that moment, that she is in pain, whereas, since you cannot have her pain, you cannot be certain that she is in pain. From this and related arguments (about the human capacity for feigning pain, for instance), the Skeptic draws the general conclusion that we can never know with certainty whether another person is in pain. The Skeptic's argument really amounts to a complaint, one could say, about the human condition as such: the Skeptic's apparent discovery is that we lack proper wiring for "real knowing" (wiring that, if we possessed it, would allow us to feel what another person feels). It is through such arguments that modern skepticism reveals itself to be not so much a school of thought as a voice of doubt that haunts the Western theorist of knowledge.

I want to outline Stanley Cavell's response to this Skeptic, most notably in Cavell's early article "Knowing and Acknowledging,"[15] since it is crucial to understanding his interest in the notion of acknowledgment and its affinity with Wang Yangming's notion of *zhenzhi*. Cavell's engagement with skepticism was unique at the time it was written, in that Cavell denies that the Skeptic can be defeated by a simple appeal to what we ordinarily say—an approach that several philosophers in the last century, beginning with G. E. Moore[16] and including such followers of Wittgenstein as Norman Malcolm,[17] took to be definitive. That appeal to ordinary language is made, when directed at the Problem of Other Minds, in some such way as the following: "The Skeptic is wrong when he insists, on the way to his skeptical conclusion, that two people can't have the same pain. For clearly, we can and do speak of two people having the same pain. For example, they may each have the headache and sore throat that accompanies the swine flu." Cavell makes evident that this is not enough to defeat the Skeptic's challenge. To see why not, consider how we ordinarily talk about cars. If you and I each own 2003 Honda Civic LXs, then we can and do say that we both own the same car (the same descriptively, as we might put it). But when yours develops a flat tire on the highway or is hit by a rock that cracks the windshield, then it seems important (to me) that it is *your* 2003 Honda Civic LX, not mine, that has a flat tire or a cracked windshield. It may be that pains, like cars, are such that it makes sense to say both that we have the same (when we do) and that nonetheless we do not have the same (the same numerically)—that is, if there are contexts in which it matters to distinguish, say, your swine flu headache from mine. But if it sometimes matters, and we do sometimes distinguish your pain from mine, then we are back to the Skeptic's challenge to our claim to know that another is in pain, since we cannot have the other's pain in that sense demanded by the Skeptic (the sense of numerically the same pain).

But Cavell goes further in his diagnosis of this mistaken appeal to ordinary speech. The fundamental error in this appeal, Cavell says, is that, by insisting that we can have the same pain (while failing to convince us that we can have it in the sense that seems required), this ordinary language respondent to the Skeptic perpetuates the idea that whether we have the same feeling is *relevant* to whether we can know what another is feeling. But if having the same feeling were relevant, then clearly the way that I can have the same feeling as you—by our both having the headache and sore throat that accompanies the swine flu, say—is insufficient to make me certain that I know what you are feeling at a given moment. Cavell's very different tack in responding to skepticism, differently inspired by Wittgenstein (or by a different reading of Wittgenstein) from Malcolm's, is to argue that the Skeptic is deceiving himself when he imagines that "feeling the same pain" is relevant to "knowing what another is feeling." To show this, Cavell sketches a scenario in which the Skeptic gets his wish—that is, in which someone is able to feel another's pain as the other feels it; and yet, as Cavell allows us to see, we would not want to say that this someone is knowing another's pain in the way that *we* want to know it.

Cavell's imagined scenario is derived from the 1941 Hollywood film *The Corsican Brothers*, itself based loosely on Alexandre Dumas's 1845 novella of the same name.[18] We are to imagine two brothers, one of whom ("Second") suffers only and exactly whatever happens to his brother ("First"). The important feature here is that Second feels First's pain not out of sympathy, by seeing First suffer, but through an (unexplained) automatic mechanism, so that Second feels pain when First accidentally slices his finger in another room, or on another continent—that is, when First is no more in view than the knife that slipped. In addition, we are asked to imagine that Second suffers *only* if First does, so that if Second had sliced his own finger, or if First had been anesthetized, Second would in either case feel nothing. In short, let it be the case that First is Second's access to the feeling (touching) world.

What we have here is thus rightly described as a situation in which pain is felt by someone (Second) *because another feels it.* This answers to the Skeptic's observation or complaint that "any pain that I can possibly feel is still my own," since in this example Second has no pain of his own: every pain he feels is First's. (If there is a remedy for the pain, one applies it to First, even as one might comfort Second.) It also answers to our sense of what "having numerically the same pain" would mean if it meant anything; for here, the pain in First's body and the pain in Second's body are literally (and so numerically) the same pain. In effect, we have made the Skeptic's claim—that there is a kind of access to another human being which no human being can have—intelligible, by describing a case in which someone *could* have such access (to at least one other human being) if only he were wired like Second. *The Corsican Brothers* scenario is thus one in which our present, actual human condition is viewed as a constraint, as a falling short of the best case for knowing others. But even so, as Cavell argues, what we are imagining with this scenario does not satisfy our wish to know another's pain. The scenario still misses what the skeptic in us wants, and in doing so it demonstrates that nothing we can imagine *of this sort* will satisfy us.

To see why, first we must ask: does First (the one who has sliced his finger) know Second's pain? One might feel that he must know this if he knows how his brother is wired, since it guarantees that their pains are identical and simultaneous. But recall that First does not feel Second's pain as Second is said to feel First's; whatever pain First feels is *his*. And that now presents itself as a problem: First's pain, rather than serving as an indication of what Second is feeling, stands in the way of his considering what Second is feeling. As Cavell says, "First's knowledge of Second's pain—if based on his own pain—is somehow too intellectual to be called 'knowledge that Second is in pain.'"[19] For First, "Knowing that Second is in pain" requires a deduction, albeit from his own condition. (He must think: since I am in pain, Second must also be in pain.) If I am Second, this will not strike me as having a regard for my being in pain. Can I be blamed for thinking, "First doesn't know what I'm suffering"? Perhaps someone will need to remind me that First is not uncaring (if he is not) but that he is, after all, *in pain* exactly and always whenever I am in pain. On the other hand, if First shows regard for Second's suffering *despite* his pain, he does so the way that any of us would. What one might have taken to be evidence for knowing another's feelings turns out to be an obstacle to what we want to call "knowing another's feelings."

But next we must ask: does Second know First's pain? We have imagined not only that Second feels the same pain as First but that the pain he feels *is* First's, so that he knows First's pain directly, *by* feeling it. One may decide that this is a case of knowing in some sense, but one should also recognize that it is not what we mean by, or want from, "knowing another's pain." For if I am Second, then what I mean by "First is in pain" is indistinguishable from what I mean by "*I* am in pain." First's pain is no longer different enough for me to be able to identify it as *his*. I have lost the space between us in which I can answer to his pain; it filibusters my experience. What would count as "knowing another's pain" goes missing because First is not, or not sufficiently, an "other" to Second. Cavell says of Second that his knowledge is "'too immediate'; his 'having' First's pain is more like an effect of that pain than a response to it."[20]

Such thinking is what leads Cavell to his Wang-like conclusion, that our knowledge of another is bound up necessarily with how we respond to him, or fail to, and that "knowing what another is feeling" means, not: feeling what he feels, but: *acting* toward him in a certain way—for example, in response to his expressions of pain. Notice that this does not defeat the skeptical conclusion in the way that the Skeptic pictured it being defeated. The other whose pain we would know may still suppress his expressions of pain; or he may express his pain to which we, occupied by what Wang calls our selfish desires, fail to attend. This happens frequently enough: people see but do not act. Wang says such people "simply do not yet know" what the presence of the other calls from them.[21] Their knowledge is *changzhi*, a falling short of real knowing (*zhenzhi*). Cavell speaks of such people *forgoing* their knowledge of the other.

While this sketch of Cavell's analysis of the Skeptic's argument is all too brief, it is perhaps sufficient to shed light on what in the human condition drives the Skeptic of other minds to his confused questioning. If the demand to respond to what we know of others can at times, or as a timeless metaphysical fact, be burdensome to us, then the possibility that we might escape the demand, through the discovery that we can never be certain what another feels, begins to show its appeal. Cavell does not deny that appeal or the metaphysical facts that inspire it, including the deep fact of our human separateness. He simply shows that, when talking about our knowledge of others' pains, or of their thoughts and feelings generally, the problem is not that certainty is forever beyond our reach but that certainty is not enough. When I wonder whether my parents are cold or whether that child is in danger, my condition is captured not by the concept of certainty but by the concept of acknowledgment. And my relevant options are not: being certain that this person is in pain or else falling short of certainty, but rather: acknowledging this person's pain or else failing to acknowledge it (attending to her pain or else failing to attend to it). It is important to stress that acknowledging as here described is not a lesser standard than propositional knowing. Consider the situation in which I am late for class and my students are all waiting. Can I know that I am late without acknowledging it? Certainly. Can I, on the other hand, acknowledge that I am late without knowing it? Clearly not. As Cavell puts it, "Acknowledgment goes beyond knowledge. (Goes beyond not, so to speak, in the order of knowledge, but in its requirement that I *do* something or reveal something on the basis of that knowledge.)"[22]

But does this "goes beyond" imply, contrary to my opening claim, that acknowledging just is ordinary or propositional knowing *plus* action? Perhaps this is where Cavell shows the articulation of his thinking to be shaped by the challenge of philosophical skepticism, much as Wang's articulation of his thinking is shaped by the overly theoretical Confucianism of his day.[23] To that extent they seem to be aimed at different intellectual errors, medicines for distinct diseases. And yet, in the first half of the above parenthetical sentence, Cavell all but says that acknowledging is not the same *in kind* as propositional knowing (they are not part of the same "order of knowledge"); to that extent his distinction matches Wang's contrast between *zhenzhi* and *changzhi*. Neither Cavell nor Wang denies that propositional knowing—for example, showing filial piety "in words"[24]—may be a precondition for real knowing; but that is no more revealing than saying that talking is a precondition, or that having sight is a precondition for knowing the beautiful color. Perhaps the temptation to say that ordinary or propositional knowing is an element of real knowing stems from this thought (shared by Wang and Cavell): to unite knowing and acting, to acknowledge the other, what is needed is something, some ability, that I already possess. It demands only my present capacity for knowing/acting—though it may lie in me in some state of denial or repression or obscuration. And so I can fail to acknowledge, just as someone with a stuffy nose fails to know the bad odor.[25] Something in me keeps me from responding with sympathy (so that I respond instead with silence), or keeps me from responding with patient silence (so that I respond instead with distracted talk).[26] The manifestations of acknowledgment, and particularly of the avoidance of acknowledgment, illustrated in Cavell's readings of *King Lear* and *Othello*, and less directly but no less significantly in his readings of *The Winter's Tale* and *The Philadelphia Story* and *The Awful Truth*, among others,[27] underscore how the tragedy or dissolution of various crises of the soul (in Lear, Othello, Leontes, Tracy, Jerry) is linked to the failure or success of one's realigning the self with one's perception of, and one's care and affection for, others. Cavell's readings of these works serve, in addition, as so many demonstrations of the place of acknowledgment and its avoidance in the long tradition of philosophical skepticism about other minds.

IV. Acknowledging-That, Acknowledging-As, and Acknowledging You

I now turn to what this consideration of Cavell's notion of acknowledgment can reveal about Wang's doctrine of the unity of knowing and acting and about *zhenzhi* or "real knowing."

Perhaps the best way to bring this out is to compare Cavell's thought with Antonio Cua's reading of one of the remarks from the *Chuanxilu* that we examined earlier. Wang had said: "Suppose we say that so-and-so knows filial piety and so-and-so knows brotherly respect. They must have actually practiced filial piety and brotherly respect before they can be said to know them."[28] Cua's initial reading of this passage seems to draw the contrast between "ordinary knowing" and "real knowing" in much the way Cavell does. Cua explains that "in the moral case mere knowledge by acquaintance is not enough. The sense of recognition involved is more a sense of *acknowledgment*.... There is no gap, properly speaking, between acknowledging [person] *A*, in the normative sense, as my father and acting toward *A* in the filial way."[29] As with Cavell, Cua seems to suggest that our knowledge of others, properly speaking, is always already wrapped up in our responsiveness to them. And I have argued for this interpretation of Wang's view. For Wang, to overlook or fail at the appropriate response, whether in philosophizing or in our day-to-day affairs, is to engage, like the Skeptic, in a form of self-deception. It is to be captive to a picture of knowing that abdicates our part in the world, our relation to others and our responsibility to them (specifically, in the Wang passage, to our parents and brothers).

But later in Cua's discussion it becomes clear that he has not united knowing and acting enough—I mean that he continues to be guided by notions of "knowing" and "acting" in moral contexts that in fact bring about their separation, exhibiting merely a more refined form of self-deception. Here is the relevant passage from Cua's book:

> Having moral knowledge in the required sense involves not merely a recognition that such-and-such is a duty but also an *acknowledgment* or acceptance of the duty as a guide to actual conduct—that is, as having an actuating import in one's life.... If I acknowledge, for example, filial piety as my duty, this involves not merely a recognition of what constitutes acts of filial piety but also an endeavor to perform these acts.[30]

Here the work of acknowledgment, which in the earlier passage seemed to require my response to another (to my father, say), consists of the effort to observe merely an antecedent commitment *to filial duty*. That is, Cua shifts the emphasis to my acknowledging *that* thus-and-such is my duty rather than—as Wang emphasizes in response to the scholars of his day—overcoming my self-deceiving view of actions as guided by duties that need to be first discussed and learned before being put into practice.[31] To think of duties (to parents, to rulers, etc.) as what wait on my acknowledgment is to place one more obstacle before my learning how to respond here and now to another (to my father, say). It pictures the intellectual action as happening elsewhere than in "the effort of concrete practice," and thus is, in Wang's words, to "pursue shadows and echoes."[32] And it seems to identify real knowing as affective responsiveness *added to* ordinary knowing, rather than as something distinct enough to warrant Wang's speaking of the ancients' wish to "restore the original substance" of knowledge and action[33] and his claiming that ordinary knowing is not a species of knowing at all. (Here is one place where coming to see what "knowing" and "acting" mean is learning how to unite knowing and acting in one's life.) That's not to deny that having some general sense of filial duty can figure in educating me on how to remove my selfish desires and act appropriately toward my father. What it denies is that "a recognition of what constitutes acts of filial piety" as precursor to "an endeavor to perform these acts" figures in the lesson we are to draw from Wang's doctrine of the unity of knowing and acting.

To see the extent of Cua's confusion over the kind of acknowledgment that talk of the unity of knowing and acting should encourage, consider how he describes the change in seeing that it inspires. This is Cua commenting on what he labels Wang's "aesthetic analogy," that "true knowledge and action . . . are like loving beautiful colors":[34]

> As soon as one sees an object as beautiful, one has already loved it in the sense that one has spontaneously responded to the object as a beautiful object. . . . As in the aesthetic case, when I am directly aware of, or recognize, a person A as my father or my brother, I may be said to have already "responded" to A in the way characteristic of a filial son or respectful brother; that is, I have already *acted* toward A in a filial or fraternal way.[35]

Cua is here offering, as an instance of my overcoming the false separation of knowing and acting, the case of my "directly" seeing "a person A as my father or my brother," borrowing (as he makes explicit) the locution of "seeing something as something" from Wittgenstein's remarks on "aspect-seeing" late in his *Philosophical Investigations*.[36] Cua's suggestion appears to be that such aspectual seeing—seeing this (a human being) as that (my father)—is a realization of the unity of knowing and acting. And aspectual seeing is the concept of experience by which Cua explicates not only Wang's "aesthetic analogy" but Cua's initial (that is, his more Cavell-like) sense of "acknowledgment," a kind of "acknowledgment-as." Recall the passage cited earlier: "There is no gap, properly speaking, between acknowledging A, in the normative sense, as my father and acting toward A in the filial way."[37]

What, in my view, is confused here is not the appeal to some concept that removes the sense of a "gap" between recognition and response (the absence of a gap is what "the unity of knowing and acting" implies and calls for) but Cua's conviction that the concept of seeing-as clarifies *how* to unite knowing and acting. The first indication that something is amiss is Cua's interpretive claim that "we may replace 'seeing beautiful colors' [in Wang's 'aesthetic analogy'] by 'seeing colors *as* beautiful.' "[38] This "way of making explicit the [conative] attitude" involved in "seeing beautiful colors" leads Cua immediately to draw the lesson of Wang's analogy by speaking of a case "when I am directly aware of ... a person A as my father" and by speaking of "acknowledging A ... as my father."[39] But there is a difference in kind between "seeing beautiful colors" and "seeing colors as beautiful." Specifically, the latter case implies that, as with any aspect-seeing experience, there is some (at least one) *other* way of seeing the colors in question (seeing them, for example, as pallid or lurid or garish). However uncertain we may be about the former possibility of "seeing beautiful colors" directly, or about ascribing to Wang "a sort of phenomenology of value perception,"[40] my interest is in the analogous cases of aspect-perception (namely "seeing a human being as my father" and "acknowledging a human being as my father") that Cua develops from his interpretive claim.[41]

Consider first what it means to fail to see a human being as my father. Is this what I do when I claim (as in Xu Ai's example) that I know my father should be served with filial piety but that I cannot put this into practice? If it is, the implication is that (again) there is some other way I am seeing this human being. But is that what either Xu Ai or Wang imagine—that my failure to act appropriately toward my father is the result of my seeing this human being as, say, my brother or ruler or neighbor, rather than as my father? Cua might reply that my failure is in seeing my father as no one in particular: I see him, at most, simply as a human being. But is that really coherent? Here I simply note that my father *is* a human being, and that it is consequently not clear how I could (claim to) see him *as* one. "One doesn't '*take*' what one knows as the cutlery at a meal *for* cutlery."[42] Of course, it is equally true that he *is* my father. Is it any more clear how

I could (claim to) see him *as* my father? Perhaps; if, that is, "seeing my father as my father" is a (not quite coherent or fully meant) description of a change in attitude from one in which I would habitually disown my knowledge of him, and so fail to respond to him appropriately, if at all.[43]

But in that case, my problem was not that I had been seeing something else, some *other* aspect of my father. Rather, my problem was that I had been missing something, something Wang might call the harmony (*he*) between my feelings and my father, a recognition of my connection to him.[44] Cavell, in a section of *The Claim of Reason* that can be read as an extended meditation on the concept of acknowledgment, speaks in an analogous case of such a person "missing something about himself, or rather something about his connection with these people, his internal relation with them, so to speak."[45] Now it is true that to see an aspect of a thing is, similarly, to perceive "an internal relation between it and other objects."[46] But to see an aspect of a thing is not, typically, to perceive a thing's internal relation *to me*. (To see its relation to me, to be brought back to myself by what I see, is at best an extension of the notion of "noticing an aspect.") I want to say: in the case of seeing my father, my brother, my ruler, my neighbor, or in general, another human being, what expresses the effort to unite knowing and acting in myself is not my trying to see this person in a new way (*as* my father, etc.) so much as my seeing what in me is blocking the recognition of my internal relation to him or her (Cavell)—that is, blocking my realizing a harmony between my feelings and him or her (Wang). If you wanted to maintain that this is no more than a difference in emphasis from Cua, my reply would be that it is the difference between being receptive to self-knowledge or self-revelation (Cavell's picture)[47] versus aiming to make something happen (bringing about the "change of aspect" in Cua's version). Such a difference can be all the difference between realizing a teaching in one's life and failing to realize it.

A parallel set of concerns arises if we consider the differences between "acknowledging this human being as my father" (Cua) and "acknowledging my father" (Cavell). If we imagine the former voiced in the first person ("I acknowledge you as my father"), what it conveys is some sort of appeal to convention. The appeal might be filled out in various ways: as an appeal to a rule, or to a ritual understanding, or to a (possibly implicit) prior agreement about how things stand between us. While it is harder to imagine a context where we would say "I acknowledge you" (or "I acknowledge you, father"), the impulse or idea behind acknowledging *this person* (my father, say), as distinct from acknowledging him *as* my father, seems to be precisely what "the unity of knowing and acting" calls for:

namely that I not interpose a conventional *way* of seeing the other, that I leave myself open to receive what the other shows of himself and respond to *that*. This does not mean that I treat all persons equally or that I forgo my particular commitment, my internal relation, to this other—as a son, say. On the contrary: for me to acknowledge someone is always also to acknowledge my relation to him or her. (Only a son can adore his father in *this* way, can be embarrassed by or for him in *that* way, can lead him away from his wife's deathbed in *that* way, etc.) Goneril's and Regan's opening speeches in *King Lear* present us with a picture of two daughters who acknowledge Lear *as* their father ("As much as child e'er loved, or father found"). But in Cordelia's "I cannot heave / My heart into my mouth: I love your majesty / According to my bond; nor more nor less," what we are given—and what Lear fails to acknowledge— is a daughter who acknowledges Lear, her father.[48]

I have offered parallel critiques, it seems, of Cua's reading of Wang's doctrine and of the Skeptic who craves to "really know" another's pain. Our knowing the needs of others with whom we are in relation, their pains and their joys, is not, as the Skeptic imagines, a matter of gaining access to some inner sensation that we lack, nor, as Cua imagines, of extending our present acknowledgment of rules or relations to their realization in performance. If I imagine that real knowing consists in adding something to or doing something with our ordinary knowing— that is, our false understanding of "knowing"—I am perpetuating the separation of knowing from acting. A reading of Cavell suggests that to really know my father, I must learn to acknowledge him. My aim here has been to show that this is Wang's view—whatever the differences between how he and Cavell acknowledge their fathers—and that this view is revelatory of my relation to others—however little I have said here about how I learn to acknowledge others. But if I *can* do that, then knowing what my father is feeling—which is to say, responding to him appropriately—will take care of itself.

LE MOYNE COLLEGE
Syracuse, New York

Endnotes

The present article is a slightly revised version of my article in *Journal of Chinese Philosophy* 39, no. 2 (2012): 174–91. I appreciate the opportunity to republish with very minor corrections.

1. This is the original acknowledgment that appeared in the aforementioned issue of this journal: "A draft of this article was read at the 2009 International Symposium on Chinese Philosophy and Analytic Philosophy at East China Normal University in Shanghai on June 19, and at the 2009 Eastern Division Meeting of the American

Philosophical Association in New York City, December 29. I wish to thank the participants at each of these gatherings for their questions and comments. I also wish to express my gratitude to the Editor-in-Chief, Chung-ying Cheng, for his helpful comments on an earlier draft; to the Managing Editor, Linyu Gu, for her careful guidance in preparing the final draft; and to Mathew Foust for organizing both the APA special session and this special issue of the Journal devoted to new comparisons of Chinese and American philosophies. I am especially grateful to Stephen Angle, not only for his comments on an earlier draft but also for introducing me to the thought of Wang Yangming at the NEH Summer Seminar 'Traditions into Dialogue: Confucianism and Contemporary Virtue Ethics' held at Wesleyan University in 2008."

2. Wing-tsit Chan, trans., *Instructions for Practical Living and Other Neo-Confucian Writings of Wang Yang-ming* (New York: Columbia University Press, 1963), no. 5, 10; citations from Chan's translation of the *Chuanxilu* are given by passage number followed by page number.
3. See Philip J. Ivanhoe, *Ethics in the Confucian Tradition: The Thought of Mengzi and Wang Yangming*, 2nd ed. (Indianapolis: Hackett Publishing, 2002), 103, 179, note 55; Ivanhoe, *Confucian Moral Self Cultivation*, 2nd ed. (Indianapolis: Hackett Publishing, 2000), 60–61.
4. See A. S. Cua, *The Unity of Knowledge and Action: A Study in Wang Yang-ming's Moral Psychology* (Honolulu: University Press of Hawaii, 1982).
5. See Warren Frisina, *The Unity of Knowledge and Action: Toward a Nonrepresentational Theory of Knowledge* (Albany: State University of New York Press, 2002).
6. See Ivanhoe, *Ethics in the Confucian Tradition*.
7. See Yang Xiaomei, "How to Make Sense of the Claim 'True Knowledge Is What Constitutes Action': A New Interpretation of Wang Yangming's Doctrine of Unity of Knowledge and Action," *Dao: A Journal of Comparative Philosophy* 8, no. 2 (2009): 173–88.
8. *Instructions for Practical Living*, no. 5, 11.
9. Ibid., no. 133, 93; emphasis added.
10. Ibid., no. 5, 10.
11. Ibid.
12. Ibid.
13. This is where Antonio Cua introduces his distinction between "prospective" and "retrospective" moral knowledge, or between knowledge anterior to and knowledge posterior to action; see Cua, *Unity of Knowledge and Action*, 14–16. I mean to be introducing what will prove to be a contrasting significance in Wang's remark, in preparation for stating, at the end of this article, my disagreement with Cua's application of the notion of "acknowledgment" to Wang. For Cua's appeal to the notion of acknowledgment, see Cua, *Unity of Knowledge and Action*, 11–17.
14. *Instructions for Practical Living*, no. 5, 10.
15. Stanley Cavell, "Knowing and Acknowledging," in *Must We Mean What We Say? A Book of Essays* (Cambridge: Cambridge University Press, 1969), 238–66. Cavell's notion of acknowledgment introduced in "Knowing and Acknowledging" guides his thinking about our response to Shakespearean tragedy and the conventions of theatre and the movies generally, as well as (and because these are illustrative of) the skeptical problem of others. See, for example, "The Avoidance of Love: A Reading of *King Lear*," in *Must We Mean What We Say?* 267–353; "Sights and Sounds," "Photograph and Screen," and "Audience, Actor, and Star," in *The World Viewed: Reflections on the Ontology of Film* (Cambridge: Harvard University Press, 1971), 16–29; and "Between Acknowledgment and Avoidance," Part IV of *The Claim of Reason: Wittgenstein, Skepticism, Morality, and Tragedy* (Oxford: Oxford University Press, 1979), 329–496.
16. See Moore's "A Defense of Common Sense" and "Proof of an External World," in G. E. Moore, *Selected Writings*, ed. Thomas Baldwin (London: Routledge, 1993), 106–33 and 147–70.
17. See Norman Malcolm, "The Privacy of Experience," in *Epistemology: New Essays in the Theory of Knowledge*, ed. Avrum Stroll (New York: Harper and Row, 1967), 129–58.
18. See Cavell, "Knowing and Acknowledging," 251–53.
19. Ibid., 252.

20. Ibid., 253. Again, if Second is able to sympathize with First's experience of pain—despite rather than because of his own experience of pain—then we would want to say that Second knows First's pain.
21. *Instructions for Practical Living*, no. 5, 10.
22. Cavell, "Knowing and Acknowledging," 257.
23. See *Instructions for Practical Living*, no. 5, 11–12; no. 218, 197–98.
24. Ibid., no. 5, 10.
25. Ibid.
26. If I am angry with someone who then falls and is injured, and I refuse to help or to call for help, I fail to acknowledge him. Still, you might say to me, "But you *really know* that person is in pain!"—as a way of insisting that I am not ignorant of his pain, that I am in fact ignoring his expressions of pain. Does this show that (Cavell's notion of) acknowledgment is distinct from (Wang's notion of) real knowing (*zhenzhi*)? No, for when you say "But you *really know* that person is in pain!" you're not saying that I have *zhenzhi*; someone with *zhenzhi* would not ignore that person's expressions of pain. What this shows is no more than that such uses of "really know" don't translate or carry the pedagogical force of Wang's notion of *zhenzhi*. (My thanks to the Editor for raising this point.)
27. For Cavell's article on *King Lear*, see Note 15. For his interpretation of *Othello*, see Part IV of *Claim of Reason* (mentioned in Note 15); a version of these pages appears as "Othello and the Stake of the Other," in *Disowning Knowledge: In Six Plays of Shakespeare* (Cambridge: Cambridge University Press, 1987), 125–42. For *The Winter's Tale*, see "Recounting Gains, Showing Losses: Reading *The Winter's Tale*," in *Disowning Knowledge*, 193–221. For *The Philadelphia Story* and *The Awful Truth*, see *Pursuits of Happiness: The Hollywood Comedy of Remarriage* (Cambridge: Harvard University Press, 1981), 133–60 and 229–63.
28. *Instructions for Practical Living*, no. 5, 10.
29. Cua, *Unity of Knowledge and Action*, 11.
30. Ibid., 12.
31. Cf. *Instructions for Practical Living*, no. 5, 11.
32. Ibid.
33. Ibid., no. 5, 10.
34. Ibid.
35. Cua, *Unity of Knowledge and Action*, 10–11.
36. Ludwig Wittgenstein, *Philosophical Investigations*, eds. G. E. M. Anscombe and R. Rhees, trans. G. E. M. Anscombe, 2nd ed. (New York: Macmillan, 1958), Part II, section xi. For a recent assessment of Wittgenstein's remarks on the concept of aspect-seeing, see William Day and Victor J. Krebs, eds., *Seeing Wittgenstein Anew* (Cambridge: Cambridge University Press, 2010).
37. Cua, *Unity of Knowledge and Action*, 11.
38. Ibid., 10.
39. Ibid., 10–11.
40. Ibid., 105, note 11.
41. More recently, Stephen Angle has adopted this same aspectual revision of Wang's analogy: "The idea . . . is that when we see a color *as beautiful*, we thereby love it." Stephen C. Angle, *Sagehood: The Contemporary Significance of Neo-Confucian Philosophy* (Oxford: Oxford University Press, 2009), 119. Angle does not, however, follow Cua in extending the language of aspect-seeing to "seeing this person as my father," etc.
42. Wittgenstein, *Philosophical Investigations*, 195c.
43. What of the case where I don't, at first, recognize that person *A* is my father—I see him at a distance, or I see him plainly enough but don't know, haven't been told, my relation to him: I am Telemachus. When *A* says, "I am the only Odysseus who will ever come back to you," and I fold him in my arms and weep, haven't I come to see *A as* my father and shown this knowledge in appropriate action? Might Wang call this Cua-like alternative a unity of knowing and acting? I think he could, but it is more important to notice that this sort of example is not Wang's concern. It is not, again, like Xu Ai's example of (ordinary) "knowing" how to serve one's father with

filial piety but finding that one cannot act appropriately. What prevented Telemachus from exhibiting the unity of knowing and acting was not the absence of appropriate action; it was the absence of his father. The missing fact ("*A* is my father") is again no more than a precondition for, not an element of, real knowing (see the paragraph concluding Part III, above). (My thanks to the Editor for pressing the question raised here.)

44. For the role of harmony (*he*) in Wang Yangming's thinking, see Angle, *Sagehood*, 69–74 and 117–31.
45. Cavell, *Claim of Reason*, 376.
46. Wittgenstein, *Philosophical Investigations*, 212a.
47. Compare Cavell, "Ending the Waiting Game: A Reading of Beckett's *Endgame*," in *Must We Mean What We Say?*, 128–29, and "The Avoidance of Love: A Reading of *King Lear*," 272–89. Harmony (*he*)—that is, the discovery of coherence (*li*) within ourselves—is the comparable self-revelatory aim in Wang; compare Angle, *Sagehood*, 49, 69–71, 117. (My thanks to the Editor for pressing this point of comparison.)
48. Lear's "avoidance of love," his "disowning knowledge" of Cordelia's love (among others), is not proof against the role of acknowledgment in our knowing of others, but Lear's all-too-human expression of that role: "the concept of acknowledgment is evidenced equally by its failure as by its success. It is not a description of a given response but a category in terms of which a given response is evaluated." See Cavell, "Knowing and Acknowledging," 263–64. (My thanks to the Editor for raising this point.)

TAO JIANG

ISAIAH BERLIN'S CHALLENGE TO THE ZHUANGZIAN FREEDOM

Abstract

Isaiah Berlin is known for articulating two competing notions of freedom operative within the modern Western political philosophy, negative and positive. He provides a powerful defense of modern liberal tradition that elevates negative freedom in its attempt to preserve personal space for one's actions and choices while regarding positive freedom as suppressive due to its potentially collective orientation. This article uses Berlin as an interlocutor to challenge Zhuangzi, known for his portrayal of spiritual freedom in the Chinese tradition, prodding modern Zhuangzians to bring the Zhuangzian spiritual freedom into the sociopolitical arena by reimagining new possibilities about politics.

I. Introduction

As Chinese exposure to various Western ideologies and institutional practices increases, some scholars trained in the Chinese intellectual tradition, both in China and in the West, have attempted to locate indigenous Chinese resources that might be analogous to those Western ideas and practices. Such a comparative approach to ideas across cultural boundaries and historical genealogies can be very effective in reaching a better understanding of both China and the West through the vantage point of their representative voices while enlarging the conceptual repertoire of a particular idea.

Moreover, from a Chinese perspective, engagement with modern Western thinkers can be a fruitful way to confront new problems and issues that emerge in the context of modernization because the West has a longer experience in modernity and the Western thinkers have had more opportunities to think through some of the issues that have

---

TAO JIANG, Associate Professor and Chair, Department of Religion, Rutgers University. Specialties: early Chinese philosophy, Mahāyāna Buddhist philosophy, comparative philosophy. E-mail: tjiang@rci.rutgers.edu

arisen in the process. Even though Chinese modernity inevitably follows a different trajectory, globalization means that many experiences and problems are shared in an increasingly interconnected world. Neither traditional Chinese thought nor modern Western philosophy has ready-made answers to the complex issues facing Chinese modernity. Vigorous intellectual engagement between traditional Chinese thought and modern Western philosophy can generate new ideas to address new problems confronting China today more effectively. This article is written from such a perspective. It uses a leading contemporary Western philosopher's deliberation on the idea of freedom as a way to push the limits of traditional Chinese meditations on this concept of critical importance in the contemporary world.

The Latvian-born British philosopher Isaiah Berlin is a major contemporary Western thinker on the subject of political freedom, best known for articulating and crystallizing two competing notions of liberty/freedom (Berlin uses the two terms synonymously) operative within the modern Western social and political philosophy, namely negative and positive freedom. His framework provides the most powerful defense of the modern Western liberal tradition that tends to elevate the ideal of negative freedom in its attempt to preserve personal space for one's actions and choices, while regarding positive freedom as suppressive due to its potentially collective orientation as opposed to the individualistic orientation of negative freedom. Creative dialogue with such a leading voice in the contemporary Western reflections on freedom can be very fruitful in motivating thinkers in the Chinese tradition to reexamine their own cultural premises, confront certain blind spots within the traditional intellectual framework, and address new questions that originate from the modern and global context.[1]

For this purpose, there is probably no better conversation partner than Zhuangzi on the Chinese side. Among traditional Chinese thinkers, Zhuangzi stands out as the most powerful advocate for freedom, and the *Zhuangzi* provides rich conceptual resources for a Chinese version of freedom, thus affording us with a great opportunity to engage the two thinkers for a potentially edifying and enriching dialogue on freedom. Let me briefly summarize their respective projects before engaging the two. This critical engagement will highlight some of the problematic implications in the Zhuangzian conception of spiritual freedom from a Berlinian perspective and make the case that the Zhuangzian *imaginaire* of spiritual freedom needs to be expanded into the social and political arena so as to make a greater contribution to the Chinese political discourse on freedom.

II. Berlin's Negative and Positive Freedom

In his famous essay, "Two Concepts of Liberty," Berlin defines negative freedom as "the area within which a man can act unobstructed by others."[2] Here the obstruction or coercion "implies deliberate interference of other human beings within the area in which I could otherwise act."[3] Clearly, negative freedom is primarily concerned with various external constraints placed on a person while living in a society. On the other hand, positive freedom "derives from the wish on the part of the individual to be his own master."[4] Put differently, positive freedom pays more attention to the internal dynamics of a person, valorizing the ideal of self-determination and self-realization. Despite the appearance that the two are simply two sides of the same thing, they do come into conflict due to their historically divergent development.[5] His essay offers a powerful defense of the modern liberal project of democracy with its entailment of negative freedom while casting an unflattering light on various conceptions of positive freedom, both Western (e.g., Stoic) and Eastern (e.g., Buddhist).[6]

Berlin's deliberation of freedom and his valorization of negative freedom over positive freedom are grounded in his acute observation that many ultimate human values are incommensurable. He defends the superiority of negative freedom by offering a spirited critique of the various ways positive freedom has been perverted and abused in the service of political suppression and tyrannical governance under the banner of achieving "higher" political and social ideals, whether genuine or cynical, making a powerful case for the necessity of privileging negative freedom over positive freedom in a liberal democracy. He provides a sobering observation that the effort to realize various ideals of positive freedom has often led to the most catastrophic human disasters and suppression of individuals in modern history, both on the left and on the right. Berlin asks, "What can have led to so strange a reversal—the transformation of Kant's severe individualism into something close to a pure totalitarian doctrine on the part of thinkers, some of whom claimed to be his disciples?"[7] According to Berlin, the line between the ideal of individual freedom and totalitarian doctrines is much more blurred than their apparent incongruity, both philosophically and historically.

Berlin lays the blame for this ghastly perversion of freedom squarely on the impulse toward a philosophically and emotionally gratifying moral monism on the part of many philosophers,[8] with disastrous unintended consequences. Moral monism is understood as the conviction that "[a]ll true solutions to all genuine problems must be compatible: more than this, they must fit into a single whole: for this is what is meant by calling them all rational and the universe harmonious."[9] Given the apparent diversity and plurality of human values, in order to make them compatible with each other, moral thinkers invariably employ various theoretical schemes to distinguish the "higher," "true," or "rational" nature from our "lower," empirical, and "irrational" nature and argue that those "higher" and "true" values are congruous with each other in forming a perfect and harmonious system of values:

> [t]he common assumption of these thinkers is that the rational ends of our "true" natures must coincide, or be made to coincide, however violently our poor, ignorant, desire-ridden, passionate, empirical selves may cry out against this process. Freedom is not freedom to do what is irrational, or stupid, or wrong. To force empirical selves into the right pattern is no tyranny, but liberation.[10]

Once distinctions are made between the higher and the lower, the true and the empirical, and the rational and the irrational, the next logical step is to find ways to achieve the former in the pair and suppress the latter, despite the suffering such a process has often caused. This is how the value of individual freedom is metamorphosed into the obedience to an authority, typically an authoritarian or even totalitarian state, which claims to speak on behalf of such "higher" and "true" values.

As Berlin sees it, there are four problematic premises that have led to the subversion of freedom into totalitarianism:

> first, that all men have one true purpose, and one only, that of rational self-direction; second, that the ends of all rational beings must of necessity fit into a single universal, harmonious pattern, which some men may be able to discern more clearly than others; third, that all conflict, and consequently all tragedy, is due solely to the clash of reason with the irrational or the insufficiently rational—the immature and undeveloped elements in life—whether individual or communal, and that such clashes are, in principle, avoidable, and for wholly rational beings impossible; finally, that when all men have been made rational, they will obey the rational laws of their own natures, which are one and the same in them all, and so be at once wholly law-abiding and wholly free.[11]

Berlin goes on to make a passionate case against moral monism that is based on some a priori conviction, instead of an investigation into how real lives are lived and negotiated in the real world. Such a conviction is also demonstrably false. He observes that "[t]he world that we encounter in ordinary experience is one in which we are faced with choices between ends equally ultimate, and claims equally absolute, the realization of some of which must inevitably involve the sacrifice of others."[12] Given this incompatibility of various ultimate values, Berlin argues that social and personal conflict and tragedy is not simply a contingent fact of life, but rather its very constitution: "[t]he necessity of choosing between absolute claims is then an inescapable characteristic of the human condition."[13]

To treat this incompatibility of ultimate values as the inescapable human condition seriously, Berlin turns to pluralism, with the negative freedom it entails, as a truer and more humane way to accommodate the differences and to affirm our conviction that human beings are free agents. Otherwise, "[t]o say that in some ultimate, all-reconciling, yet realizable synthesis, duty *is* interest, or individual freedom *is* pure democracy or an authoritarian state, is to throw a metaphysical blanket over either self-deceit or deliberate hypocrisy."[14] This means that negative freedom, with pluralism as its positive corollary, is a potent way to keep various forms of positive freedom in check so that the monistic orientation of the latter does not overwhelm the pluralistic orientation of the former. Berlin ultimately justifies this on the ground of incompatibility of values, trying to preserve, within the social and political arena, a space for the individual with the idea that certain personal space *within* the social and political domain is inviolable. It enshrines the primacy of the *ordinary* individual and the inviolability of her choices as a human being.

Charles Taylor is arguably the most prominent critic of Berlin's formulation of freedom and the latter's elevation of negative freedom at the expense of positive freedom. In his article "What's Wrong with Negative Liberty," Taylor decries Berlin's caricature of "the whole family of positive conceptions"[15] as well as Berlin's espousal of "a corresponding caricatural version of negative freedom."[16] As Taylor points out, Berlin's formulation tilts heavily toward safeguarding against external hurdles to individual freedom but does not take as seriously obstacles to individual freedom that originate from within, such as "lack of awareness, or false consciousness, or repression."[17] To make his case, Taylor argues that behind the formulation of positive/negative freedom lie some deeper differences of doctrines:

> [d]octrines of positive freedom are concerned with a view of freedom which involves essentially the exercising of control over one's life. On this view, one is free only to the extent that one has effectively determined oneself and the shape of one's life. The concept of freedom here is an exercise-concept.
>
> By contrast, negative theories can rely simply on an opportunity-concept, where being free is a matter of what we can do, of what it is open to us to do, whether or not we do anything to exercise these options.[18]

Taylor uses what he regards as the more fundamental distinction between an opportunity-concept and an exercise-concept to expose the one-sidedness in Berlin's formulation. According to Taylor, the problem with Berlin's formulation is that it aligns negative freedom solely with an opportunity-concept and positive freedom with an exercise-concept. Such an alignment does not encapsulate the ideal of freedom:

> [w]e can't say that someone is free, on a self-realisation view, if he is totally unrealised, if for instance he is totally unaware of his potential, if fulfilling it has never even arisen as a question for him, or if he is paralysed by the fear of breaking with some norm which he has internalised but which does not authentically reflect him. Within this conceptual scheme, some degree of exercise is necessary for a man to be thought free.[19]

This means that negative freedom can, and must, also be aligned with an exercise-concept.[20] Taylor argues that Berlin, by denying the combinability between positive theories and opportunity-concept on the one hand and between negative theories and exercise-concept on the other, only recognizes the value of opportunity concepts and "leaves no place for a positive theory to grow."[21]

Furthermore, Taylor makes a passionate case that the fear of "Totalitarian Menace," as is evident in Berlin's argument against potential abuses of positive freedom, has led many liberal political thinkers to abandon one of the major sources of freedom in modern Western intellectual tradition, namely Romanticism and its progenies. Calling such an impulse "Maginot Line mentality," Taylor argues that it is indefensible as a view of freedom,[22] as it would have a stifling effect on a powerful source of the modern conception of freedom.

According to Taylor, the appeal of Berlin's formulation of freedom is its simplicity. However, freedom is never simple and always involves various kinds of discrimination and distinction that require evaluations of purposes and values: "our attributions of freedom make sense against a background sense of more and less significant purposes, for the question of freedom/unfreedom is bound up with the frustration/fulfillment of our purposes."[23] Without making such distinctions in weighing the difference in the significance of various human purposes (e.g., between traffic rules and abortion rules that compromise our exercise of freedom), freedom becomes trivial and spiritless, instead of being the powerful drive that motivates human self-realization and fulfillment. In this article, Taylor does not address the issue of the incompatibility of values Berlin raises in his essay, even though he deals with this subject more directly in his other works.[24]

To sum up, the value of negative freedom lies in that it does not offer prescriptive and normative claims about what the individual agent should or should not do, hence saving the critical space for the individual agent for her own self-determination and self-realization. But critics of Berlin, such as Charles Taylor and others, have argued that making no positive claims about the positive content of freedom completely leaves out the critical scholarly examination of what constitutes a good and fulfilling life, and hence is ultimately detrimental to the political project of liberal democracy.

In some sense, Taylor's critique of Berlin validates Berlin's argument about the incommensurability of values and the necessity of choice among such values, even though the necessity of choice also appears to echo Taylor's contention that freedom has to involve both an opportunity-concept and an exercise-concept.[25] It seems that when facing the "totalitarian menace" posed by conceptions of positive freedom due to their monistic orientation, Berlin decides to simply bite the bullet and reject the project of positive freedom in the political and social arena. Taylor on the other hand wants to maintain a middle ground that leaves room for the public discourse on positive freedom while remaining loyal to the project of modern liberal democracy with its entailment of negative freedom.[26]

Although Berlin's article does not directly engage Chinese intellectual traditions, much of his critique of positive freedom is very much relevant within the Chinese context. Thinkers trained in Chinese thought need to take such critiques seriously in order to confront similar issues. In general, the Chinese intellectual traditions tend to focus on positive freedom, requiring a person to engage in moral/spiritual cultivation to achieve self-realization and self-mastery. However, the *Zhuangzi* is an intriguing exception in that it clearly exhibits distinct traits of negative freedom, showing a deep appreciation for personal space and a profound skepticism toward moralistic certainty as well as embracing value-pluralism, even though it still assumes the primacy of self-cultivation. Let us take a closer look at the Zhuangzian project of freedom before engaging Berlin on this subject.

III. Zhuangzian Freedom (*Xiaoyao* 逍遙)

Against the general grain of the Chinese intellectual tradition that cherishes the relational nature of the world, especially the human society (e.g., the Confucians tend to emphasize the nurturing aspect of human relationality), Zhuangzi[27] is deeply ambivalent about what he perceives to be the inherently relational nature of existence. Unlike any other classical Chinese philosophical texts, the *Zhuangzi* problematizes the aspect of entanglement in relationality. In many ways, the Zhuangzian project of freedom is how to overcome such entanglements.

Zhuangzi's uneasiness about the relational nature of existence in the world is vividly captured in a well-known story from "The Mountain Tree" (*Shanmu* 〈山木〉) Chapter. A cicada is about to be preyed upon by a mantis who is oblivious of its own imminent danger of being attacked by a magpie who itself does not realize that it is the target of a bird-catcher, with the latter in each pair taking advantage of the former's self-deception and illusory sense of safety.[28] When Zhuangzi sees this, he is alarmed: "[i]t is inherent in things that they are tie[d] to each other, that one kind calls up another."[29] He remains gloomy for three days. Clearly, the relational nature of being in the world is deeply troubling for Zhuangzi. Consequently, how to effectively negotiate various domains of relationality lies at the heart of the Zhuangzian project of freedom.

The Zhuangzian freedom (*xiaoyao*) can be articulated in the cluster of three related concepts, transformation (*hua* 化), roaming (*you* 遊), and forgetting each other and letting each other be (*wang* 忘). More specifically, the Zhuangzian freedom is grounded in the "transformation of the self" (*hua*) such that the transformed self can gracefully roam (*you*) within the complexity of the world as well as beyond the constraint of worldly entanglements, forget each other and let each other be (*wang*). Let us briefly examine these aspects.

The condition of the self is front and center in Zhuangzi's meditation on freedom in that he takes personal cultivation and transformation, *hua*, as the point of departure. The stories of personal cultivation and transformation abound in the text.[30] One of the most important occurrences of *hua* appears in Zhuangzi's signature butterfly story. Here Zhuangzi tells us about being a butterfly in a dream; once awakened, he cannot tell whether he is Zhuang Zhou who dreams he is a butterfly or the butterfly who dreams it is Zhuang Zhou. As he is musing on the difference and the connection between him as Zhuang Zhou and the butterfly in the dream, he invokes the notion of "transformation between things" (*wuhua* 物化).[31] What does *wuhua* mean in the *Zhuangzi*?

There are several notable stories of *wuhua* in the text. Besides the story about the dramatic transformation between Zhuangzi and a butterfly, between dreaming and awakening, there is also the famous story about the fantastic transformation of a huge fish Kun into a giant bird Peng at the start of the opening chapter, "Roaming with Ease" (*Xiaoyao You* 〈逍遙遊〉). These stories suggest that, as A. C. Graham perceptively observes, "the Taoist does not permanently deem himself a man or a butterfly but moves spontaneously from fitting one nature to fitting another."[32] The *Zhuangzi* dramatizes a highly cultivated daemonic state in which all of our sense organs are perfectly attuned to the way of the world such that it enables us to roam along with the myriad creatures by acclimatizing ourselves to the world. For Zhuangzi, such a state is not so much a mystical union as a nimble mind that is attuned to the way of the world. The Zhuangzian cultivation transforms the self such that it is aligned with the "axis of the Dao" (*daoshu* 道樞) and becomes a daemonic[33] self. Zhuangzi portrays in some detail the daemonic in the *Xiaoyao You* Chapter:

> [i]n the mountains of far-off Ku-yi there lives a daemonic man, whose skin and flesh are like ice and snow, who is gentle as a virgin. He does not eat the five grains but sucks in the wind and drinks the dew; he rides the vapour of clouds, yokes flying dragons to his chariot, and roams beyond the four seas. When his spirit is concentrated, it keeps creatures free from plagues and makes the grain ripen every year.[34]

Many commentators interpret this passage "mystically," and it is indeed tempting to do so. However, if we do not treat the passage literally, but rather metaphorically, we can characterize the daemonic (*shen* 神) in terms of the images invoked here: lofty (mountain), disentangled from the world (far-off), cool (ice and snow), gentle and pure (virgin), refined and subtle (sucking in the wind and drinking the dew instead of eating five grains), not limited by space (roaming beyond the four seas), cultivated and nurtured (concentration), and potent (keeping creatures free from plagues and making the grain ripen every year). Interpreted this way, the *Zhuangzi* can be seen as describing this daemonic being as a spiritual dimension within us, characterized by its subtlety, purity, potency, and free-spiritedness.

Another famous example of the transformation of the self is captured in a dialogue in "The Teacher Who Is the Ultimate Ancestor" (*Da Zong Shi* 〈大宗師〉) Chapter between Confucius and his favorite disciple, Yan Hui 顏回. Here Yan Hui describes the stages of his spiritual progress to Confucius, from forgetting benevolence (*ren* 仁) and rightness (*yi* 義), to forgetting ritual (*li* 禮) and music (*yue* 樂), and finally to sitting and forgetting (*zuo wang* 坐忘). Yan Hui explains the experience of *zuo wang* as: "I let organs and members drop away, dismiss eyesight and hearing, part from the body and expel knowledge, and go along with the universal thoroughfare."[35] Confucius is stunned by Yan Hui's achievement, "If you go along with it, you have no preference; if you let yourself transform, you have no norms,"[36] and asks to be Yan Hui's disciple.

If we juxtapose these accounts of personal transformation, it should be clear that the daemonic cultivated through various practices described in the *Zhuangzi* transcends the worldly constraints and limitations. The transformed, daemonic self, when negotiating with the world, takes one of two routes, either beyond the norms and boundaries or within them. This is captured in the two kinds of roaming (*you*) depicted in the *Zhuangzi*. The first kind of roaming, namely roaming beyond the boundaries, is the paradigmatic Zhuangzian *you* and it has been duly noted by traditional commentators as well as modern interpreters, for example, roaming between heaven and earth (*you hu tiandi zhi yi qi* 遊乎天地之一氣), into the infinite (*You wuqiong* 遊無窮), beyond the four seas (*You hu sihai zhi wai* 遊乎四海之外), beyond the dust and grime (*You hu chen'gou zhi wai* 遊乎塵垢之外), beyond the norm (*You fang zhi wai* 遊方之外), and so on.

The second kind of *you*, roaming within boundaries, is subtler and less prominent in the Inner Chapters. This aspect of the Zhuangzian freedom represents "the freedom that *roams in between* constraints."[37] The celebrated story of the butcher Cook Ding is the ultimate example of the second kind of *you*, supremely attuned senses and daemonically guided actions in roaming between the constraints within an ox. As the butcher describes it, at the beginning he sees the whole ox, and gradually he is able to discern bone and muscle patterns and eventually he discovers what are normally invisible paths inside the ox. The butcher describes how he does it this way: "[a]t that joint there is an interval, and the chopper's edge has no thickness; if you insert what has no thickness where there is an interval, then, what more could you ask, of course there is ample room to move the edge about."[38]

What is extraordinary in this description is Cook Ding's discernment of an interval in a joint (*You jian* 有間) and his realization of thicklessness of his chopper's edge (*wu hou* 無厚). Neither is apparent from the ordinary perspective. Clearly in the butcher's long years of practice, both he himself and the ox are transformed such that he can run his chopper as if its edge had no thickness while at the same time the intervals of the ox's joints are brought into the open. Put differently, in his cutting, or rather disentangling, of an ox the butcher is no longer his ordinary self while the ox is no longer an ox to an ordinary person. He is transformed in such a way that neither the butcher nor the ox stands in the way of the other. This is in line with our interpretation that self-transformation is foundational in the Zhuangzian project of freedom.

Here Zhuangzi paints a picture of perfect attunement with nature,[39] with the transformed self perfectly aligned with the axis of the Dao, to use the Zhuangzian language. The ox is a metaphor for the intricacy and complexity of the world, which explains the lesson, on how to nurture life, learned by the king from the butcher's performance and explanation. Zhuangzi calls this state "the Great Thoroughware"[40] (*datong* 大通) or "the Great Openness."[41] As a result, the world opens itself up and any resistance drops away. Hence the butcher does not need to hack his way through the ox; instead, his chopper roams between the joints inside the ox, staying intact for more than nineteen years and counting. Analogously, a perfected Zhuangzian sage can roam the world without having to force his way through, by exploring route and ways invisible and unavailable to the uncultivated.

The transformed self is internally and externally realigned with the axis of the Dao such that it attunes perfectly to the vicissitudes of the world. For Zhuangzi, the ordinary relational self is misaligned such that self and the world stand in the way of each other's movement. The solution lies in realigning the human agency in a way that relationality of the world no longer constitutes an obstacle in one's actions. This is the immanent dimension of the freedom in the *Zhuangzi*, as opposed to the transcendent dimension of the freedom understood in terms of roaming beyond norms and boundaries mentioned previously. In this connection, it is interesting to note that the immanent *you* is almost always used in a situation where there is potential danger in dealing with various external constraints, especially when facing the state. This is particularly clear in expressions like "roaming within his (the ruler's) cage" (*You qi fan* 遊其樊). We will come back to this point later in the article.

Socially, the ideal state of freedom is understood as one wherein everybody is no longer consciously upholding morals and values. Instead, they just forget each other and let each other be (*wang*). *Wang* is a prominent theme in the *Zhuangzi*. We have already seen its usage in connection with sitting (*zuo wang*) in describing a rarified state of self-cultivation wherein the everyday cognition drops away and the daemonic comes in. *Wang* also has a social aspect. The most famous instance of forgetting in a social context is pronounced, ironically and playfully of course, through the mouth of Confucius on the spuriousness of morals and values:

> [w]hen the spring dries up and the fish are stranded together on land, they spit moisture at each other and soak each other in the foam, but they would be better off forgetting each other in the Yangtse or the Lakes. Rather than praise sage Yao and condemn tyrant Chieh, we should be better off if we could forget them both and let their Ways enter the transformations. As the saying goes, "Fish forget all about each other in the Yangtse and the Lakes, men forget all about each other in the lore of the Way."[42]

Commentators usually interpret the Zhuangzian forgetting as the manifestation of an un-self-aware spontaneity, a consummate virtue in classical Chinese thought. However, this interpretation under-appreciates the social and political aspects of the idea of *wang*. Socially, it can be interpreted as leaving each other alone or letting each other be. Such an interpretation is supported by the use of *wang* in the peculiar Zhuangzian discourse on friendship.

The *Da Zong Shi* Chapter describes an interesting group of friends, Zi Sanghu 子桑戶, Meng Zifan 孟子反, and Zi Qinzhang 子琴張, whose take of friendship is rather unusual, to say the least:

> [w]hich of us can be *with* where there is no being with, be *for* where there is no being for? Which of us are able to climb the sky and roam the mists and go whirling into the infinite, living forgetful of each other for ever and ever?
>
> The three men looked at each other and smiled, and none was reluctant in his heart. So they became friends.[43]

What is of special interest to us here is the peculiar way ideal Zhuangzian friendship is depicted as friends forgetting each other and letting each other be who they want to be. Apparently, even friendly entanglement for Zhuangzi should be resisted and rejected.

In many ways, letting each other be is a core Zhuangzian social value, in contrast with what he regards as the meddling and intrusive ways of the Confucian or Moist moralists. This is a clear indication of value-pluralism in the *Zhuangzi*. It celebrates excellence in all walks of life as well as in all forms of life. It does not seek to impose a fixed perspective on what is worthy and respectable.

However, this does not mean that Zhuangzi is a moral relativist. Interpreters of Zhuangzi have struggled with various passages in the text that seem to advocate some form of relativism. If we couch the Zhuangzian project within the context of the classical Chinese debate on human nature, we can see that nature poses a limiting condition for the range of possibilities for what is considered valuable in the text. This can be explained by what P. J. Ivanhoe points out,

> Zhuangzi believed there are ways of living that are contrary to the way the world is: that is, which violate our nature and set us against the natural patterns and processes to be found in the world. Moreover, he further believed that there are ways of acting that enable us to accord with the nature of both ourselves as creatures—things among things in Nature's vast panorama—and Heaven's patterns and processes. People who act in such a way are paragons for human living.[44]

For example, Zhuangzi observes that a damp environment is unhealthy for humans but is perfectly fine for eels. Clearly nature poses a limit for the range of possibilities to flourish for Zhuangzi. But since we do not always know the limits and the possibilities (in fact more often than not we simply do not know), it makes more sense to be open-minded about the world. Hence I would characterize Zhuangzi as a value-pluralist, rather than a relativist. Zhuangzi is pushing against the Mencian tactics to justify the Confucian moralism by their selective treatment of various natural inclinations. For Zhuangzi, moralism damages the integrity and authenticity of natural human endowments, hence crippling the natural development of those endowments. The *Zhuangzi* is full of fantastic tales celebrating the extraordinary accomplishments of people in various professions and social status, like a butcher, a fisherman, a social outcast, and others. The key lies in staying "authentic to their nature" (*zhen* 真).[45] The Zhuangzian authenticity is non-formulaic and serves as a way to resist the darker sides of moralism, namely dogmatism, hypocrisy, narrow-mindedness, close-mindedness, moral aggressiveness, and moral aggrandizement.

The idea of letting each other be is also carried into Zhuangzi's discussion about politics. In the last of the Inner Chapters, "Responding to Emperors and Kings" (*Ying Diwang* 〈應帝王〉), the *Zhuangzi* offers some thoughts on governance. As Graham points out, this is clearly not the kind of subject Zhuangzi devotes his time and effort to.[46] The most relevant passage to our discussion here in that chapter addresses the ideal of an enlightened kingship:

> When the enlightened king rules
> His deeds spread over the whole world
>   but seem not from himself:
> His riches are loaned to the myriad things
>   but the people do not depend on him.
> He is there, but no one mentions his name.
> He lets things find their own delight.[47]

This represents the Daoist ideal that a sage-king who rules the least and is not imposing rules the best. He just lets everybody be. The *Laozi* has a similar take on the ideal governance and is much more developed than the *Zhuangzi* in discussing the ideal Daoist sage-ruler.

It is obvious that Zhuangzi does not enjoy discussing politics, at least not directly and explicitly. He is much more interested in spiritual freedom in all of its subtle and fantastic dimensions. His general attitude toward politics, by contrast, is that of futility and aversion. This explains the limited contribution the *Zhuangzi* makes to the traditional Chinese political discourse. In other words, for those who want to get away from politics (e.g., hermits) or are frustrated in their political ambitions (e.g., exiled scholar-officials), the *Zhuangzi* is their counsel and comfort.[48] Other than that, the *Zhuangzi* has not been a major voice in traditional Chinese political discourse, especially the political discourse on freedom where it could have made the most contribution. This has far-reaching ramifications, which will become even more problematic when we bring in Berlin.

IV. Berlin and Zhuangzi on Negative Freedom

The Zhuangzian freedom, insofar as it is predicated upon what Charles Taylor calls an exercise-concept, namely self-transformation, is more in line with Berlin's definition of positive freedom. However, in some critical respects, Zhuangzi's idea of freedom, in its effort to push against the suffocating and crushing relationality of being in the world, also resonates with Berlin's negative freedom. Both Zhuangzi and Berlin cherish the personal space and celebrate the value of pluralism. Like Berlin's negative freedom, the Zhuangzian freedom thrives in personal space with its characteristic ambivalence toward the state. Zhuangzi's antipathy toward moral monopoly, social conformity, and political tyranny is evident throughout the text. This makes Zhuangzi unique among traditional Chinese thinkers most of whom are more interested in exploring positive freedom, e.g., Xunzi. Nevertheless, the centrality of self-transformation in the Zhuangzian project of freedom and its lack of political engagement are problematic for Berlin. Let us examine these aspects in greater detail.

In his discussion of the two concepts of freedom, Berlin devotes significant effort to debunking the social and political implications of various ideals of spiritual freedom cherished in some religious and non-religious traditions, such as the Stoic and the Buddhist. At the heart of such conceptions of freedom lies what Berlin describes as a "strategic retreat into an inner citadel—my reason, my soul, my 'noumenal' self—which, do what they may, neither external blind force, nor human malice, can touch."[49] Berlin is clearly troubled by this approach to freedom and is at times even hostile to it by calling it a form of the doctrine of sour grapes: "[i]t is perhaps worth remarking that in its individualistic form the concept of the rational sage who has escaped into the inner fortress of his true self seems to arise when the external world has proved exceptionally arid, cruel, or unjust."[50] This is the doctrine that "maintains that what I cannot have I must teach myself not to desire; that a desire eliminated, or successfully resisted, is as good as a desire satisfied."[51] We can understand Taylor's accusation of Berlin's sweeping caricaturization of all expressions of positive freedom mentioned previously.

To be fair to Berlin, he is not arguing against the doctrinal integrity or the spiritual values of those expressions of freedom per se, but rather their social and political ramifications and potential abuses. In this respect, he views them as antithetical to the project of political freedom: "[a]scetic self-denial may be a source of integrity or serenity and spiritual strength, but it is difficult to see how it can be called an enlargement of liberty. . . . Total liberation in this self (as Schopenhauer correctly perceived) is conferred only by death."[52]

The Zhuangzian freedom exhibits some of the traits Berlin critiques. For example, one instance of roaming (*you*) within boundaries is found in the expression "roaming free inside his (the king's) cage" (*You qi fan* 遊其樊). This appears in the discussion of the fasting of the heartmind[53] (*xin zhai* 心齋) between Confucius and Yan Hui in the "Worldly Business among People" (*Ren Jian Shi* 〈人間世〉) Chapter. The context of this is a discussion of how a Daoist sage can live an enlightened life while trying to bring his wayward ruler closer to the Way. Zhuangzi, through the mouth of Confucius, proposes the fasting of the heartmind so that the enlightened person "no longer has deliberate goals, the 'about to be' at the center of him belongs to the transforming processes of heaven and earth. Then he will have the instinct for when to speak and when to be silent, and will say the right thing as naturally as a bird sings."[54] In other words, an enlightened Zhuangzian has to learn how to navigate within the dangerous confines of the king's cage.

Here it seems as though Zhuangzi is guilty of advocating a retreat to the inner citadel of oneself in order to avoid confronting the complexity and the danger of the world. However, that is not quite true. This case involves a Zhuangzian attempt to engage with the world in its most perilous and risky endeavors, namely how to guide an all-powerful monarch away from his waywardness with no protection. Zhuangzi is not advising against engaging the king, but is rather trying to find a more effective way to do so. He is explicit in justifying such a worldly engagement:

> [t]o leave off making footprints is easy, never to walk on the ground is hard. What has man for agent is easily falsified, what has Heaven for agent is hard to falsify. You have heard of using wings to fly. You have not yet heard of flying by being wingless; you have heard of using the wits to know, you have not yet heard of using ignorance to know.[55]

As Graham points out insightfully here, Zhuangzi is making the point that "it is easy to withdraw from the world as a hermit, hard to remain above the world while living in it."[56] This is precisely the kind of roaming that takes place within the boundaries of the worldly affairs without being bound by them, as opposed to transcending such boundaries by leaving behind worldly affairs.

However, although Zhuangzi does not advocate simply retreating into the inner citadel of oneself in his advice on how to navigate inside the king's cage, he is not challenging or even questioning the legitimacy of the cage, either. His advice on how to deal with it rests on accepting the king's cage as an unalterable, if hopeless, political reality. He does not ponder the possibility of enlarging the proverbial cage or destroying it. Not even as a matter of *imagination*. Given the richness of the Zhuangzian *imaginaire*, it is puzzling and, indeed, unfortunate that it has a rather limited imagination about the state and politics. The advice given in the text is either on how to operate within the cage or how to stay out of it. When operating within the cage of the state, the Zhuangzian imagination is devoted to the discernment of potentials that lie in the invisible or even the undesirable realms of the world in order to "*roams in between* constraints"[57] with greater efficacy and ease. Zhuangzi's discussion of the fasting of the heartmind mentioned above and the wonderful story about Cook Ding are both such cases.

When living outside the cage of the state, Zhuangzi enjoys life at the margin of society, being left alone. The most famous example of the Zhuangzian advice to stay out of the king's cage can be found in the "Autumn Floods" (*Qiu Shui* 〈秋水〉) Chapter wherein Zhuangzi compares someone who serves the state to an enshrined dead tortoise and asks the king's two emissaries: "[w]ould this tortoise rather be dead, to be honored as preserved bones? Or would it rather be alive and dragging its tail in the mud?"[58] Once the two emissaries reply that the tortoise would prefer the latter, Zhuangzi demands that they leave him alone, "Away with you! I shall drag my tail in the mud."[59] As opposed to trying to find an effective way to engage politics and the state, Zhuangzi only wants to be left alone here.

However, from Berlin's perspective, the political implications of leaving the society behind are deeply problematic:

> [t]his is the traditional self-emancipation of ascetics and quietists, of stoics or Buddhist sages, men of various religions or of none, who have fled the world, and escaped the yoke of society or public opinion, by some process of deliberate self-transformation that enables them to care no longer for any of its values, to remain, isolated and independent, on its edges, no longer vulnerable to its weapons.[60]

As such, it is not really a political doctrine, even though it has clear political implications.[61] It is not particularly useful as a way to engage politics and enlarge the realm of freedom *within* society and politics. This particular criticism is clearly relevant to the *Zhuangzi*. The Zhuangzians,[62] with their general antipathy toward politics, tend to cede the ground of political discourse to others, mostly the Confucians, in premodern China. Aside from obvious historical and cultural reasons, this also reflects a limitation of the Zhuangzian ability to imagine a kind of polity that can accommodate the desire for personal space and allow for individual freedom *within* society and politics, not outside.

From Berlin's perspective, at the root of the inadequacy of the Zhuangzian imagination of political freedom lies the axiomatic primacy of self-cultivation in the traditional Chinese discourse on personhood. As Gerald MacCallum perceptively observes, advocates of negative freedom "hold that the agents whose freedom is in question (for example, 'persons,' 'men') are, in effect, identifiable as Anglo-American law would identify 'natural' (as opposed to 'artificial') persons"[63] and the defenders of positive freedom "sometimes hold quite different views as to how these agents are to be identified."[64] This means that Berlin's negative freedom is articulated from the perspective of an ordinary person with natural cognitive endowments. This is clear from Berlin's fight against the monistic conviction of moral philosophers that all true values are ultimately commensurable. Berlin proposes that "we must fall back on the ordinary resources of empirical observation and ordinary human knowledge"[65] and takes seriously "[t]he world that we encounter in ordinary experience"[66] in understanding the human society. The valorization of an ordinary "natural" person with her ordinary knowledge and ordinary experience is at the heart of Berlin's deliberation on freedom. In many ways, negative freedom safeguards the "ordinariness" of a free and natural moral agent against the encroachment by others.

So the obvious question is: does the concept of an ordinary natural person exist as the focus of intellectual deliberation, aside from the need for cultivation and education, in traditional Chinese philosophy? The *Zhuangzi*, with its celebration of ordinary folks, might seem like a good place to locate a discourse on a natural person, but the "ordinary" folks in the text are not ordinary at all. They are often exemplars of unique virtues and paragons of special skills, even though their social status varies widely. This points to the assumed primacy of self-cultivation in the *Zhuangzi*.

At this juncture, it is important to point out that Berlin does not reject the project of self-transformation. In fact, as John Gray convincingly argues, the value of negative freedom for Berlin lies in its being "a condition of self-creation through choice-making."[67] Berlin's powerful defense of negative freedom is precisely to enable our self-creation through the choices we make as free agents. However, what is different between Zhuangzi and Berlin is that Berlin theorizes from the perspective of an ordinary "natural" person and the choices available to her, instead of reasoning from the vantage point of a perfected sage or the paragon of skills and the range of possibilities for him as in the case of Zhuangzi.

So what does this discussion amount to if we hope to make the *Zhuangzi* more relevant to the modern discourse on political and social freedom?[68] To develop a Zhuangzian *imaginaire* of political freedom that safeguards an individual against the encroachment of others and the state, thinkers in the Chinese tradition need to think through the implications of such a world from the vantage point of an ordinary, average person. This requires a paradigm shift, away from the axiomatic premise of self-cultivation and epistemic superiority of a cultivated sage, an assumption that is shared by all traditional Chinese thinkers, including Zhuangzi.

From a traditional Zhuangzian perspective, an ordinary person cannot be really free from various entanglements due to the intrinsic interconnectedness of beings in the world; only a cultivated and daemonic person can be genuinely free in this sense. That is, only a cultivated person can obtain through cultivation the kind of personal space that is invisible, hence unavailable, to others wherein one can enjoy freedom from any entanglement and thrive. However, there is no reason that a Zhuangzian cannot imagine a political system wherein such valued personal space is actually brought out in the open as a political space for individuals that is institutionally protected. In other words, if it is indeed possible for an accomplished Zhuangzian paragon to gain access to the precious personal space through his vigorous cultivation, there should be nothing inherently prohibitive that prevents the Zhuangzian from envisioning a more effective way to enlarge such personal space so that more people can enjoy and thrive. Such a protected political space for individuals is Berlin's negative freedom. The conception of this political space requires a new social and political imagination, entirely consistent with the Zhuangzian spiritual *imaginaire*. If such a move is possible for a modern Zhuangzian, he can certainly embrace some idea of political rights as the institutional guarantor of an individual's freedom against the interference by other people as well as the state. Put differently, for a Zhuangzian breakthrough in the political and social arena, there needs to be a new imagination of what is politically and socially possible, instead of simply accepting the political reality of whatever era or rejecting politics as an unworthy cause.

Importantly, venturing into the social and political arena does not compromise the lure of the Zhuangzian project. As I pointed out earlier, Zhuangzi and Berlin share many concerns with regard to moral monism, social conformity, and political tyranny and share their advocacy of value pluralism and epistemic humility. Their difference has to do with where they see the viable and attractive solutions lie. Clearly, Berlin's ultimate concern is political with the spiritual regarded as a suspect at best whereas Zhuangzi's case is exactly the opposite. More specifically, for Berlin, the political should be the ultimate arbiter for any spiritual claim whereas for Zhuangzi the spiritual should be vigorously pursued whereas the political is to be put up with.

However, as Charles Taylor perceptively argues in his critique of Berlin, negative freedom without spiritual inspiration is impoverished and self-defeating.[69] On the other hand, as Berlin powerfully demonstrates, escapist spirituality and monistic positive freedom often pervert the project of individual freedom. The Zhuangzian spiritual freedom can potentially bridge the gap between the two. The value of the Zhuangzian spiritual freedom lies precisely in its cultivation of personal space, its pursuit of disentanglement from the world, its advocacy of value-pluralism, and its epistemic humility. This very much resonates with Berlin's political project of negative freedom. What worries about Zhuangzi for Berlin is its antipathy toward politics, but there is nothing intrinsically anti-political in the Zhuangzian project. In fact, Berlin can well supplement the Zhuangzians with a viable and attractive political *imaginaire*. On the other hand, in Zhuangzi, we see a spirituality that is non-aggressive and non-imposing. It is a kind of negative spirituality that can serve as the spiritual corollary of the political and social project of negative freedom Berlin so powerfully articulates and defends. Moreover, Berlin's negative freedom enhances the Zhuangzian spiritual freedom in the political and social arena. Here we see a genuine opportunity for potentially fruitful cross-fertilization on the project of negative freedom between Berlin's political interest and Zhuangzi's spiritual pursuit. Indeed, it can even be argued that to be a Berlinian politically is to be a Zhuangzian spiritually.

V. Conclusion

In this article, I have used Isaiah Berlin as the interlocutor to reexamine the Zhuangzian project of spiritual freedom in order to raise new questions and expand the traditional horizon.[70] It is clear from our comparative study that for Zhuangzi freedom is first and foremost a spiritual problem that can only be resolved through spiritual cultivation hinted at in the text. On the other hand, for Berlin, freedom is primarily a social and political problem that can be dealt with only within the social and political realm. That is, for Berlin a political system should be set up in such a way that an ordinary person can make her own choices in her self-realization and self-actualization. Both Berlinian and Zhuangzian negative freedoms are achievement: for Berlin negative freedom is a political project, a constitutional achievement; for Zhuangzi, negative freedom is a spiritual project, an inner accomplishment.

Berlin argues against two troubling tendencies in some of the moral and spiritual traditions in the West: moral monism and political disengagement. Berlin's solution is political negative freedom and value pluralism, accomplished through a constitution of the political institution in modern liberal democracy. Although Zhuangzi shares Berlin's concern about moral monism and advocates moral pluralism, it is rather unfortunate that the Zhuangzian expressions of negative freedom are mainly confined to the spiritual domain and are not forcefully carried into the political discourse in reimagining new possibilities with regard to the state. It never happens to Zhuangzi[71] that the state can be reconstituted in such a way that its ability to intrude upon people's personal freedom can be kept in check. Therefore, what is lacking in the classical Chinese tradition is not so much the discourse of negative freedom itself but rather its limitation to the spiritual matter with little direct engagement with the mainstream political discourse. It is no surprise that we do not find any codification of negative freedom in institutional building in traditional China. Consequently, it is left to individuals themselves to cultivate a personal space, instead of its being codified in a constitution as in modern liberal democracy.[72]

We hope this comparative engagement between Berlin and Zhuangzi has made it clear that the challenge to Zhuangzi from Berlin's perspective is how the Zhuangzian project of freedom can have bigger voice in the political discourse on freedom, aside from its spiritual values. This is where the Zhuangzian tradition can learn from the West, and Berlin in particular, namely to develop a new kind of political *imaginaire* about the state which is capable of leaving people alone and giving room for them to realize and actualize themselves, consistent with the Zhuangzian *imaginaire* of spiritual freedom. On the other hand, Zhuangzi's spiritual negative freedom can help to mitigate Taylor's critique of Berlin. Such a cross-cultural conversation can indeed be promising in enriching our conceptual resources in dealing with various issues of our time.

RUTGERS UNIVERSITY
New Brunswick, New Jersey

Endnotes

This article partially builds on the argument I put forward in my 2011 article, "Two Notions of Freedom in Classical Chinese Thought: The Concept of *Hua* 化 in the *Zhuangzi* and the *Xunzi*" (*Dao: A Journal of Comparative Philosophy* 10, no. 4: 463–486). That article was originally inspired by Isaiah Berlin's articulation of two concepts of freedom in modern Western social and political philosophy, negative and positive. Berlin's discussion and articulation was instrumental in helping me to conceptually realign key ideas in classical Chinese thought in order to tease out and construct credible Chinese notions of freedom that are not confined to the modern Chinese translation of the word freedom, namely *ziyou* 自由. Since the two reviewers of the article in the *Dao* expressed the hope that I dealt with Berlin's argument more fully and systematically rather than simply using it as a framing device to construct Chinese notions of freedom, the current article gives me an opportunity to do exactly that. I am indebted to those two reviewers for pushing me in this direction. I appreciate it that the *Journal of Chinese Philosophy* has provided me this opportunity to do it. I am grateful for the helpful and often challenging philosophical and editorial comments and suggestions offered by Editor-in-Chief, Chung-ying Cheng, Managing Editor, Linyu Gu, and one of the coeditors for this special issue, Eric Nelson. A Chinese version of this article was presented at the Centennial Celebration Conference of the Philosophy Department at Peking University in October 2012. I appreciate the comments from the conference participants, especially Chenyang Li and Robin Wang. However, all possible errors remain mine alone.

1. In March of 2011, there was an international symposium on Isaiah Berlin and contemporary Chinese thought held at Tsinghua University in Beijing, China. This is a clear indication of the importance Chinese thinkers attach to Berlin's thought.
2. Isaiah Berlin, "Two Concepts of Liberty," in *Four Essays on Liberty* (New York: Oxford University Press, 1969), 122.
3. Ibid.
4. Ibid., 131.
5. The conflict between the two will be elaborated later in this essay.
6. Berlin specifically mentions the stoics and Buddhist sages as examples of positive and spiritual freedom: "There are two methods of freeing myself from pain. One is to heal the wound. But if the cure is too difficult or uncertain, there is another method. I can get rid of the wound by cutting off my leg. If I train myself to want nothing to which the possession of my leg is indispensable, I shall not feel the lack of it. This is the traditional self-emancipation of ascetics and quietists, of stoics or Buddhist sages, men of various religions or of none, who have fled the world, and escaped the yoke of society or public opinion, by some process of deliberate self-transformation that enables them to care no longer for any of its values, to remain, isolated and independent, on its edges, no longer vulnerable to its weapons. All political isolationism, all economic autarky, every form of autonomy, has in it some element of this attitude. I eliminate the obstacles in my path by abandoning the path; I retreat into my own sect, my own planned economy, my own deliberately insulated territory, where no voices from outside need be listened to, and no external forces can have effect. This is a form of the search for security; but it has also been called the search for personal or national freedom or independence." Berlin, *Four Essays on Liberty*, 135–36.
7. Ibid., 152.
8. Ibid., 170.
9. Ibid., 147.
10. Ibid., 148.
11. Ibid., 154.
12. Ibid., 168.
13. Ibid., 169.
14. Ibid., 171.
15. Charles Taylor, "What's Wrong with Negative Liberty," in *The Idea of Freedom: Essays in Honour of Isaiah Berlin*, ed. Alan Ryan (Oxford: Oxford University Press, 1979), 175.
16. Ibid., 176. Taylor seems to have softened his critique of Berlin later on, e.g., *A Secular Age* (Cambridge: The Belknap Press of Harvard University Press, 2007), 685.
17. Ibid., 176.
18. Ibid., 177.
19. Ibid.
20. John Gray defends Berlin against Taylor's charge by arguing that negative freedom is "*choice among alternatives or options that is unimpeded by others*" (John Gray, *Isaiah Berlin* [Princeton: Princeton University Press, 1997], 15, original italics), instead of simply the unobstructed pursuit of one's desires as Taylor alleges.
21. Taylor, "What's Wrong with Negative Liberty," 178.
22. Ibid., 179.
23. Ibid., 191.
24. Taylor agrees that we should examine whether a view of freedom can only be realized within a certain form of society and whether this pursuit necessarily leads to justifying the excess of totalitarian oppression in the name of liberty. But he dismisses any attempt to evade the question "by a philistine definition of freedom which relegates

them by fiat to the limbo of metaphysical pseudo-questions." Ibid., 193. It is not clear whether the issue of incompatibility of values falls under the category of "metaphysical pseudo-questions" or not. Taylor's later works acknowledge this issue more forcefully.
25. Defenders of Berlin, such as John Gray, argue that choice is essential to Berlin's conception of negative freedom and reject Taylor's charge that Berlin's negative freedom is purely an opportunity-concept.
26. This is more apparent in Taylor's later works, such as *Sources of the Self* (Cambridge: Cambridge University Press, 1992) and *A Secular Age* (Cambridge: The Belknap Press of Harvard University Press, 2007).
27. For the purpose of discussions in this essay, I will not differentiate between the historical Zhuangzi's own writings and later additions to the text bearing his name. There is enough cogency and internal coherence of the text, as well as the way it was received historically, that warrant this approach. My focus here is on what the text represents within the Chinese intellectual tradition, not the historicity of its different layers.
28. This is the source of a popular Chinese saying, "*Tanglang buchan huangque zai hou* 螳螂捕蟬黃雀在後."
29. A.C. Graham, trans., *Chuang Tzu: The Inner Chapters* (Indianapolis: Hackett, 2001), 118.
30. I have argued elsewhere that to properly the Zhuangzian idea of freedom we need to move away from the idea of choice or from the focus on *ziyou* 自由, usually translated as freedom in modern Chinese, and instead examine the concepts of *hua* 化 (transformation or to transform) and *you* 遊 (to roam or to navigate). I have made the case that *hua* and *you* in the *Zhuangzi* points to a vision of transformative freedom as the result of spiritual transformation. The paradigmatic expression of this transformative freedom is Confucius's autobiographical note that at the age of seventy he could follow his heartmind's (*xin* 心) desire without overstepping the boundary of propriety (*Analects*, 2: 4). Put differently, at that point in Confucius's life, his heartmind's desire is so well aligned with the norm of propriety that there is no struggle on his part to follow the norm of what is right. This sense of freedom exemplified in Confucius's life at seventy is an achievement, not a natural state he is born into. Such an accomplishment requires sustained effort in personal cultivation (*xiushen* 修身) on the part of the agent that transforms himself from the state of uncouth nature to the state of moral refinement. In this essay, I will expand my earlier discussion of the Zhuangzian freedom.
31. Translators of the *Zhuangzi* almost uniformly gloss *wuhua* as the transformation of things. Brook Ziporyn puts it somewhat differently as "the transformation of one thing into another." Brook Ziporyn, trans., *Zhuangzi: The Essential Writings with Selections from Traditional Commentaries* (Indianapolis: Hackett, 2009), 21. I will adopt Ziporyn's rendition as it does not have the ambiguity with the phrase "transformation of things," and modify it as "transformation between things."
32. Graham, trans., *Chuang Tzu: The Inner Chapters*, 61.
33. Here "daemonic" is used synonymously with "spiritual," distinguished from "demonic" that carries a negative meaning.
34. Graham, trans., *Chuang Tzu: The Inner Chapters*, 46. The last sentence is revised at the suggestion of Chung-ying Cheng. The original translation is: "When the daemonic in him concentrates it keeps creatures free from plagues and makes the grain ripen every year."
35. Graham, trans., *Chuang Tzu: The Inner Chapters*, 92.
36. Ibid.
37. Scott Cook, "Zhuang Zi and His Carving of the Confucian Ox," *Philosophy East and West* 47, no. 4 (1997): 540, original italics.
38. Graham, trans. *Chuang Tzu: The Inner Chapters*, 64.
39. Although, as Chung-ying Cheng points out to me, the ox might disagree. I interpret the ox as a metaphor for the intricacy and complexity of the world, echoing the view advanced by Robert Eno in his essay "Cook Ding's Dao and the Limits of Philosophy," in *Essays on Skepticism, Relativism and Ethics in the Zhuangzi*, eds. Paul Kjellberg and Philip J. Ivanhoe (Albany: State University of New York, 1996).

40. Burton Watson, trans., *The Complete Works of Chuang Tzu* (New York: Columbia University Press, 1968), 90.
41. Brook Ziporyn, trans., *Zhuangzi: The Essential Writings with Selections from Traditional Commentaries*, 49 fn. Graham translates it as "the universal thoroughfare." Ziporyn renders *datong* as "Great Openness" even though he amends it as *huatong* (化通) by adopting a parallel in the *Huainanzi*. Mair's translation as "the Transformational Thoroughfare" follows the same textual change (Victor Mair, trans., *Wandering on the Way: Early Taoist Tales and Parables of Chuang Tzu*, [Honolulu: University of Hawaii Press, 1997], 64).
42. Graham, trans., *Chuang Tzu: The Inner Chapters*, 90.
43. Ibid., 89, Graham's italics.
44. Philip J. Ivanhoe, "Was Zhuangzi a Relativist?" in *Essays on Skepticism, Relativism, and Ethics in the Zhuangzi*, 201.
45. One reviewer raised the issue concerning the social implications of this claim. The Zhuangzian authenticity can open the door to resignation, rather than freedom, and passivity of an indirect acceptance or even affirmation of social conformity and hierarchy. Such troubling implications will be dealt with when we critique the Zhuangzian conception of freedom from Berlin's perspective later in the essay.
46. Graham, trans., *Chuang Tzu: The Inner Chapters*, 94.
47. Ibid., 96.
48. Berlin calls this the "doctrine of sour grapes." Berlin, "Two Concepts of Liberty," 139. More on this later in the essay.
49. Berlin, *Four Essays on Liberty*, 135.
50. Ibid., 139.
51. Ibid.
52. Ibid., 140.
53. The Chinese term *xin* 心 is usually translated as heart or heart-mind. But as many modern commentators have correctly pointed out, there is no distinction between the heart and the mind in classical Chinese thought. Therefore, I have decided to coin the term "heartmind" to translate *xin* in order to highlight such a non-distinction implied in it.
54. This is from Graham's note, *Chuang Tzu: The Inner Chapters*, 69.
55. Ibid.
56. Ibid.
57. Cook, 540, original italics.
58. Graham, trans., *Chuang Tzu: The Inner Chapters*, 122.
59. Ibid.
60. Berlin, *Four Essays on Liberty*, 135–36.
61. Ibid., 139.
62. These can include those who are lifelong hermits who live at the margin of society or those whose political ambitions are frustrated.
63. Gerald C. MacCallum, Jr. "Negative and Positive Freedom," *The Philosophical Review* 76, no. 3 (1967): 321.
64. Ibid.
65. Berlin, *Four Essays on Liberty*, 168.
66. Ibid.
67. John Gray, *Isaiah Berlin*, 21.
68. I would like to thank Chung-ying Cheng for pushing me to clarify the implications of my discussion of Berlin and Zhuangzi here.
69. Taylor, "What's Wrong with Negative Liberty," 179, 192.
70. Several people have raised the objection that my critique might have been too demanding, too harsh, or even unfair, to Zhuangzi. While I agree that this essay might be more critical of Zhuangzi than celebratory, my purpose is to make better use of the unique aspects of the Zhuangzian freedom, namely its negative aspect, as a possible indigenous intellectual resources for the development of a liberal polity in China. Since there are few traditional Chinese thinkers who demonstrate a profound appreciation of negative freedom, Zhuangzi deserves to be taken more seriously in the contemporary political discourse, not just being elevated, but confined, to the spiritual domain.

71. I do not mean to fault Zhuangzi alone for the lack of political imagination here. Imagination is socially and culturally conditioned even as it tries to transcend such conditions, with varying degrees of success. The limitation of the Zhuangzian political imagination is in many ways the product of a lack of alternative forms of political systems in early China.
72. I do not mean to imply that the lack of a political discourse on negative freedom alone is responsible for the lack of development in the democratic institution building in traditional China. The historical circumstances are of course too complicated to be reduced to a single cause. But the lack of intellectual interest and popular *imaginaire* in this direction must have played some role.

STEPHEN R. PALMQUIST

MAPPING KANT'S ARCHITECTONIC ONTO THE *YIJING* VIA THE GEOMETRY OF LOGIC

Abstract

Both Kant's architectonic and the *Yijing* can be structured as four perspectival levels: $0 + 4 + 12 + (4 \times 12) = 64$. The first, unknowable level is unrepresentable. The geometry of logic provides well-structured maps for levels two to four. Level two consists of four basic *gua* (2, 64, 63, 1), corresponding to Kant's category-headings (quantity, quality, relation, modality). Level three's twelve *gua*, derived logically from the initial four, correspond to Kant's twelve categories. Level four correlates the remaining 48 *gua* (in twelve sets of four) to Kant's theory of the four university faculties (philosophy, theology, law, medicine), and to four categorially organized (twelve-fold) domains comprising his philosophical system.

I. Geometrical Figures as Maps for the Four Levels of Perspectives

In a recent issue of this journal I briefly sketched a framework for comparing the architectonic structure of Kant's philosophy with that of the 64 hexagrams (*gua* 卦) that constitute the *Yijing* 《易經》.[1] The core claim is that both systems of thought can be understood in terms of four perspectival "levels," each exhibiting an increasingly complex systematic structure. Previously I explained (though only briefly) how Kant's system, organized around twelve categories, corresponds *exactly* to the *Yijing* on the first three levels, given a nonstandard method of arranging the 64 *gua*[2] that I shall call the "Compound *Yijing*."[3] I then *predicted* that some of Kant's metaphysical applications of his Critical theories could be interpreted in such a way that they would correspond to the 48 *gua* that comprise the outer, or fourth level of the Compound *Yijing*. My purpose in this follow-up article is to provide a more detailed explanation of the initial idea by showing exactly how the first three levels of both systems can be

STEPHEN R. PALMQUIST, Professor, Department of Religion and Philosophy, Hong Kong Baptist University. Specialties: Kant studies, philosophy of religion, logic of symbolism. E-mail: stevepq@hkbu.edu.hk

"mapped" onto a set of simple geometrical figures that have a direct structural correspondence to certain basic logical relations, then to sketch a possible way to fulfill the prediction made in the previous article.

As I have previously introduced the mapping technique called "the geometry of logic" in numerous other contexts,[4] I begin here in §I with only a brief explanation of the procedure and its guiding rules, together with an account of the simplest (first) level of systemization. I proceed to apply the technique in §II to the second level, by mapping both the four basic *gua* and Kant's four category headings onto two intersecting line segments, and in §III to the third level, by mapping both the twelve intermediate *gua* and Kant's two main categorial tables[5] onto a set of four triangles arranged (roughly) in a circle. The article concludes in §IV by offering some tentative suggestions as to how the fourth level, the remaining 48 *gua* that constitute the outer circle of the Compound *Yijing*, might be discerned as operating in some of the key features of Kant's philosophical system, and by proposing a map that could assist in examining such correlations more deeply at some later stage.

The first (or grounding, core) level for both Kant's architectonic and that of the Compound *Yijing* is pre-systematic: just as Kant's "thing in itself" is by definition unknowable,[6] so also the "Dao" that underlies the *Yijing*'s complex distinctions ultimately cannot be named;[7] as a result, neither plays any constitutive role in the architectonic forms that shape the content of what *can* be known within its respective system. (That is, the thing in itself is *not* a representation; and there is no *gua* called "The Dao.") In classical (Aristotelian) logic, this grounding level corresponds to the principle of identity: A = A. Those unaccustomed (or opposed) to metaphysical thinking often have difficulty appreciating why such a principle should be employed at all. Functioning as the necessary starting point for any (philosophically complete) discussion of reality, it corresponds to what Parmenides called "the One"—that is, the principle that "what is, is".

The geometry of logic maps this essential starting-point onto the geometrical *point*—a figure that technically cannot be represented, since it occupies a *position* without being *extended* in space.[8] Just as a mathematical point is indivisible, no *system* (as such) has yet arisen when one refers *only* to "the thing in itself" (in Kant's philosophy) or to "the Dao" (in the *Yijing*). The system begins to arise in each case only when the initial (postulated) unity becomes *two*, a logical relation called "analysis" in western logic and corresponding to the basic distinction between *yin* and *yang* in Chinese philosophy. This transformation of 1 (what is) into 2 (the distinction between what is and what is not) completely describes the first level of the geometry of logic, and can be mapped onto a straight line segment with the opposite components of the system situated at the two end-points. (Placing an arrowhead at either end of the line segment depicts the fact that neither component of a first-level analytic relation is "prior" to the other; from a purely logical point of view, *opposites arise together*.) To maximize simplicity, I normally use "+" to represent positivity (or the *yang* force—i.e., what *is*) and "–" to represent negativity (or the *yin* force—i.e., what *is not*). However, the solid and broken lines of the *Yijing* convey the same logical distinction; employing two sets of identical terms would be redundant, so in this article I shall normally let the traditional forms of the 64 *gua* replace my customary "+/–" apparatus. With this overview as a basic introduction, let us now proceed in the next two sections to examine the precise correlations between the second and third levels of Kant's categorial system and the Compound *Yijing*.

II. Correlating Kant's Category Headings with the Four Basic *Gua*

The key to recognizing within the *Yijing* a pattern of relations that is more than just binary ($2^6 = 64$), but *compound* $(4 + 12 + [4 \times 12] = 64)$—that is, a pattern that contains *triadic* relations as well as *dyadic* relations because, as we shall see in §III, the "12" consists of four sets of *three*—is to put aside the time-honored tradition of grouping the 64 hexagrams into eight (*ba* 八) "houses." Treating the *trigram* as the fundamental unit, the latter tradition takes the eight *gua* that consist of an identical trigram on the top and bottom and regards each of these as the heading for a unique set of eight *gua*. The resulting $8 \times 8 = 64$ pattern has become so deeply entrenched that it takes quite an effort to be open to the possibility of using other ordering patterns. But if the goal is to identify an overlap between the *Yijing* and any *twelvefold* architectonic, such as Kant's, then identifying an alternative to the *bagua* 八卦 is essential. Ironically, we shall see in §IV that the traditional *bagua* form an intriguing pattern within the Compound *Yijing*.

In place of the *bagua* the Compound *Yijing* identifies the first and last pair of *gua* as being the most basic, for they serve (explicitly) as the starting-points and the end-points of the system. The first two—*gua* 1 (☰), called *qian* 乾 ("the creative"), and *gua* 2 (☷), called *kun* 坤 ("the receptive")—are the only two that are completely "pure" (i.e., composed entirely of either *yang* lines or *yin* lines). Since they are both composed of identical trigrams on the top and bottom, they are included in the traditional *bagua*. A crucial weakness of the *bagua* is

that it does *not* include the dual *end-points* of the system: *gua* 63 (䷾),
called *jiji* 既濟 ("after completion"), and *gua* 64 (䷿), called *weiji* 未濟
("before completion"). One of the main arguments for regarding the
Compound *Yijing* as an architectonically richer way of ordering the
overall system than the traditional ordering in terms of eight houses is
that the former properly acknowledges the importance of this unique
pair of *gua*, the only two in the entire *Yijing* that are thoroughly
"mixed" (i.e., where the *yin* and *yang* lines *alternate*, so that the same
type of line never appears twice in succession).

Once we have identified the inner (fourfold) core of the Compound
Yijing, relating it to Kant's categorial system is quite straightforward.
For Kant likewise organizes his Table of Categories (and the initial
table of logical functions in judgment) around four headings: the
distinction between *quantity*, *quality*, *relation*, and *modality* colors
virtually every theory he defends, in much the same way that *gua*
numbers 1, 2, 63, and 64, define the ultimate starting and ending points
of the *Yijing*. Moreover, in his discussion of how the categories are
applied to objects in the form of "principles of pure understanding,"
Kant groups his basic fourfold classification into "mathematical"
(quantity and quality) and "dynamical" (relation and modality)
types.[9] While we might be tempted to associate this distinction with
the distinction between the first two *gua* and the last two (since *gua* 1
and 2 depict absolute and therefore an apparently mathematical
opposition, while *gua* 63 and 64 express the system's only entirely
relative and therefore apparently most dynamical opposition), I shall
argue that Kant's distinction is more complex.

In Chapter II of the first *Critique's* Analytic of Principles Kant
defines "mathematical" principles as conditions for the possibility of
the "intuitive" (i.e., immediately *experienced*) content of an experience, while "dynamical" principles are conditions for the possibility of
the "discursive" content (i.e., content mediated by our thinking about
a thing's *existence*).[10] The second distinction that defines this fourfold
relation is between principles (and so also, original category classes)
that are "extensive" (cf. quantity and relation) versus those that are
"intensive" (cf. quality and modality).[11] I have argued elsewhere[12] that
the latter distinction should be given priority, with the category headings corresponding to "extensive" principles best being mapped
onto the horizontal (−) axis of a cross, while those corresponding to
the "intensive" principles are mapped onto the vertical (+) axis.
The "intuitive" (−) versus "discursive" (+) distinction then defines the
polar oppositions at the end-points of each axis: whereas *quantity* is
extensive and intuitive (− −), *relation* is extensive and discursive (− +);
likewise, *quality* is intensive and intuitive (+ −), while *modality* is
intensive and discursive (+ +). Using the conventions of placing posi-

tive (*yang*) terms *above* and/or to the *left* of negative (*yin*) terms, and of depicting arrows as pointing *from* pure *to* mixed components, we can now easily correlate Kant's four classes with the four basic *gua* of the Compound *Yijing*, as shown in Figure 1.

At this level (as in every diagram throughout this article), lines 1 and 6 determine the position of each *gua* on the cross. So, *gua* 1 is placed at the top because it begins and ends with *yang* (+) lines; it points to and is completed by *gua* 64, placed at the lowest position, because the latter has *yang* (+) as line 1 and *yin* (–) as line 6; etc. The significance (i.e., the architectonic function) of the inner four lines will emerge at the next two levels; their only function here is to confirm the distinction between the pure (initial) *gua* and the completely mixed (final) *gua*.

Considerable attention could be given to the question of whether or not the correlations shown in Figure 1 are anything more than arbitrary. In order to reserve sufficient space to discuss the third and fourth levels, I shall here offer only a few observations. First, associating quantity (i.e., the extended nature of the basic "stuff" that we intuit in our day-to-day experiences) with "the receptive" seems virtually self-evident, from Kant's perspective. Kant famously calls sensibility (the human power that gives rise to sensible intuition) the faculty of "receptivity," in contrast to understanding (the human power to think) as the faculty of "spontaneity."[13]

Second, this comparative map suggests that the role of modality in Kant's system *just is* the understanding. Indeed, the fact that Kant concludes his discussion of the Principles of Pure Understanding with the principle corresponding to this class is no accident: the *Yijing* could not be more succinct in identifying this position as "the creative," for understanding *begins* only when the mind acknowledges its modes (i.e., the specific ways that intuition and conception are internally related). We shall explore this further in §III, when we discuss the correlations that emerge at the third level of both systems.

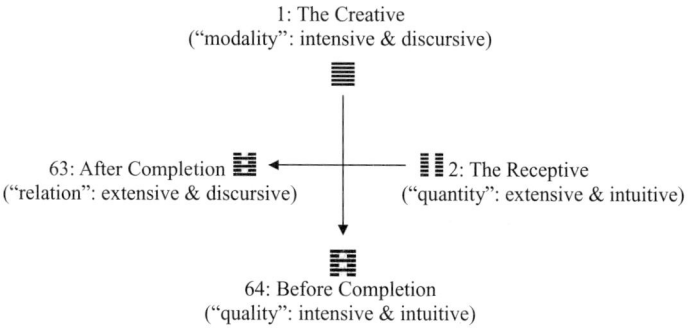

Figure 1.

Third, just as the two *gua* that define each fundamental pair are themselves exact opposites (i.e., each *yin* changes to *yang* and vice versa), so also the map highlights the fact (often neglected by interpreters) that the absolute opposite of Kant's "quantity" is not "quality" (the latter being its *polar* opposite, since it shares the characteristic of being "intuitive," just as *gua* 2 and 64 share three lines and are opposite in three lines), but "modality," as represented by the fact that *gua* 1 and 2 have no lines in common.

Fourth, this comparison also sheds light on aspects of the *Yijing* that might otherwise remain mysterious, such as why "before completion" comes *after* "after completion": the arrangement shown in Figure 1 suggests that *gua* 64 has a *logical* priority over *gua* 63, even though the understanding only reaches completion when it *extends* into the realm of actual relationships. That is, the last *gua* is derived from the first one, with this pair defining the abstract axis of intensional creativity; but like modality and quality, these features of human thought do not become *real* until they interact with the extended quantities (objects of receptivity) that are genuinely completed when they enter into *relation* with other things.

III. Correlating Kant's Twelve Categories with the Third-Level *Gua*

To unpack the full range of (potentially rich) implications that arise out of a comparison of the architectonic structure of Kant's philosophy with that of the Compound *Yijing* would require a book-length work. Our focus here is more limited: to identify the *rules of mapping* that enable us to display such correlations clearly. This is why I have grounded the discussion in the geometry of logic, whose rules I have already elaborated in detail elsewhere, as explained in note 4. All too often interpreters tend to think of both Kant's categories and the progression of the *Yijing*'s *gua* as a merely random aggregate of features that just happen to add up to a certain number. A cursory glance at the traditional numbering of the *Yijing*, for example, shows that, although the *gua* appears in ordered pairs (with every even-numbered *gua* mirroring the odd-numbered *gua* that precedes it, with one or more *yang* line changing to a *yin*, and/or vice versa), the arrangement appears random beyond this obvious pattern. Without claiming that Kant's categories provide a key that unlocks a secret order for the entire system, I shall provide a set of *rules* that demonstrate how every *gua* can be generated directly from the basic four, whose order, as we saw in §II, is anything but random. Drawing out all the potentially rich implications of the resulting correlations, however, lies beyond the scope of this article.

Just as Kant derives his twelvefold table of categories from his four basic category headings, with each heading giving rise first to a set of opposites (i.e., a thesis and an antithesis) followed by a third term that combines key features of the first two (i.e., a synthesis), so also the mapping rules applied to the third level of the Compound *Yijing* employ a triadic structure. In order to derive a third-level *opposition* from each of the basic *gua*, we merely change the top line (from *yang* to *yin*, or vice versa) to generate the first new *gua*, then change the bottom line to generate the second. In each case this produces two derivative *gua* that are opposites in lines 1 and 6. To form a synthesis between these two derivative *gua*, we merely perform *both* operations at the same time, so that both the top and bottom lines of the second-level *gua* are changed into their opposites. Thus, for example, in Figure 2, *gua* 1 (☰) changes first to *gua* 43 (☱), called *guai* 夬 ("break-through [resoluteness]"), and then to *gua* 44 (☴), called *gou* 姤 ("coming to meet"), with this pair being synthesized to produce *gua* 28 (☳), called *daguo* 大過 ("preponderance of the great"). Once these

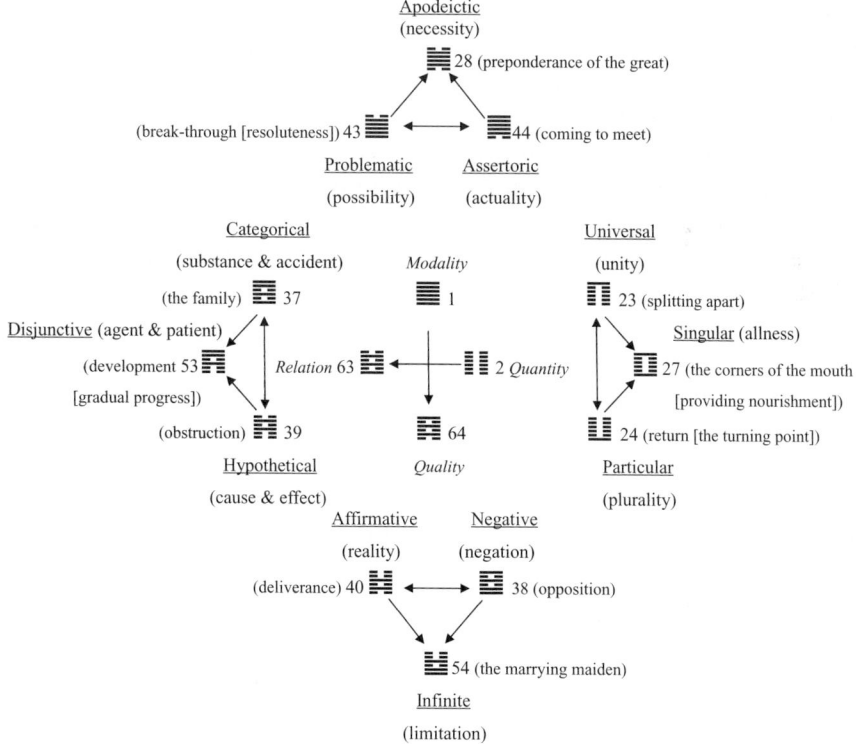

Figure 2.

rules of synthesis are recognized, the ordered relations of the entire system of twelve third-level *gua* are easy to see.

The structural identity of Kant's table of categories with the third level of the Compound *Yijing* becomes evident once we realize (a point often overlooked in the secondary literature on Kant) that in his official presentation of the initial tables (of categories and of logical functions), Kant does not count the basic four headings as *members* of the system as such. Clearly identifying the twelvefold table as delineating a distinct *level* of Kant's architectonic enables us easily to correlate its components with those of the third level of the Compound *Yijing*. Given the mapping rules set out above, and following the correlations between the basic classes that were shown in Figure 1, we can construct Figure 2 as a proposal for correlating the twelve third-level *gua* with Kant's twelvefold tables. Because Kant introduces his twelve terms in *two* tables, as the logical functions *in* any judgment and then as the twelve *categories*, I include both sets of terms in Figure 2, with the logical functions underlined and the category names provided in parentheses.

I shall now make some tentative observations about the various correlations that emerge on this third level of the Kantian/*Yijing* architectonic, as depicted in Figure 2. In so doing, I shall focus on one "quadrant" at a time, where a quadrant is defined (at this level) as the set of three components that arise out of one of the four basic *gua*; on the fourth level, as we shall see in §IV, each quadrant will be extended to twelve additional *gua*, with a set of four being derived from each third-level *gua* in that quadrant. As we shall see, lines 3 and 4 remain the same for each *gua* that appears in a given quadrant, so that each quadrant can be named after these two inner lines. (To facilitate seeing these connections, Figure 2 includes the four second-level *gua*.) Obviously, we should not expect a perfect fit between the conceptual *content* of these two very different systems. My goal in this section is to demonstrate that their *architectonic structure* is identical on this third level; any resonance between their respective contents will be a pleasant surprise.

Before proceeding to a detailed analysis of the correlations between Kant's categories and the twelve third-level *gua*, we should take note of two types of pattern that first emerge at this level of the Compound *Yijing*. First, we must understand how the third term in each triad shown in Figure 2 constitutes a *genuine synthesis* of the first two terms, because this synthesis is what transforms this ordering of the *Yijing* into more than just a simple system based on binary (analytic) relations. Indeed, understanding how the triads are composed is a necessary requirement for understanding why this system of ordering is properly called "compound." The synthetic component (i.e., each *gua* that has two arrows pointing to it) can be derived from the initial analytic pair (i.e., each pair of *gua* with a double-headed arrow between them) in two ways. One method of constructing the synthetic *gua* is to put the *top* trigram from the first *gua* (i.e., the *gua* that appears either on the left or on top) together with the *bottom* trigram of the second *gua* (i.e., the *gua* that appears either on the right or on the bottom). The other method yields the same result, because each set of three *gua* on the third level (and, incidentally, also its corresponding second-level *gua*) all share the same four internal lines: to construct the synthetic *gua*, use the top line from the first *gua* and the bottom line from the second *gua*, keeping the four internal lines the same for all *gua* in that quadrant.

Second, if each second-level *gua* is taken together with the three third-level *gua* derived from it, then (as just noted) the resulting set of four *gua* all share exactly the same four internal lines. As we shall see in §IV, the same holds true for *every* set of four *gua* that are mapped onto a cross in the entire Compound *Yijing*. That is, every time a set of four *gua* appears, they will share the same four inner lines; these lines can therefore be treated as a *label* for that set—the only exception being the first-level quaternity, which as we saw in §II is derived not from the identity of inner lines, but from the selection of the first two (totally pure) and last two (totally mixed) *gua* in the overall system of 64. What is common to *every* quaternity that will be mapped onto a cross, including the basic four, is that the top and bottom lines of each *gua* follow the pattern previously stipulated by the geometry of logic (i.e., + + or *yang-yang* being at the top and pointing downward to + – or *yang-yin*, and – – or *yin-yin* being at the right and pointing leftward to – + or *yin-yang*).

Of all the correlations shown in Figure 2, probably the most striking is that between the three categories of quantity and the three *gua* that are directly derived from *gua* 2 (the receptive). No set of three *gua* serves to *depict* more obviously than in this triad the nature of the three categories in Kant's table: just as universal judgments (e.g., "All bodies have weight") employ "top-down" reasoning and particular judgments (e.g., "This book weighs a pound") employ "bottom-up" reasoning, *gua* 23 and 24 place the only *solid* line at the top or at the bottom, respectively, of the set of otherwise broken lines. The *names* assigned to these two *gua* might seem inappropriate at first; but for anyone who grasps the internal logic that guides the naming of the *Yijing*'s *gua*, the names also make good sense. When a concept expresses *unity* (or a judgment, *universality*), it has nowhere else to *go*, should any change be required, but to "split apart" (*bo* 剝), just as a concept that expresses *plurality* (or a judgment, *particularity*) must be viewed (if faced with any future *change*) as beginning a "return" (*fu* 複) to the universal. That the *synthesis* of these two categories expresses concepts of "allness" or "totality" ("*Allheit*" in German) (or judgments, *singularity*) is symbolized by the actual shape of the corresponding *gua*, the only hexagram in the *Yijing* that resembles a square. The Chinese name, *yi* 頤 ("the corners of the mouth"), derives in part from the shape of the *gua* (reminiscent of an open mouth), and more literally means "providing nourishment," in the sense of being *receptive to what is good*. The judgment relating to *gua* 27 clarifies that this is the character and life situation of the "superior man"—the person who has achieved the perfect balance of universality and particularity in such a way as to have become a *singular individual*, or what might nowadays be called a "whole person."

A similarly intriguing set of resonances occurs in the modality quadrant of Figure 2, between Kant's terms for the three modal categories and both the *image* and the *name* of each corresponding *gua*: just as "problematic" judgments express concepts of *possibility* and "assertoric" judgments express concepts of *actuality*, *gua* 43 depicts the strength of pure *yang* opening up into a single *yin* gap (as if to suggest a new possibility just emerging into view), while *gua* 44 depicts this single *yin* gap at the bottom (as if to suggest that the possibility has now become *fully actualized*). The names for these *gua* also dovetail nicely with Kant's categories: one must possess "resoluteness" to "break-through" (*guai* 夬) old barriers in order to be open to a new *possibility*; and the experience of transforming a possibility into an *actuality* just *is* "coming to meet" (*gou* 姤) the object in one's own experience. The connection between the synthetic components in this quadrant is not entirely obvious, but is nevertheless detectable: just as Kant thinks concepts of *necessity*, as conveyed by apodeictic judgments, somehow *combine* aspects of possibility with aspects of actuality (yet move beyond both), so also *gua* 28 depicts the excessive strength of pure *yang* in the inner four lines being eclipsed by (or necessarily bound up in) two outer *yin* lines. Claims to have achieved *apodeictic certainty* (such as Kant makes for some of his own theories) are undoubtedly the "highest" judgment-claims in all of philosophy, and can hardly be described with a more appropriate phrase than "preponderance of the great" (*daguo* 大過).[14]

The third-level components of the quadrant opposite to modality, the three categories of quality, also resonate with the corresponding *gua*, though not as clearly as those considered above. For example, affirmative judgments (those that attribute concepts of *reality* to an object) are not obviously judgments of "deliverance" (*jie* 解), the name of *gua* 40. The further explanation of this *gua* in the *Yijing*, however, does connote a significant emphasis on *affirming* one's current situation: based on a conditional, it links both sides to an assessment of where one finds *reality*. "If there is no longer anything where one has to go, / Return brings good fortune. / If there is still something where one has to go, / Hastening brings good fortune."[15] Either way, the value of one's current project is being affirmed: if the job is done, affirm its reality and go home; if the job is still ongoing, affirm its worth and bring it to full fruition quickly. By contrast, negative judgments (those that attribute concepts of *negation* to an object) resonate quite obviously with "opposition" (*kui* 睽), the name of *gua* 38. The two trigrams that compose this *gua* represent a flame on top of a lake[16]—fire and water being the two most strongly *opposed* members of the traditional Chinese five elements. The synthesis in this quadrant seems rather remote from Kant's corresponding category: infinite judgments (those that attribute concepts of *limitation* to an object) seem wholly unrelated to "the marrying maiden" (*gui mei* 歸妹), the name of *gua* 54. Yet even here some indirect correlation can be discerned, once we realize that this is one of four *gua* that are typically taken as symbolizing the relationship between a man and a woman. Indeed, this *gua* is the only one emphasizing the importance of establishing appropriate boundary-conditions: through the institution of a marriage that recognizes proper limits, the infinite value of love can be nurtured.[17]

The remaining quadrant, consisting of the three categories of relation, conveys the most tenuous correlations of all those that emerge at this level. One of the problems is that, because of the nature of this classification of judgment (i.e., as *relating* one thing to another), the *concepts* each type expresses always come in pairs. Thus, categorical judgments (e.g., "Duty must always be obeyed") express concepts of *both* substance and accident, while hypothetical judgments (e.g., "If the readers are bored, they will stop reading") express concepts of both cause and effect. Attempting to correlate the former to *gua* 37, called *jia ren* 家人 ("the family"), seems at first like comparing apples and oranges. However, once again, consulting the text reveals some intriguing resonances, for the emphasis here is on the *laws* that govern family relationships, and in Chinese culture there is no closer correlate to Kant's categorical imperative than the principle of filial piety.[18] Correlating the latter, with its emphasis on causal relationships within the empirical world (as opposed to the moral world constituted by the relations between persons), to *gua* 39, called *jian* 蹇 ("obstruction"), is more straightforward. For here, the two trigrams represent (following traditional Chinese symbolism) "a dangerous abyss lying before us and a steep, inaccessible mountain lying behind us."[19] What better imagery could depict the transcendentally mysterious (yet inescapable) relationship between cause (the inaccessible mountain) and effect (the dangerous abyss)? Just as the advice provided in the *Yijing* text focuses on how to *deal with* such obstructions, so also Kant's treatment of the principle of cause and effect does not encourage us to climb the mountain (much less jump over the abyss), but focuses on how to cope with the inevitable obstruction that the phenomenal world places along the path of the moral agent. The synthetic component in this quadrant, disjunctive judgment (e.g., "Authorities should be obeyed, but without neglecting one's own well-being"), expresses conceptual relations between an "agent" and a "patient" (i.e., one who experiences the *effect* of another's actions). In the same way that Kant portrays this classification as a synthesis of the categorical and hypothetical forms of judgment, and as the direct opposite of infinite judgments (since what is disjunctive by definition cannot approach a limit), so also the *Yijing* conveys *gua* 53, called *jian* 漸 ("development" [gradual progress]) as placing the "tree" trigram from *gua* 37 on top of the "mountain" trigram from *gua* 39, yet also as representing the direct opposite to *gua* 54 (the synthetic component in the quality or *yang-yin* quadrant of Figure 2). Before marriage (*gua* 54), one must experience a gradual progress of development in a relationship; the "agent" perspective of morality must be merged with the "patient" perspective of causality, if such a disjunction (i.e., a marriage, in the *Yijing*, or the reciprocity of nature's wholeness, in the first *Critique's* Third Analogy) is to emerge.

My main reason for noting these resonances between Kant's categories and the *gua* that constitute the third level of the Compound *Yijing* is not to argue that the *Yijing* somehow foreshadowed Kant's philosophy, nor that Kant's philosophy reveals the "true meaning" of the *Yijing*'s ancient symbolism. That any significant historical linkage exists between these two systems is extremely unlikely. Rather, such resonances suggest that both Kant and the *Yijing* have appealed to *one and the same architectonic backdrop* that is determined by the structure of reason itself and therefore influences the way the human mind tends to organize its experience of the real world; only the existence of such a backdrop could explain how two such different systems of thought have independently arrived at theories with such strikingly similar structural features. But the most challenging question is whether this structural parallelism continues when we examine the fourth level of the Compound *Yijing*. In the final section I shall sketch a possible way of meeting that challenge.

IV. Overview and Implications of the Fourth Level

The fourth level of the Compound *Yijing* arises directly out of each of the twelve *gua* that make up the third level, by following one additional mapping rule. To avoid confusion, let us first review the basic rules introduced in §§II–III: (i) the core quaternity consists of the first two ("pure") *gua* and the last two (perfectly "mixed") *gua*; (ii) lines 3 and 4 of each *gua* within the same quadrant remain fixed and thus establish the *identity* of all *gua* on every level of that quadrant; (iii) positions of the *gua* on each third-level triad are derived from the corresponding second-level *gua* by changing first its top line (to define the "thesis" *gua*), then its bottom line (to define the "antithesis" *gua*), then both its top and bottom lines (to define the "synthesis" *gua*); and finally (iv) the variation in lines 1 and 6 determines the position where each *gua* is placed on the cross, regardless of where the cross appears in the overall system, such that *yang* (+) always appears above and/or to the left of *yin* (−).

The new rule that explains how the fourth-level *gua* is derived from those on the third level is that lines 2 and 5 of the corresponding third-level *gua* determine which set of four inner lines will define the corresponding quaternity at the level of the outer 48 *gua*, with the line next to the one that did *not* change (when deriving the third-level *gua*) now changing. The exact application of this rule *seems* to differ, depending on which position the third-level *gua* occupies in its quadrant; but that is only apparent, because each third-level *gua* was composed by changing a *different line* of its corresponding second-level *gua*. (Recall rule 3, above.) For example, to generate the first quaternity in the *yang-yang* (+ +) quadrant, start with *gua* 43 (☰); this *gua* was derived from *gua* 1 by changing the *top* line (i.e., line 6), so now *line 2* changes in order to derive the inner four lines shared by all four *gua* in the corresponding fourth-level quaternity. The complete Compound *Yijing* is generated by following the same procedure with each of the twelve third-level *gua*, as shown in Figure 3.

Significantly, each quadrant in Figure 3 includes *two* of the traditional *bagua* mentioned in §I, as indicated by the eight underlined numbers. In both pure quadrants, one of these eight key *gua* appears as the basic (second-level) *gua* initiating the whole quadrant (i.e., *gua* 1 and 2), while the other appears at the outer extremity of the fourth level, at the furthest point beyond the synthetic *gua* (i.e., *gua* 30 and 29, respectively). In both mixed quadrants, by contrast, the two representative *bagua* appear in the same position on opposite fourth-level crosses—on the vertical axis for the quadrant stemming from the second-level horizontal axis, and on the horizontal axis for the quadrant stemming from the vertical level. Far from ignoring the significance of the *bagua*, therefore, the Compound *Yijing* demonstrates that their positions in the overall system follow nonrandom rules of *balance*.

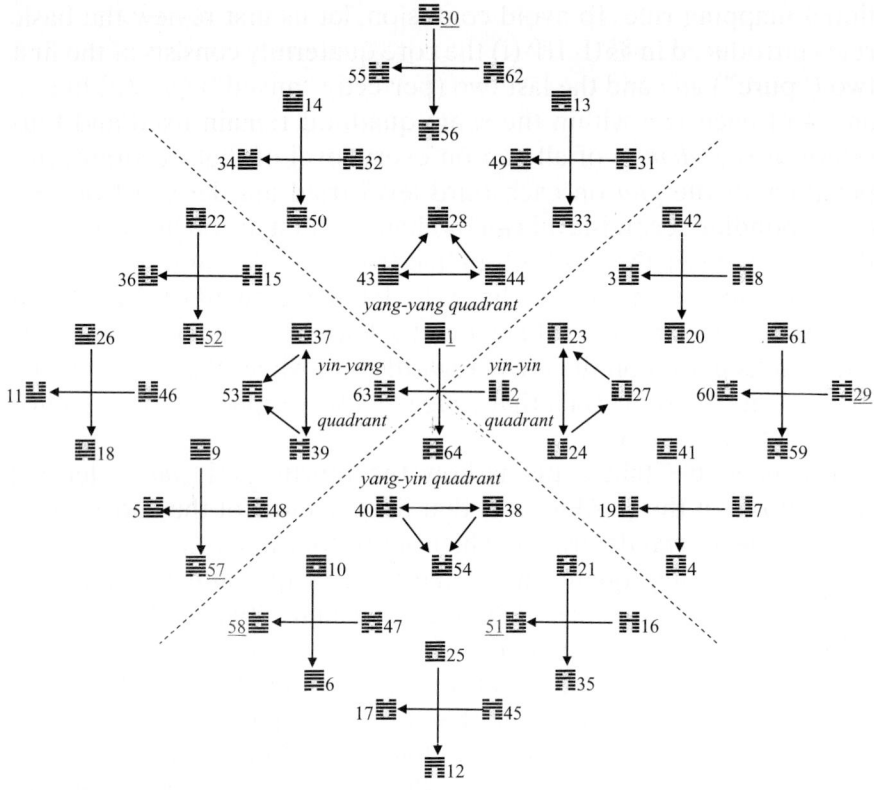

Figure 3.

The remaining challenge is to find a way of correlating this fourth level of the Compound *Yijing* with the architectonic structure of Kant's broader philosophical system. While there may be several plausible ways of doing this,[20] one good approach is to identify each quadrant with one of the four university *faculties* that Kant discusses in his 1798 book, *The Conflict of the Faculties*:[21] my hypothesis is that philosophy, being the "lower" faculty, corresponds to the *yin-yin* (– –) quadrant; theology, being the highest of the three "higher" faculties, corresponds to the *yang-yang* (+ +) quadrant; law (theology brought down to earth, so to speak) corresponds to the *yang-yin* (+ –) quadrant; and medicine (the philosophy of the body) corresponds to the *yin-yang* (– +) quadrant. This application has the advantage of being simple, complete, and fully grounded in Kant's text. Its disadvantage is that it appears to leave out of consideration quite a large proportion of Kant's philosophical writings. However, if we stretch what is covered by each faculty just slightly, fruitful ways of making the relevant correlations emerge. Confirmation of this hypothesis would require identifying twelve basic sets of (fourfold) categorial principles, each introduced within (or at least implied by) Kant's writings, each serving to guide our understanding of concrete human situations related to one of the four university faculties, and each corresponding to one fourth-level quaternity in Figure 3.

Since the second and third levels of the Compound *Yijing* both correspond to Kant's main tables of categories and logical functions, as introduced and applied in the first *Critique's* Transcendental Analytic, fulfilling this remaining task requires locating correlations within *other* areas of Kant's philosophy. In the next four paragraphs, each heading correlates one of the four university faculties to the relevant quadrant of the Compound *Yijing*, following the order of quadrants as presented in §III (i.e., *gua* 2, 1, 64, and 63)—the *same order* Kant follows in *Conflict*. In each case I shall then suggest three areas of Kant's philosophy (and, where readily discernible, the four principles presented therein) that correlate with the three quaternities in that quadrant. In each case, I derive the first area from later sections of the first *Critique*, the second from Kant's explicitly moral/metaphysical writings, and the third from other post-1781 writings. *Justifying* these tentative hypotheses will have to wait for another occasion.

The philosophy faculty: yin-yin (– –) *quadrant*. My hypothesis is that the first *Critique's* distinction between the four categories of nothing, which serves as a propaedeutic to Kant's whole critique of metaphysics in the "Transcendental Dialectic," corresponds to the quaternity consisting of *gua* 3, 8, 20, and 42.[22] The second *Critique's* table of the categories of freedom[23] should then correspond to the quaternity consisting of *gua* 4, 7, 19, and 41, with the third *Critique's* distinction between the four "moments" of beauty[24] corresponding to the quaternity consisting of *gua* 29, 59, 60, and 61.

The theology faculty: yang-yang (+ +) *quadrant*. The main purpose of the theology faculty, according to Kant, is to train professionals to take care of people's spiritual needs. Here and in each higher faculty, one quaternity (corresponding to the first third-level *gua* that arises in that quadrant) should correlate with an idea of reason discussed in the first *Critique's* Dialectic—in this case, the idea of *God*. Kant's distinction between three ways of proving God's existence (the ontological, cosmological, and physic-theological), taken together with his own "possibility proof,"[25] should correspond to the quaternity consisting of *gua* 14, 32, 34, and 50. Since religion for Kant must be grounded not only in good theology but also in good *ethics*,[26] the opposite quaternity, consisting of *gua* 13, 31, 33, and 49, should correspond to a quaternity in the second part of the *Metaphysics of Morals*, the Doctrine of Virtue. My initial suggestion is that the fourfold "Schema of Duties of Virtue"[27] might fulfill that role, while the four categorial principles establishing the guidelines for a "true church" in the Third Piece of *Religion within the Bounds of Bare Reason*[28] correspond to the synthetic quaternity, *gua* 30, 55, 56, and 62.

The law faculty: yang-yin *(+ −) quadrant*. Here the purpose is to train lawyers to take care of people's property rights, both during life and after death; so the relevant idea of reason is *immortality*. The main quaternity proposed in the corresponding area of metaphysics, *rational psychology*,[29] distinguishes between the fourfold nature of the soul, as substantial, simple, unified, and related to spatial objects. My hypothesis, therefore, is that this set corresponds to the quaternity consisting of *gua* 6, 10, 47, and 58, with the opposite quaternity, consisting of *gua* 16, 21, 35, and 51, corresponding to four principles established in the first part of the *Metaphysics of Morals*, the Doctrine of Right. The division of the objective relation of law to duty[30] seems to be the best candidate presented in Kant's text. For the synthetic quaternity, four basic principles from Kant's vision of the ultimate political situation, in *Toward Perpetual Peace*, should correspond to *gua* 12, 17, 25, and 45; and here I propose the three "Definitive Articles," with the "Secret Article" as the fourth component.[31]

The medicine faculty: yin-yang *(− +) quadrant*. The purpose here is to train doctors to care for people's *physical* well-being, as free agents imbedded in nature; so the relevant idea of reason is *freedom*. The corresponding area of metaphysics, *rational cosmology*, as treated in the Dialectic's Antinomy of Reason,[32] examines four irresolvable issues: whether the world has a beginning in time; whether composite substances consist of simple parts; whether a causality of freedom operates in the natural world; and whether an absolutely necessary being exists. I suggest that these should correspond to the quaternity consisting of *gua* 15, 22, 36, and 52, with the opposite quaternity, consisting of *gua* 5, 9, 48, and 57, corresponding to the four ways of understanding *motion*, in *Metaphysical Foundations of Natural Science*: phoronomy, dynamics, mechanics, and phenomenology. The best place to search for four basic principles describing Kant's vision of the ultimate unity of nature and freedom, corresponding to the synthetic quaternity consisting of *gua* 11, 18, 26, and 46, is his final (uncompleted) work, known as *Opus Postumum*. Unfortunately, Kant's notes are so sketchy and contain so many fourfold distinctions (usually with little or no explanation) that identifying the most important quaternity would be extremely difficult, if not impossible.

The next step would be to assess whether and to what extent the *names* for the four *gua* in each of these twelve fourth-level quaternities resonate with Kant's descriptions of the corresponding principles, as suggested above (or with others, if better candidates emerge). This task is well beyond the scope of the current essay; but carrying it out would require being prepared sometimes to employ the names and/or symbolism of the *Yijing*'s *gua* to revise Kant's selection of terms, and at other times to use Kant's terms to suggest refinements of how the Chinese name for a specific *gua* is traditionally understood. As the suggested correlations presented in §III illustrate, however, resonances between the two systems may be more readily available than one first expects, once the full text of the *Yijing* is consulted.

I make no claim here to have discovered *the* "correct" way to order the *Yijing*; rather, I claim only that *this* way of arranging the 64 *gua* has the advantage of displaying a systematic structure very similar (if not identical) to that employed by Kant. To those who disapprove of Kant's architectonic to begin with, this exercise will merely bolster their confidence in downplaying any theory or concept that seems to be introduced "merely" to fill a gap in the architectonic structure. Yet it would be wrong to view the correlations I have demonstrated, especially in §III, as *merely* coincidental. Nor, as explained above, is it likely that the *Yijing* and Kant exhibit such striking structural parallels as a result of some unknown historical connection. Rather, the foregoing evidence should encourage others interested in exploring the vast field of East-West dialogue to focus on developing some of these specific correlations in further detail.[33] Indeed, for those who share Kant's bias in *favor* of architectonic reasoning, this effort to forge a deep connection between two apparently disparate systems of thought should provide numerous seeds for further fruitful application.

HONG KONG BAPTIST UNIVERSITY
Hong Kong, China

Endnotes

I would like to thank Lok Yuen Ching, whose interest in the *Yijing* relates mostly to its application to Chinese medicine, for assisting me at various stages in the development of this project, especially in constructing Figure 3 and in the ongoing task of exploring the various interpretive possibilities contained therein. Thanks also to Eric Nelson for inviting me to contribute to this important collection of essays. My thanks furthermore go to Chung-ying Cheng, Linyu Gu, a blind reviewer, and the whole editorial team of *JCP* for their substantial comments and generous assistance.

1. See "Introduction: Levels of Perspectives in Kant and Chinese Philosophy," *Journal of Chinese Philosophy* 38, no. 4 (2011): 505–8. Immanuel Kant defines "architectonic" as "the art of systems" in *Critique of Pure Reason*, trans. Werner S. Pluhar (Indianapolis: Hackett, 1996), A832/B860. For a detailed discussion of Kant's concept of architectonic as such (rather than as *structuring* his own system) and an argument that the *Yijing* adopts a similar approach to philosophizing, see my article, "Architectonic Reasoning and Interpretation in Kant and the *Yijing*," *Journal of Chinese Philosophy* 38, no. 4 (2011): 569–83.
2. Peter D. Hershock, "The Structure of Change in the *Yijing*," in *Philosophy of the Yi: Unity and Dialectics, Journal of Chinese Philosophy* 36, Supplement (2009): 48–72, organizes the 64 *gua* into what he calls a "three-leveled order" (not counting "the common, empty center of all three levels") by identifying *gua* numbers 1, 2, 63, and 64

as the system's fundamental core (56; see also 69–72), a set of twelve secondary *gua* as generated directly from these basic four (using one of four different types of rule for determining the changes), and the remaining 48 *gua* as forming an outer core that can be similarly arranged as twelve sets of four *gua* each (with lines 2–5 being identical for each set of four). My detailed account of this way of organizing the *Yijing* (unnamed by Hershock) follows this same pattern, but rearranges the order of the *gua* using slightly different (and much simpler) mapping rules. In a nutshell, Hershock uses what he calls "inner linking," whereby one starts at the level of the outer 48 *gua* and derives each of the twelve middle-level *gua* from a corresponding set of four: the top trigram is defined by lines 2–4 of the four outer-level *gua*, and the bottom trigram by lines 3–5 of that set. What this ignores is that the time-honored tradition of the *Yijing* philosophy is that *some lines change while others remain constant*. In the revised ordering I shall adopt, by rearranging only two pair of *gua*, each quadrant retains a rigorous systematic identity not exhibited by any of the maps Hershock presents.

3. I derive this name as follows. Hershock's (unnamed) method identifies four basic *gua*, forming what I elsewhere (see note 4, below) refer to as a "second-level *analytic* relation," and posits a *synthetic* (threefold) relation between certain other *gua*; the geometry of logic calls any combination of analytic and synthetic relations a "compound" relation.

4. I first applied the geometry of logic to Kant's system in "The Architectonic Form of Kant's Copernican Logic," *Metaphilosophy* 17, no. 4 (1986): 266–88, revised and reprinted as Chapter III in my book, *Kant's System of Perspectives: An Architectonic Interpretation of the Critical Philosophy* (Lanham: University Press of America, 1993). For applications outside the realm of Kant studies, see my article "Analysis and Synthesis in the Geometry of Logic," *Indian Philosophical Quarterly* 19, no. 1 (1992): 1–14, and my book, *The Tree of Philosophy: A Course of Introductory Lectures for Beginning Students of Philosophy*, 4th ed. (Hong Kong: Philopsychy Press, 2000), especially Lectures 13 and 14.

5. Kant introduces his standard twelvefold division as a table of the "logical functions in judgment" (*Critique of Pure Reason*, A70/B95), then uses these to construct his official "Table of Categories" (A80/B106) that eventually becomes the basis for his defense of the Principles of Pure Understanding (A148/B188-A235/B294); cf. note 11, below.

6. See my article, "The Radical Unknowability of Kant's 'Thing in Itself,' " *Cogito* 3, no. 2 (1985): 101–15; revised and reprinted as Appendix V of Palmquist, *Kant's System of Perspectives*.

7. The namelessness of the Dao is implied throughout the *Yijing*, but is stated explicitly (though paradoxically) in Chapter 1 of Laozi's *Dao De Jing*.

8. Euclid's definition (in *Elements*, Book I, Definition 1) is: "A point is that of which there is no part." Pythagoras' definition was "a monad having position" (quoted in Leslie Jaye Kavanaugh, *The Architectonic of Philosophy: Plato, Aristotle, Leibniz* [Amsterdam: Amsterdam University Press, 2007], 106).

9. Kant, *Critique of Pure Reason*, A160-161/B199-200.

10. Ibid., A160-162/B199-201.

11. Kant defines "axioms" (the principles corresponding to quantity) as "extensive magnitude" (ibid., A162f/B202f) and "anticipations" (those corresponding to quality) as "intensive magnitude" (A166f/B207f). His definitions of "analogies" (the principles corresponding to relation) and "postulates" (those corresponding to modality) imply a similar distinction by referring to the external "connection of perceptions" (A176-177f/B218f) and the internal agreement or "coherence" of intuition and conception (A218f/B265-266f), respectively.

12. Palmquist, *Kant's System of Perspectives*, III.3; see especially Figure III.4 and Table III.7 (83,89).

13. Kant, *Critique of Pure Reason*, A50/B74. Chung-ying Cheng has suggested associating *yin* with quality and *yang* with quantity. With a different set of mapping rules to define the onto-epistemic correlation between these sets of terms, such an alternative would certainly be plausible. However, as I shall explain further in §III, I am here adopting the mapping rules employed in my previous publications on the geometry of logic, and these rules make the choice of correlations shown in Figure 1 nonarbitrary. An

intriguing question would be to ask what is at stake when the mapping rules change. Different rules could certainly be established, for example, that would require quantity to be associated with "the creative" (pure *yang*) and quality with "the receptive" (pure *yin*). Perhaps what is at stake in this case is whether one considers the point of the creation of all things to begin with the determination of their quantity (as in traditional realism) or with the determination of their modality (as I am claiming Kant's transcendental idealism requires). Unfortunately, the intriguing question of how one's choice of mapping rules relates to one's underlying worldview is beyond the scope of this article.

14. Another interesting implication of these correlations is that a singular judgment (e.g., "Socrates is mortal") is *never* apodeictic, just as *gua* 27 and 28 are exact opposites (cautious attention to nourishment and bold claims to greatness being mutually exclusive in any system that values *balance*).
15. *I Ching or Book of Changes*, 3rd edition, trans. Richard Wilhelm and Cary F. Baynes (London: Routledge & Kegan Paul, 1968 [1951]), 154.
16. Ibid., 147.
17. Ibid., 208–9.
18. Ibid., 143.
19. Ibid., 151.
20. In *Kant's System of Perspectives*, X.1, for example, I present a diagram (Figure X.1) whose structure closely resembles that of Figure 3. I there present that diagram as a possible way of laying bare "the idea [of Kant's philosophical system] as a whole" that Kant says his readers must grasp in order to resolve his book's apparent inconsistencies (*Critique of Pure Reason*, Bxliv). It defines the four main quadrants as those belonging to Critique (– –), analytic restatement of Critique (+ –), the realms of experience dealt with by the three *Critiques* (– +), and (Kantian) metaphysics proper (+ +).
21. While Kant's book applies this fourfold distinction to the "faculties" (i.e., departments or schools) of the university, it closely parallels the distinction he makes throughout his mature works between the four faculties (i.e., powers or abilities) of the human mind: sensibility (– –), understanding (+ –), judgment (– +), and reason (+ +).
22. See Kant, *CPR* A290-292/ B346-349.
23. See *Critique of Practical Reason*, 66 (Academy Edition pagination), where Kant provides a table listing twelve categories of freedom, but does not specify any special heading for each.
24. See *Critique of the Power of Judgment*, 203–40 (Academy Edition pagination); for summaries of how Kant explicitly links these "moments" to the four categories, see Palmquist, *Kant's System of Perspectives*, IX.2.A (295–297) and *The Tree of Philosophy*, Lecture 29.
25. See my book, *Kant's Critical Religion: Volume Two of Kant's System of Perspectives* (Aldershot: Ashgate, 2000), Chapter V.
26. See ibid., Chapter VI, especially Figure VI.2 (126).
27. See Immanuel Kant, *Metaphysics of Morals*, trans. Mary J. Gregor (Cambridge: Cambridge University Press, 1996), 398.
28. See Palmquist, *Kant's Critical Religion*, VII.3.A and VIII.3.A, especially Figure VII.5 (171).
29. As treated by Kant in the first *Critique's* Dialectic, A341–405/B399–432.
30. Kant, *Metaphysics of Morals*, 240–41.
31. Immanuel Kant, *Toward Perpetual Peace: A Philosophical Project*, trans. Mary J. Gregor in *Practical Philosophy*, eds. Mary J. Gregor (Cambridge: Cambridge University Press, 1996), 349, 354, 357, 368.
32. Kant, *CPR* A405–567/B432–595.
33. My attention has been limited almost exclusively to the structural patterns themselves and the *names* traditionally assigned to the 64 *gua*; when appealing to the text of the *Yijing*, I have gone no further than to consult the introductory explanation and "Judgment" section. This leaves open a huge area of potential further research, into the question of whether a more thorough examination of the *Yijing* (including, especially, the Commentaries) would reveal *still further* insights into the depth of its consistency with (or in some cases, perhaps its challenge to) Kant's architectonic system.

GRAHAM PARKES

LAO-ZHUANG AND HEIDEGGER ON NATURE AND TECHNOLOGY

Abstract

Many of our current environmental problems stem from damage to the natural world through excessive use of modern technologies. Since these problems are now global in scope, it is helpful to take a comparative philosophical approach—in this case by way of Laozi, Zhuangzi, and Martin Heidegger. Heidegger's thoughts on these topics are quite consonant with classical Daoist thinking, in part because he was influenced by it. Although Zhuangzi and Heidegger warn against the ways technology can impair rather than promote human flourishing, they are not simply anti-technological in their thinking. Both rather recommend a critical stance that would allow us to shift to a more reflective employment of less disruptive technologies.

The context is a practical one: as the twenty-first century begins we face environmental problems on an unprecedented and global scale, yet neither the politicians nor most of the people in the developed world show the courage or will to change the behavior that is causing the problems. From a Daoist point of view, the government of the People's Republic of China toward the end of the twentieth century had the right idea in resisting the encroachment of the evils of capitalism and consumerism. Now that these evils are being welcomed as agents of China's transformation into a world economic power, and one-and-a-quarter billion Chinese aspire to the high level of consumption of the more developed nations, the prospect of global environmental devastation looms ever larger and more grimly.[1]

But if we reflect on the terms in which environmental problems are currently discussed—terms deriving from the Cartesian-Newtonian underpinnings of "the modern Western scientific worldview" which enabled the development of technology—it is clear that they are extremely parochial, having become current only in Europe and less than four hundred years ago. For if we look beyond the Cartesian

---

GRAHAM PARKES, Professor, Department of Philosophy, University College Cork. Specialties: comparative philosophy (Europe and East Asia), environmental philosophies, aesthetics. E-mail: g.parkes@ucc.ie

Journal of Chinese Philosophy, Supplement to Volume 39 (2012) 112–133
© 2013 Journal of Chinese Philosophy

understanding of the natural world as inanimate matter to previous eras and other cultures, we find a multitude of quite different ways of understanding the human relation to nature, most of which conduce to less destructive behavior toward the environment. One of the more interesting of these ways comes from philosophical Daoism.

Though many of these salutary understandings of nature stem from non-Western traditions—the Australian aboriginal, Polynesian, Japanese Buddhist, and Native American cultures, to name a few—they are also consonant with some non-mainstream currents of thinking in the West, which have resurfaced recently in the "deep ecology" movement.[2] Since deep ecology invokes both Daoist ideas and Heidegger's thought, it may be instructive to undertake a comparison. Having already discussed the earlier Heidegger in relation to Lao-Zhuang, I now extend the comparison to themes in some later works.[3] The point is less a philosophical analysis of each side than a bilateral illumination of ideas that might help us in our thinking about environmental issues.

Since environmental problems often derive from social, political, and economic conditions, their solutions depend on an alteration of these conditions along lines suggested by writers in political and social ecology. Nevertheless, as Marx surely realized (and Nietzsche made explicit), one of the most effective ways of changing the world is by interpreting it so compellingly as to alter other people's interpretations of it, and this often has to be done through transformations of individual awareness, one at a time.[4] The emphasis in what follows is on this second approach.

Let us proceed from the premise that the understanding of the human relation to the cosmos that we find in the classics of philosophical Daoism, the *Laozi* and *Zhuangzi*, naturally conduces to a respectful attitude and behavior toward the natural world. Although the occasional dissenting voice has been raised (from positions of flawed understanding), Daoist ideas have been justifiably invoked as being helpful in thinking about the environment. Although the *Laozi* is primarily a text of political philosophy addressed to the ruler of a state, it can also be taken as being directed toward the individual as the ruler of the smaller body politic of the human being—and on this level the Daoist sage as depicted in the *Laozi* can be taken as a model for living life in general.[5] Rather than being an exercise in the history of philosophy, the present essay understands philosophy as "a way of life" and so approaches the Lao-Zhuang texts as sources of ideas about how to live.[6]

One might nonetheless question the practical helpfulness of Daoist ideas by pointing to the gap between theory, or belief, and practice, thanks to which the right ideas and good intentions fail to be translated into appropriate behavior. For instance, the C.E.O. of a large manufacturing company may be a professed believer who subscribes to the Christian conception of the natural world as God's creation (and so worthy of respect and veneration), as well as to the Biblical notion of the impossibility of a rich man's entering the kingdom of heaven. Yet at the same time he may dedicate his energies to maximizing profits for the shareholders and himself, while regarding the pollution of the environment as one of the "costs of doing business" rather than a desecration of God's handiwork. The same might be true, *mutatis mutandis*, of a good Muslim or a good Hindu—though not of a good philosophical Daoist.

The reason for this is that Daoism is one of those practice-based philosophies of self-transformation in which new understanding goes hand in hand with a change not only in attitude but also in behavior.[7] Because somatic practice (whether in breathing techniques or more active physical skills) is an integral part of the philosophical discipline, getting onto or staying on the Way necessarily involves a transformation in one's activity (though perhaps less in what one does than in how one does it).[8] This will be true of any philosophy and/or religion based in somatic practice, two salient examples being Kūkai's Shingon Buddhism and Dōgen's Sōtō Zen.[9] Thus any belief-system that emphasizes somatic practice for the purpose of an experiential realization (of in this case the intrinsic worth of nature) will ensure a similarly tight connection between attitude and activity on the part of the practicing believer. If Heidegger rarely emphasizes *somatic* practice as such, it is because he regards genuine thinking not as a theoretical but a manual activity:

> Meditative thinking now and then demands greater exertion [than calculative thinking]. It demands a longer period of practice. It requires even more subtle care than every other genuine hand-work. But it must also know how to wait, as the farmer waits to see whether the seed will sprout and come to fruition.[10]

This essay will show that the affinities between Heidegger's and Daoist ideas are sufficiently deep—in part because he was influenced by his reading of the Daoist classics—for his thinking to harmonize with and complement Daoist understandings of the human-nature relationship.[11] Naturally Heidegger is in a better position than the Daoists (through having a larger stretch of history to survey) to appreciate the extent to which "nature" is a historical and cultural construct, and he is especially illuminating on what he calls "the mathematical projection of nature" that arose in the seventeenth century and enabled the development of modern technology.[12] But there are also grounds on both sides for supposing that it may be possible to get around such constructions and projections to some unmediated experience of the natural world (even if for such an experience to be communicated it has to be mediated by language). Consider the Daoist sage who has transcended all partial perspectives so as to be able to "open things up to the light of heaven," since "once the axis is found at the center of the circle there is no limit to responding with either [It or Other]," and so the sage "stays at the point of rest on the potter's wheel of Heaven ... letting both alternatives proceed."[13] Or the Heideggerian thinker who is able to contemplate things as "they rest in the returning to the whiling of the farness of their self-belonging ... as long as resting is the hearth and sway of all movement."[14]

The themes to be compared can be specified with respect to the following features of the Daoist attitude toward nature:

1. It is realistic, rather than sentimental or romanticizing. "Nature is not humane: it regards the ten thousand things as straw dogs";[15] "Heaven is impartial to everything it covers, earth to everything it carries."[16]
2. It is non-anthropocentric. The *Laozi* names four "great processes" in the world: *dao* 道, heaven and earth (nature), and the king.[17] The king, as greatest among human beings, is only one of four and is named last, and the last sentence of *Laozi*, 25 encourages the human being to emulate the three prior processes.
3. One respect in which the human being is to emulate nature is by being self-effacing—"To retire when the task is accomplished is the way of nature"[18]—and knowing when to stop—"even heaven and earth cannot go on for ever."[19] Numerous passages in the *Laozi* advocate living modestly and without extravagance, reducing one's desires, taking the middle way and avoiding extremes—"It is the way of nature to take from what has excess in order to make good what is deficient."[20]
4. In emulating the three greater processes (earth, heaven, *dao*) the human being will attain *ziran* 自然, "spontaneous self-unfolding," and thereby flourish along with the other myriad processes.
5. Humans thrive when they practice *wuwei* 無為, activity that doesn't disrupt the spontaneous unfolding of natural forces and phenomena.
6. Technology is OK when *wuwei*, suspect when *youwei* 有為 (*youwei* being activity disruptive of, or not in harmony with, the forces of heaven and earth).
7. To let the human (*ren* 人) overwhelm the natural (*tian* 天) brings trouble.[21]

I

Our talk of "nature" and what is "natural" is prefigured in two distinct terms in Daoist discourse: *tian* and *ziran*. The Daoists understand *tian*, which is often used for the compound *tiandi* 天地 (heaven-earth), as the natural world, including the forces of nature that both surround us and work through us as natural impulses and autonomous functions of the body. Human beings are a part of nature and dependent upon it for their survival—the "way of heaven" is said to "benefit without harming"[22]—even though nature exhibits no special interest in the human species—it is "not humane" and "impartial."

Ziran means something like "spontaneous self-unfolding," and although the *zi* component means "self," the Daoists always understand the self-unfolding of any particular process as occurring in the context of the myriad things in general.[23] Thus although the *ziran* of each particular in a sense curtails the *ziran* of others lower on the food chain, it does so only within limits. If a herbivore begins to overconsume the plants on which it lives, its numbers will correspondingly diminish and its self-unfolding come to an end. The notion of *ziran* is thus connected with an idea of "natural limits."

Taken together, these two aspects of the natural according to Daoism are consonant with Heidegger's understanding of the ancient Greek notion of *phusis*, which he understands as "what emerges from out of itself (e.g., the emergence of a rose), self-opening unfolding."[24] Just as *ziran* takes place within the larger patterning of *dao*, so *phusis* for Heidegger refers not only to all particular beings, "heaven as well as earth, the stone as well as the plant, the animal as well as the human and human history as the work of humans and gods, and finally and primarily the gods themselves under fate," but also to "Being itself, thanks to which beings can be observable and remain." Something corresponding to *fate* is also included, as we shall see, in the Daoist understanding of *tian*.

Heidegger's conception of natural unfolding also includes an idea of natural limits, as evidenced in this passage, which is strikingly reminiscent of the *Laozi*:

> The imperceptible law of the earth preserves it in the sufficiency of the arising and perishing of all things within the allotted circle of the possible, a law that each thing follows yet none is aware of. The beech tree never oversteps what is possible for it. The bee colony dwells in what for it is possible. Only the will that sets itself up ubiquitously in technology devours the earth in the exhaustion and consumption and alteration of what is artificial.[25]

II

Daoism is one of the world's least anthropocentric philosophies, as evidenced in the *Zhuangzi* as well as *Laozi*. Numerous passages in the *Zhuangzi* aim to relativize the human perspective on the world by showing the validity of the perspectives of other beings (from animals and insects to birds, fish, and trees). Daoists acknowledge that a certain amount of "centrism" characterizes all species, and that the human perspective of utility is necessary for survival. But this does not mean that the perspective of utility is alone valid, or that it alone conduces to human *flourishing*—not to mention to the flourishing of the entire cosmos. All the authors of the *Zhuangzi* regard more and broader perspectives as better than fewer and narrower.[26]

Heidegger's explicit opposition to humanism, as well as his constant calls for a reopening of "the question of Being" as the major task confronting philosophy, likewise take him far from anthropocentrism.[27] Although some commentators, among them the perceptive Michael Zimmerman, worry about "Heidegger's perceived anthropocentrism," such concerns are surely unfounded.[28] From the time of *Being and Time* Heidegger's thinking has been explicitly non-anthropocentric, and there is no reason to question his explicitness on this topic. Near the beginning of that text he distinguishes his analysis of Dasein from anthropology, psychology, and biology; and if that distinction has been obscured by glossing the term *Dasein* as "human being," the consequence is to be ascribed to careless commentators rather than the author of the original text.[29] There the term *Mensch*, "human being," is conspicuous by its (almost total) absence.

Some critics seem to be put off by the emphasis in *Being and Time* on the instrumental attitude toward the world, but this derives simply from Heidegger's desire to consider Dasein in its "everydayness." As a being whose being is an issue for it at the practical level as well as existentially, Dasein *has* to adopt an instrumentalist attitude toward nature to some extent, being dependent on the natural world for its survival. What is significant from the Daoist viewpoint about Heidegger's analysis of instrumentality is that it exemplifies a thoroughly *relational* understanding of the self: Dasein "*is* its world" and its world is a matrix of dynamic relationships. Moreover, Heidegger does allow at several points for an attitude toward nature that is neither instrumentalist nor abstractly objective, even though he declines to elaborate this theme.[30]

What *is* problematic in the early Heidegger, as Zimmerman and others have remarked, is his insistence on an abyssal difference between human beings and animals—and, by extension, plants and the inorganic realm.[31] This insistence distances him from Daoism, which grants that humans are distinct from other beings but affirms our continuity with them as well. As Hans Jonas has pointed out, there is an undeniable Gnostic strain in Heidegger's early thinking, as evidenced in his claim that through its Angst-mediated relationship with nothingness and death Dasein is fundamentally "not at home" in the world.[31] Despite all the "body" language in *Being and Time*—metaphors of standing, stepping, running, jumping, falling, grasping, holding, throwing, and so forth abound—which points up Dasein's existence as physical, it is hard not to take the "not at home" as an echo of the Orphic idea of the soul's not being at home in the body or physical world. But since the Gnostic resonances diminish as Heidegger's thinking becomes more rooted in the earth, one can perhaps take the "not at home" as pointing up the radical finitude of our being-here, in harmony with Heidegger's emphasis on the dynamic, "always underway" aspect of our existence.

As Kah Kyung Cho has shown, the gap between human and animal existence, between Dasein (as world) and other beings, becomes ever narrower after Heidegger's celebrated "turning" (*Kehre*).[33] And just as the Daoists are more concerned with *dao* than the human, so Heidegger stays away from anthropocentrism as talk of Being gives way in his later thought to discussions of "Way," "Saying," and "Nearness." As he writes in "The Nature of Language" (1958): "Perhaps there is concealed in the word 'Way,' *dao*, the mystery of all mysteries of thinking Saying [*Sage*]. . . . All is Way" (WL 92/198).[34]

III

A *locus classicus* for the Daoist ideals of simplicity and awareness of sufficiency is the beginning of the *Laozi*'s third chapter:

> Not to honor men of worth will keep the people from contention;
> Not to value goods that are hard to come by will keep them from theft;
> Not to display what is desirable will keep them from being unsettled of mind.

This last line exemplifies a basic Daoist attitude toward the major contributor to environmental degradation: rampant consumerism, which depends precisely on displaying unnecessary things as "desirable"—with the explicit aim of unsettling the minds of consumers so much that they'll buy them. In this respect the Daoist emphasis on "reducing desires"[35] anticipates Thoreau and the early Marx on the way false needs and manufactured desires alienate the modern human from genuine life. As the *Laozi* puts it: "When you have little, you'll attain much. With much, you'll be confused."³⁶ The author of this translation, Robert Henricks, aptly associates this passage with the Daoist ideal of *zhi-zu* 知足, "knowing what is enough"—which capitalist society makes inordinately difficult.³⁷

Heidegger, too, is a great advocate of simplicity and modest living, as evidenced in his own life, especially after the War, and in his increasing fondness for the term *gering* (small, simple). An important way to attain simplicity for the Daoists, which Heidegger seems to follow, is through "emptying" the heart-mind of all clutter (extraneous desires, irrelevant calculations, and so forth).³⁸

IV

The Daoist idea of *ziran*, "spontaneous self-unfolding," characterizes all of the "ten-thousand things" except the civilized human being. Different kinds of natural phenomena have different ways of coming into being, developing, and declining, though all such phases are in accord with, because generated and patterned by, *dao*.

> *Dao* gives them life, *de* 德 rears them;
> Things give them shape, circumstances bring them to maturity.
> Therefore the ten-thousand things revere *dao* and honor *de*.
> Yet *dao* is revered and *de* honored
> Not because an authority decrees so,
> but through spontaneous self-unfolding.³⁹

Human beings, however, growing up in society, are constrained by the processes of education, socialization, and acculturation to check their natural inclinations, and especially (as Freud saw so perceptively) with respect to aggressive impulses and the so-called "natural functions" of ingesting, excreting, and sex. Insofar as our spontaneous self-unfolding is inhibited or distorted by being directed into socially acceptable channels, as creatures of culture we lose our spontaneity as natural beings. We are thus distinguished by our tendency to miss, lose, or stray from the Way.

Since the dynamics of *dao* are obscure, the *Laozi* recommends emulating natural phenomena, the ways of nature, as a way of getting back to spontaneous self-unfolding. As (an alternative reading of the last sentence in) *Laozi*, 25 puts it:

> Human beings emulate earth's earthing,
> Which emulates heaven's heavening,
> Which emulates *dao*'s *dao*-ing,
> Which emulates spontaneous self-unfolding.⁴⁰

What is being recommended here is not simply a reversion to some primitive naturalness, for returning to *dao* after having strayed away affords the accomplished human being, or sage, a broader and deeper perspective than appears to be attainable by other kinds of beings.

V

When a particular individual has cultivated its powers (*de*) to the highest, it is so harmoniously integrated into the patterning of *dao* that its activity becomes *wuwei*, or "nondisruptive activity."[41] This activity is so far from being "inaction" (a common, misleading translation) that, in "listening" and responding to *dao* by engaging in *wuwei*, one acts in such a way that "nothing is left undone."[42] The quietistic reading of Daoism also understands *wuwei* as something easy, a simple "going with the flow," rather than the result of the prolonged practice required for un-doing the unnaturalness instilled by the socialization process. The good Daoist is often represented as a consummate practitioner of some physical technique or skill. After sufficient practice, one's activity contributes to and enhances the spontaneous self-unfolding (*ziran*) of other beings and processes, so that the sage is in a position to "help" or "support" the ten thousand things to be natural.[43] There's a similar idea in the *Zhuangzi*, with its talk of returning to life as "becoming a helper of Heaven [*xiang tian* 相天]."[44]

While *wuwei* does not disrupt *ziran*, it is nevertheless not assimilable to one of the "ultimate norms" of Deep Ecology, which states that "all things in the biosphere have an equal right to live and blossom."[45] While well-meaning, this tenet is ill-considered or poorly formulated—for if we had granted equal rights to the tubercle bacillus, a perfectly natural being, we would be continuing to sicken and die of tuberculosis. Although the deep ecologists draw on Daoist ideas, the one who drew up that particular norm clearly didn't acquire the Daoist distaste for universal rules or principles. In considering the present danger of the Ebola virus, for example, the Daoist would look at the larger context, foresee the decimation of the human race, and suggest that we risk a little disruption of the natural by containing the spread of something so lethal, from a sense that the flourishing of the whole might well require some human beings. The rule of thumb that says: "Be fully aware of the relevant context, and if the species is mortally threatened, do something!" is not perniciously anthropocentric, just rather sensible.

Corresponding to the distinction between *wuwei* and *youwei* activity is the distinction Heidegger makes between attitudes and behavior based in *Stellen* as opposed to *Lassen*. *Stellen* is the assertive activity of "setting, putting, placing," while *Lassen* is rather "letting" and "allowing"—and is even "the relation to Being."[46] He characterizes the Western metaphysical tradition as being based on *Stellen*, and especially on the "representing thinking" (*vorstellendes Denken*) of the subject of consciousness, by contrast with his own, open-to-the-call-of-Being thinking, as exemplified in his Meister Eckhart-inspired notion of *Gelassenheit* (releasement). Heidegger often emphasizes the limitations of representational thinking through word-plays between *Vorstellen* (representing) and *Verstellen* (disguising).[47]

In *Toward an Explanation of Releasement: Conversation on a Country Path* from 1944, Heidegger's interlocutors explicate the *lassen* in *Gelassenheit* along the lines of *wuwei*:

> Researcher: You speak unrelentingly of a letting, so that the impression arises of some kind of passivity. Yet I think I'm right in saying that it's by no means a matter of an impotent letting things glide and flow.
> Scholar: Perhaps concealed in releasement is a higher doing [*Tun*] than in all deeds in the world and in the machinations of humans . . .
> Teacher: . . . which higher doing is nevertheless no activity.
> Researcher: Releasement therefore lies . . . outside the distinction between activity and passivity . . .[48]

Heidegger may have been influenced here by Buber's edition of the *Zhuangzi*, who writes in his Afterword of "true doing" (*das wahre Tun*) as a "not-doing."[49]

In the 1955 speech "*Gelassenheit*," Heidegger distinguishes "calculative" (*rechnendes*) from "meditative" (*besinnliches*) thinking in terms reminiscent of Wilhelm's translation of the *Laozi* (where *dao* is translated as *Sinn*): "Calculative thinking is not any kind of meditative thinking, not a thinking that thinks on the sense [*Sinn*] that holds sway in all that is."[50] There is a parallel here with Zhuangzi's distinction between *bian* 辯 the kind of analytical thinking that discriminates between alternatives, and *lun* 論, "the sorting which evens things out."[51] When the Daoist sage is said to sort out "everything within the cosmos" he is engaging in an "ordering of things in their proper relations,"[52] by refraining from imposing value-judgments on them from partial perspectives. Zhuangzi would agree with Heidegger that both kinds of thinking are "in their own way justified and necessary"[53]—but they would further agree on the desirability of encouraging the ordering while keeping the calculative kind to a minimum, practicing it only when the circumstances necessitate.

VI

Let us now consider *wuwei* in relation to the employment of the fruits of technology, which might at first seem incompatible with *wuwei*. The Daoist attitude to technology is rather complex. There is certainly a nostalgic strain of thinking back to the good old days when things and people were fewer and simpler, as evidenced especially in *Laozi*, 80, which begins: "Let the country be small and the people few."[54] In this primitivist utopia, "though [the people] might have boats and carriages, no one will use them." Similar ideas are to be found in certain chapters of the *Zhuangzi* authored by someone whom A. C. Graham has aptly labeled the "Primitivist."[55]

But when we look at the most famous story in the *Zhuangzi* concerning the products of technology, about the gardener who dismisses the innovation of the well-sweep,[56] it is clear that the objection is less to the tool as such than to the calculative "mind-set" that is needed in order to invent such contraptions, and the effect on the soul of the one who relies on them. The Wilhelm translation puts the point in a vivid image that may have influenced Heidegger's ideas about the limitations and dangers of "calculative thinking" (*rechnendes Denken*): "If one has a machine-heart [*Maschinenherz*] in one's breast, one loses pure simplicity."[57]

The idea of *wuwei* can help us evaluate the effects of different kinds of technology, not by providing a universal rule concerning what should or should not be deployed, nor by providing a criterion for distinguishing "good" from "bad" technologies (universal rules and strict criteria being alien to the spirit of Daoism), but rather by offering a rough "rule of thumb." Imagine arranging various kinds of technologies along a continuum with *wuwei* at one end and *youwei* at the other. At the *wuwei* pole would be windmills, sailboats, watermills, and the like: implements that make use of the natural forces of wind, water, and gravity without abusing or using them up. (When I position my sailboat, for example, in such a way that the wind fills its sails, this in no way reduces the amount of wind available for yours.) Toward the *youwei* end we would have set-ups like the nuclear power plant, which disrupts natural processes monstrously. Although uranium occurs and degrades naturally, the reaction that powers nuclear plants can only be achieved through highly complex technical procedures, and the plutonium waste generated thereby is toxic on a whole different scale—and time-scale—from those of naturally occurring lethal poisons.

The Daoist rule of thumb would suggest that the closer to the *wuwei* pole the technology, the greater the chances of its being favorable to human flourishing and the flourishing of the whole in the long run—and vice versa. But under what circumstances does the whole flourish? Since nature is not humane, we need to protect ourselves against its lethal tendencies—but to what extent? A species' flourishing depends on its population relative to its environment and other species in it. Natural processes prevent predators from eliminating their prey completely, and parasites from killing off their hosts. Since human technology has enabled the species to eliminate an amazing number of predators (in the wide sense that includes the tubercle bacillus and Ebola virus), our population now threatens to become too large in relation to the available natural resources. If, rather than accepting these limitations of *tian*, we respond by resorting to technology that increases crop yields through genetic engineering, the Daoist would warn against such a *youwei* course of action.

Nor would *ziran* and *wuwei* mean in this context just letting things take their natural course and allowing population to burgeon. (There is no good argument for having more people on the earth—only bad arguments for the need to have more of "us" in relation to "them.") For a species to allow itself to perish from preventable overconsumption of resources is not *wuwei* but plain stupidity. If population control uses moral suasion and/or minimal technology to set limits to human reproduction, this alteration of the "natural" course of things may at first look like *youwei* behavior; but if the limits are in the service of assuring the survival (if not flourishing) of other species, it is hardly disrupting the *ziran* of the natural world as a whole.

One could entertain a contemporary version of the *Laozi* primitivist fantasy along these lines: with greatly reduced numbers, we human beings could, by means of *wuwei* technology, pursue and satisfy our genuine needs, and enjoy a respectable level of culture, while letting most—if not all—plant and animal species flourish. The natural sciences would learn much from being able to study how other species interact in the absence of undue human pressure. They would also investigate without exploiting them: causing animals suffering for the sake of cosmetics testing would be grossly *youwei*. But what about medical research that stands to save alleviate human suffering and save lives? Rather than trying to answer such a difficult question by appealing to some universal principle, the Daoist would recommend a consideration of each individual case in the widest appropriate context—while as a rule regarding with great suspicion any technology that disrupts the course of nature in major ways (cloning and genetic engineering, for example), surmising undesirable consequences in the long run.

VII

A relevant distinction here that is helpfully problematized by the *Zhuangzi* is between *tian* and *ren*, between what comes from nature and what comes from the human: "To know what is Heaven's doing and what is man's is the utmost in knowledge."[58] Likes and dislikes—and all such value judgments—imposed upon us by socialization, and then self-imposed thanks to our desire to conform, overlay our natural dispositions and curb our spontaneity: "Wherever desires and cravings are deep, the impulse which is from Heaven is shallow." Only by ignoring, seeing through, or getting rid of these superimposed desires can we find out what our natural impulses might be.

Tian as nature allots each individual a particular physical frame and a certain configuration of life-energies that condition and set limits to the particular abilities that we develop, and which is limited by a definite finitude we call "mortality":

> Death and life are destined; that they have the constancy of morning and evening is of Heaven. . . . That hugest of clumps of soil [*dao*] loads me with a body, has me toiling through a life, eases me with old age, and rests me with death; therefore that I find it good to live is the very reason why I find it good to die.[59]

Through taking up the task of living with these limitations,

> The True Men of old did not know how to be pleased that they were alive, did not know how to hate death. . . . They were pleased with the gift that they received, but forgot it as they gave it back. It is this that is called "not allowing the thinking of the heart to damage the Way, not using what is of man to do the work of Heaven."[60]

This last sentence reminds us that one of the great dangers of civilization comes from its overvaluation of discriminating consciousness, "the thinking of the heart[-mind]" (*xin* 心), which, when it holds too great sway, stultifies our deeper intuition and overrides the nobler impulses from nature.

Obviously we want to survive, and we believe that to thrive we must make use of other species: "That oxen and horses have four feet, this we ascribe to Heaven; haltering horses' heads and piercing oxen's noses, this we ascribe to man. Hence it is said: / 'Don't let man extinguish Heaven, / Don't let deliberation extinguish destiny.' "[61] For the Daoists, failing to keep in check the drive to dominate is distinctly dangerous, and so they advocate a balance between the natural and the human: "Someone in whom neither Heaven nor man is victor over the other, this is what is meant by the True Man."[62] The Zen master, who like the Daoist sage is a highly refined individual who nevertheless lives simply, would in such a balance between nature and culture be a paradigm case of the True Man. (As would someone in the Western traditions like Thoreau or Nietzsche, both of whom were influenced by Asian thought.[63])

It all depends, as always, on the particular context; but if I am unable, for example, to procreate as I would like to, or live as long as I want, owing to some lack in my natural constitution, the Daoists would encourage an acceptance of such fated limitations and be wary of going to great lengths, through the use of expensive and sophisticated technology, to have oneself create more life or postpone one's death. Of course my initial reaction is going to be, "Yes, I want that biotechnological procedure done," or "Give me that artificial/transplanted heart"; but since these procedures are so expensive and disruptive of the natural course of things, we might do well, with an eye to the flourishing of the whole, to question their desirability or necessity.

Heidegger describes how nihilism arises from the obsession with beings that is trying to compensate for the emptiness deriving from obliviousness to the broader context of Being (*dao*). As technology manufactures more and more to fill the void, its drive for control and its understanding of the natural world as mere raw material eventually extend to encompass human beings. Writing in the mid-thirties to -forties, Heidegger is prescient in envisaging how this dismal process may issue in "factories for the artificial generation of human material" and "the possibility of directing the generation of male and female organisms according to plan and need." In this light, "technology, based without knowing it on the void of Being, is mere organization of lack."[64] And when later he reads the pronouncement by a Nobel prize-winning chemist to the effect that scientists will soon be able to "synthesize, split and change living substance at will," Heidegger writes: "We are not aware that technology is here preparing an attack on the life and nature of the human being, by comparison with which the explosion of the hydrogen bomb is of little significance."[65] A salutary word for enthusiasts of bio-engineering.

VIII

In a series of essays from the early 1950s Heidegger elaborates an understanding of things that has significant implications for our relations to the environment as well as continuing resonances with Daoism. The essay "The Thing" begins with a consideration of how the fruits of modern transportation- and communications-technology are abolishing distance at an unprecedented rate—but without bringing about any genuine nearness. Heidegger is prescient (writing in

1950) concerning the power of television: "The peak of this abolition of every possibility of farness is attained by television, which will soon pervade and dominate the entire apparatus and machinery of communication."[66] The internet has carried the abolition of distance even further along such Heideggerian lines, still without creating the wished-for closeness.[67] This lack of nearness constitutes for Heidegger a fundamental and horrifying (*entsetzend*) perturbation of the human condition, in which "everything is displaced [*herausgesetzt*] from its former being."[68] On grounds like these we may find that environmental problems derive from a disturbance in our relations with things in general and not just with natural phenomena.

According to Heidegger several historical circumstances have prevented us from experiencing things as things. The ancient Greek thinkers, Plato and Aristotle in particular, advocated an understanding of everything present as an "object of production."[69] Thanks to its consonance with the creation stories in *Genesis*, this kind of "productionist metaphysics" has dominated Western thinking.[70] In those stories God creates the world from nothing; according to the myth in Plato's *Timaeus*, the Divine Craftsman makes the soul and body of the universe from materials already to-hand; on Aristotle's account things are "formed matter." The combined power of these stories tends to prevent us from seeing how culturally conditioned the question is, when faced with things we want to understand: "How (or by whom) were they made?" Such a question would never occur to a classical Chinese thinker, for whom the question would be: "How (or from what) did they grow?" The mindset implied by the former encourages manipulation of the world and eventually leads to a Newtonian "dead matter in motion" conception of the universe and modern technology; whereas the latter understanding, which finds the power of transformation inhering in the processes themselves rather than an external manipulator, is more conducive to respect and reverence for those processes and powers.

But to return to Heidegger's text: in response to "the annihilation of things as things" that scientific knowledge has promoted, he undertakes an extended consideration of what a particular thing, a jug, *is* in its thingness, *as* a thing.[71] The jug comes from the eleventh chapter of the *Laozi*, where together with two other things that require emptiness in order to function (a cartwheel and a room) it works as an image of *dao* as well as of the human being.[72] What is for Heidegger essential to the jug, the emptiness it encloses, is a phenomenon that science, which always focuses on something rather than nothing, is unable to explain. Science only tells us, unhelpfully, that the apparent emptiness is actually full of air. But Heidegger pursues his discussion of the jug's emptiness further, delineating its relations to its context, to the point where the thing is seen to "gather the fourfold" of heaven and earth, gods and mortals. In bringing about the fourfold, moreover, "the thing things world."[73] Here we arrive at a perfectly Daoist understanding of the thing in the world as *de* in the context of *dao*, a particular focus of energies in the larger force-field of the universe, in and through which the whole can be discerned.[74]

An essay of Heidegger's from the following year, "Building, Dwelling, Thinking," treats similar themes, though with more emphasis on the role of human beings dwelling on the earth as mortals, through "caring for the fourfold" in the sense of "sheltering it back into its being," and "saving the earth" in the sense of "letting it free into its own being."[75] The refusal to confront our mortality that is evidenced in the modern mania for prolonging life through such high-tech means as cryonic suspension, organ transplants, cloning, etc., has its counterpart in a resentment against the natural world for bearing with it such mortality. Instead of celebrating the creative possibilities of our impermanence by affirming the Dionysian cycles of death and rebirth with all our powers (to put it in Nietzschean language consonant with Zhuangzian practice), we attempt to negate the eternally self-renewing life of the natural world by destroying it.

A second death-defiant strategy, also recognized as such by Heidegger, is to attempt to shore up our impermanence by surrounding ourselves with more and more consumer goods, in the vain hope that our existence might become less frail if only we can possess more things. In the language of *Being and Time:* made anxious by the nothingness at the core of our being, we flee and throw ourselves into beings. Existential *Angst* intensifies the desire to consume, with the result that the population of post-industrial societies lives surrounded by a multitude of things—most of them in attics, basements, and garages, and thus rarely even seen, let alone used, and almost never befriended as companions on the way. If things are to gather the fourfold of heaven and earth, gods and mortals, they will require some room, and so they had better not be too many, since each thing "shows itself in the illumination it brings with it" and conditions (*bedingt*) and "things" (*dingt*) the worlding of the world.[76] And according to the *Laozi*, "The world is a sacred vessel."[77]

IX

Let us finish by considering a few sentences from a speech Heidegger gave in 1955 that was published under the title *Gelassenheit* (releasement). He says that in spite of the exertion that the practice of meditative thinking demands, it is still accessible to anyone: "It is sufficient if we stay with what lies near and contemplate what lies nearest: that which concerns each one of us here and now; here: on this spot of home-earth, now: in the present world-hour."[78] But thanks to modern communications-technology, many of us spend many of our hours—watching television, surfing the internet, phoning and texting—in "pseudo-worlds" far from the spot of home-earth on which we (mediately) sit.

Though some of Heidegger's lamentations over our alienation from "the field around the farm . . . the customs of the village" have an overly primitivist tone, his point is well taken that we are generally oblivious to the effects of the "displacement" that modern media exert on our existence. With this he stands in a minority tradition of philosophers (such as Rousseau, Thoreau, and Nietzsche) who have affirmed the importance of *place* in our lives, in the belief that the physical environment in which our bodies live and move conditions our existence in the profoundest ways. By comparison with Nietzsche, who remained "loyal to the earth" while wandering like a nomad, Heidegger's emphasis on *Bodenständigkeit* (ground-standingness) sometimes smacks of what the Germans so graphically call *Schollenkleberei*, the condition in which clods of earth stick to one's peasant boots. It is hard to shake the impression that true earth is to be found only around the cabin in Todtnauberg, and the best clods solely in the soil from which one sprang.

Heidegger characterizes the consequences of the hegemony of calculative thinking famously as follows: "Nature is becoming a single gigantic gas-station, a mere source of energy for modern technology and industry."[79] As he contemplates the advent of nuclear power, what disturbs him, apart from the dangers, is the unnatural independence from place: "The direct production of new energies will soon be no longer connected to particular countries and parts of the earth, as with the occurrence of coal and oil and wood from forests." But when he goes on to consider the possibility of finding "a new ground and soil" in the nuclear age, and getting once again on "the way to what is near," Heidegger dispels suspicions of being a Luddite by affirming the necessity of the technological world and saying it would be "shortsighted to want to condemn it as the work of the Devil."[80]

As the talk of "the way" suggests, the solution is Daoist in the way it "lets both alternatives proceed." The idea is to use technology but not let it "claim us exclusively and thus distort, confuse, and ultimately devastate our nature [as thinking beings]." This "simultaneous Yes and No to the world of technology" Heidegger calls "releasement toward things"—where the thing is a gathering of the fourfold. Along with this goes "openness to the mystery," where the mystery refers to the uncanny way in which the meaning of the world of technology both announces itself and withdraws into concealment at the same time.[81] These attitudes will both flourish to the extent that we engage in thinking, thereby standing us in good stead to employ the fruits of technology without being dominated by or obsessed with them.

Now that anyone without a personal stake in producing polluting, non-renewable sources of energy that aggravate global warming (oil, coal, and gas) can see the necessity of replacing them with clean, renewable sources that alleviate dangerous climate change (solar, wind, photovoltaic—all quite *wuwei*), it becomes ever more clear that new technologies, sensibly and sensitively employed in the context of scaled-back consumption, open a way to the solution of environmental problems. The words of Hölderlin that Heidegger quotes in discussing the question of technology are apposite: "Where, however, danger is, grows / The saving power too."[82] And also the Daoist injunction, *zhi-zu*: "Know when you have enough."

UNIVERSITY COLLEGE CORK
Cork, Ireland

Endnotes

This essay is a revised version of an article published in 2003 (*Journal of Chinese Philosophy* 29, no. 3 [2003]: 19–38) and, is an extension of ideas concerning nature, technology, and ecology that were presented in my essay "Thoughts on the Way: *Being and Time* through Lao-Chuang," in *Heidegger and Asian Thought* (Honolulu: University of Hawaii Press, 1987), with a new focus on some of Heidegger's later writings. A more recent treatment can be found in "Zhuangzi and Nietzsche on the Human and Nature," in *Environmental Philosophy* 10, no. 1 (2013): 1–24.

1. For a devastating account of the assault on the natural environment during the Mao era, see Judith Shapiro, *Mao's War against Nature: Politics and the Environment in Revolutionary China* (Cambridge: Cambridge University Press, 2001).
2. The most important of these currents has its source in thinkers like Giordano Bruno and Jakob Boehme and flows through Spinoza and Goethe, then through Schelling, Schopenhauer, and Nietzsche in Europe, and Emerson and Thoreau in America.
3. In my "Thoughts on the Way: *Being and Time* through Lao-Chuang," in Graham Parkes, ed., *Heidegger and Asian Thought*, see especially the sections "The Nature of Nature," "Back to Nature," "Authentic Use," and "Technology versus Ecology." What follows is only an introductory overview and not the close reading of individual texts that an in-depth comparison would require. Indeed limitations of space preclude consideration of the following relevant essays of Heidegger's: "The Question concerning Technology" (*Die Frage nach der Technik*), "The Set-up" (*Das Gestell*), "The Danger" (*Die Gefahr*), "The Turning" (*Die Kehre*), and "Science and Reflection" (*Wissenschaft und Besinning*).
4. "Philosophers have merely *interpreted* the world in various ways, whereas the point is to change it." Karl Marz, *Theses on Feuerbach*, 11.
5. Correlations between the macrocosm of the state and the microcosm of the body are central to Daoist thinking: see Kristofer Schipper, *The Taoist Body* (Berkeley: University of California Press, 1993) especially the chapters "The Inner Landscape" (100–12) and "Keeping the One" (130–59).
6. Although Western philosophies have tended to be far more theoretically oriented than East-Asian ways of thinking, Pierre Hadot has shown that, even after the "ascent

to theory" advocated by Platonism and Christian philosophy, a minority tradition of "philosophy as a way of life" has persisted in the West as well. See his *Philosophy as a Way of Life: Spiritual Exercises from Socrates to Foucault*, trans. Michael Chase (Oxford: Blackwell Publishing, 1995).

7. On this topic, see my essay "Awe and Humility in the Face of Things: Somatic Practice in East-Asian Philosophies," *European Journal for Philosophy of Religion* 4, no. 3 (2012): 69–88.
8. For references to breathing, see *Laozi*, 10 ("concentrating the breath"), 16 ("maintain tranquility in the center"), 55 ("for the mind to egg on the breath is called violent"), 56 ("mysterious sameness/profound union); and *Zhuangzi*, 2 (Ziqi's breathing-induced trance), 6 ("the breathing of the True Man is from down in his heels"), and 7 (where Huzi speaks of "impulses coming up from my heels"). For practice in physical skills *Laozi*, 54 ("cultivating the body leads to genuine power [*de*]"), and *Zhuangzi*, 12 ("By the training of our nature we recover the Power"), as well as the stories concerning consummate practitioners of physical skills in Chapters 3, 13, 19, 22.

For the *Laozi* I follow for the most part the translation of D. C. Lau, *Tao Te Ching* (Hong Kong: Chinese University Press, 1982), modifying it on occasion in the light of other translations, and abbreviating references as "L" followed by the chapter number (Wang Bi text rather than Ma Wang Dui). The other translations I find most useful are Robert G. Henricks, *Lao-tzu: Te-Tao Ching* (New York: Random House, 1993) and Hans-Georg Möller, *Laotse: Tao Te King* (Frankfurt: Fischer, 1995). The Möller translation is now available in English, as *Daodejing: The New, Highly Readable Translation of the Life-Changing Ancient Scripture Formerly Known as the Tao Te Ching* (Chicago: Open Court, 2007), as is Roger Ames and David Hall, *Dao De Jing: A Philosophical Translation* (New York: Ballantine Books, 2003). For *Zhuangzi* I used the rendering by A. C. Graham in *Chuang Tzu: The Inner Chapters* (London: Allen & Unwin, 1981). Now that Brook Ziporyn's excellent translation has appeared, *Zhuangzi: The Essential Writings, with selections from traditional commentaries* (Indianapolis/Cambridge: Hackett Publishing, 2009), I would recommend referring to that along with Graham's.
9. For some of the ecological implications of the philosophies of these thinkers, see my essay "Kūkai and Dōgen as Exemplars of Ecological Engagement," *The Journal of Japanese Philosophy* 1 (2013): 85–110.
10. Martin Heidegger, *Discourse on Thinking*, trans. John M. Anderson and E. Hans Freund (New York: Harper & Row, 1966), 47/*Gelassenheit* (Pfullingen: Neske, 1959), 13. Though translations from Heidegger are my own, references will be to extant English translations and then the original German texts.
11. For evidence of the influence of Daoism on Heidegger's work, see Reinhard May, *Heidegger's Hidden Sources: East-Asian Influences on His Work*, trans. Graham Parkes (London: Routledge, 1996).
12. See, especially, Heidegger's second book on Kant, *Die Frage nach dem Ding* (Tübingen: Niemeyer, 1962); *What Is a Thing?*, trans. W. B. Barton and Vera Deutsch (Chicago: Regnery, 1967).
13. *Zhuangzi*, 2, *IC*, 52–53.
14. Discourse on Thinking, 69/*Gelassenheit*, 41. Heidegger may have been aware that Nietzsche went beyond his customary perspectivism to a view similar to that of the Daoists in the chapter "Before Sunrise" in *Thus Spoke Zarathustra*: see my essay, "Nature and the Human 'Redivinized': Mahāyāna Buddhist Themes in *Thus Spoke Zarathustra*," in John Lippitt and James Urpeth, eds., *Nietzsche and the Divine* (Manchester: Clinamen Press, 2000), 181–99.
15. *Laozi*, 5.
16. *Zhuangzi*, 6. I follow the customary translation of *wan-wu* as "ten thousand things," with the reminder that the process worldview of the Daoists and their frequent use of *wu* as a verb should encourage us to read "thing" in a verbal or processual sense.
17. *Laozi*, 25.
18. Ibid., 9.
19. Ibid., 23.
20. Ibid., 77. See also *Laozi*, 3, 9, 12, 13, 15, 16, 22, 24, 29, 32, 36, 41, 46, 60, 63.

21. *Zhuangzi*, 6, 17.
22. *Laozi*, 81.
23. As Roger Ames puts it: "The notion of 'self' in the locution [*ziran*] has a polar relationship with 'other.' " "Putting the *Te* back into Taoism," in J. Baird Callicott and Roger T. Ames, eds., *Nature in Asian Traditions of Thought: Essays in Environmental Philosophy* (Albany: State University of New York Press, 1989), 120.
24. Martin Heidegger, *An Introduction to Metaphysics*, trans. Ralph Mannheim (New Haven: Yale University Press, 1959), 14/*Einführung in die Metaphysik* (Tübingen: Niemeyer, 1966), 11.
25. Martin Heidegger, "Overcoming Metaphysics," in *The End of Philosophy*, trans. Joan Stambaugh (New York: Harper & Row, 1973), 109/ "Überwindung der Metaphysik," in *Vorträge und Aufsätze*, 1:62–91.
26. The story of the huge gourd at the end of the *Zhuangzi*'s first chapter illustrates the restricted nature of the perspective of utility and the dangers of getting stuck in any one perspective.
27. Heidegger's opposition to humanism, owing to its neglect of Being, is most explicit in the well known "Letter on Humanism" in response to Sartre's championing of humanism.
28. Michael E. Zimmerman, *Contesting Earth's Future: Radical Ecology and Postmodernity* (Berkeley: University of California Press, 1994), 121. The third chapter of this excellent study includes a comprehensive discussion of Heidegger in relation to deep ecology.
29. Martin Heidegger, *Sein und Zeit*, 11th ed. (Tübingen: Niemeyer, 1963), § 10. Where subsequent references give pagination rather than a section number, it is of the German edition, since this is given in the margins of both English translations.
30. Heidegger, *Sein und Zeit*, 70. For a fuller discussion of this issue, see my "Thoughts on the Way," 110–20, and the "Epilogue" to that essay.
31. Zimmerman, *Contesting Earth's Future*, 115–17, and David Farrell Krell, *Daimon Life* (Bloomington: Indiana University Press, 1992), part 1, "Advanced Za-ology," 33–134.
32. "Existential-ontologically the not-at-home must be conceived as the more primordial phenomenon [than feeling at home in the world]" (*Sein und Zeit*, 189). See also Hans Jonas, *The Phenomenon of Life* (New York: Harper & Row, 1966), 232.
33. Kah Kyung Cho, *Bewusstsein und Natursein: Phänomenologische West-Ost-Diwan* (Freiburg: Alber, 1987), chapter 2, "Ökologische Suggestibilität in der Spätphilosophie Heideggers," which is a fine treatment of ecological themes in late Heidegger from a perspective aligned with Daoism.
34. Martin Heidegger, *On the Way to Language*, trans. Peter D. Hertz (New York: Harper & Row, 1971), 92 / *Unterwegs zur Sprache* (Pfullingen: Niemeyer, 1965), 198. For a discussion of Heidegger's use of these terms, see Reinhard May, *Heidegger's Hidden Sources*, Chapter 4, "*Dao:* way and saying."
35. *Laozi*, 1, 37, 64.
36. Ibid., 22.
37. Robert G. Henricks, "Introduction" to *Lao-tzu: Te-Tao Ching*, xxvii.
38. The sage is said to "empty the minds of the people" in the interests of better government (*Laozi*, 3), and the exhortation to emptiness at the beginning of ch. 16 seems to be associated with meditative techniques.
39. *Laozi*, 51.
40. This reading, suggested by Wang Qingjie, puts the comma after the second occurrences of *di, tian,* and *dao* rather than the first (*Ren fa di di, fa tian tian, fa dao dao, fa ziran*), and takes the second occurrence of each term as a verb rather than a noun. See Wang Qingjie, "On Laozi's Concept of Ziran," *Journal of Chinese Philosophy* 24, no. 3 (1997): 291–321, 297.
41. *Laozi*, 38.
42. Ibid., 48.
43. Ibid., 64.
44. *Zhuangzi*, 19, Chuang Tzu:The Inner Chapters, 182.

45. Bill Devall and George Sessions, *Deep Ecology: Living as If Nature Mattered* (Salt Lake City: Gibbs M. Smith, 1985), 66–67. For some reservations about the way deep ecology has taken over Dōgen's ideas, see my "Voices of Mountains, Trees, and Rivers."
46. An Introduction to Metaphysics, 21/16.
47. See, for example, Heidegger, *What Is a Thing?*, 73/69 (1951–52). It is not generally appreciated that Heidegger was an advocate of "letting," and especially of *sein-lassen* (letting-be) from the time of *Being and Time*: see especially section 18, and the discussion in "Thoughts on the Way," 119, 127.
48. Discourse on Thinking, 61/33.
49. Martin Buber, *Reden und Gleichnisse des Tschuang-Tse* (Leipzig: Insel Verlag, 1921), 133. A great deal of what is said in the *Conversation* about the *Gegnet* ("region"—equivalent to "Being") and things resonates with Buber's *Zhuangzi*, and especially with his "Afterword."
50. Discourse on Thinking, 46/13.
51. *Zhuangzi*, 2.
52. Chuang Tzu:The Inner Chapters, 12.
53. Discourse on Thinking, 46/13.
54. Henricks, *Lao-tzu: Te-Tao Ching*.
55. Chuang Tzu:The Inner Chapters, 195–217.
56. Zhuangzi, Ch. 12.
57. *Dschuang Dsi: das wahre Buch vom südlichen Blütenland*, trans. Richard Wilhelm (Munich: Diederichs, 1969 [first published 1912]), 136.
58. *Zhuangzi*, 6, Chuang Tzu:The Inner Chapters, 84.
59. Chuang Tzu:The Inner Chapters, 86.
60. Ibid., 85.
61. *Zhuangzi*, 17, Chuang Tzu:The Inner Chapters, 149.
62. Ibid., 6, Ibid., 85.
63. On Nietzsche's credentials as an environmental philosopher, see my essays "Floods of Life around Granite of Fate: Nietzsche and Emerson as Thinkers of Nature," *ESQ: A Journal of the American Renaissance* 43 (1997): 207–40; "Staying Loyal to the Earth: Nietzsche as an Ecological Thinker," in John Lippitt, ed., *Nietzsche's Futures* (Basingstoke: Macmillan, 1998), 167–88; "Nietzsche's Environmental Philosophy: A Trans-European Perspective," *Environmental Ethics* 27, no.1 (2005): 77–91.
64. Overcoming Metaphysics, 106–7/87.
65. Discourse on Thinking, 52/20.
66. Martin Heidegger, "The Thing," in *Poetry, Language, Thought*, trans. Albbert Hofstadter (New York: Harper & Row, 1971), 165/ "Das Ding," in *Vorträge und Aufsätze* (Pfullingen: Neske, 1967), 2:37.
67. For an insightful treatment of this issue, from a perspective consonant with Daoism, see Peter D. Hershock, *Reinventing the Wheel: A Buddhist Response to the Information Age* (Albany: State University of New York Press, 1999).
68. "The Thing", 166/38.
69. Ibid., 168/40.
70. For an excellent account of this phenomenon, see "Division Two" of Michael E. Zimmerman, *Heidegger's Confrontation with Modernity: Technology, Politics, and Art* (Bloomington: Indiana University Press, 1990): "Heidegger's Critique of Productionist Metaphysics," 137–274.
71. T, 170/42.
72. As suggested by Hans-Georg Möller in his commentary to Laotse, 11 (170). These three things are also images of the human being, which just as much needs emptiness in order to function.
73. "The Thing", 172–9/46–51.
74. For the "focus-field" understanding of *de* and *dao*, see Ames and Hall, *Dao De Jing: A Philosophical Translation*.
75. Martin Heidegger, "Building, Dwelling, Thinking," in *Poetry, Language, Thought*, 145–61 / "Bauen, Wohnen, Denken," in *Vorträge und Aufsätze*, 2:19–36.
76. "The Thing", 171, 181/43, 53.

77. *Laozi*, 29.
78. Discourse on Thinking, 47/14.
79. Ibid., 50/18.
80. Ibid., 53/21–22.
81. Ibid., 54–56/23–25.
82. Martin Heidegger, "The Question Concerning Technology," in *The Question Concerning Technology and Other Essays*, trans. William Lovitt (New York: Harper & Row, 1977) / "Die Frage nach der Technik," in *Vorträge und Aufsätze*, 1:5–36.

MARTIN SCHÖNFELD

WORLD PHILOSOPHY AND CLIMATE CHANGE: A SINO-GERMAN WAY TO CIVIL EVOLUTION

Abstract

The environmental crisis is the collision of civilization with biospherical limits. Its sign is climate change, which is brought about by a cultural maladaptation, and which threatens to lead to scarcity, displacement, and violence. The solution will have to be a global transformation—a civil evolution—to a postcarbon and sustainable world order. China and Germany, I argue, are well positioned to achieve this new adaptation to living within limits, whereas the United States may have difficulties to respond adequately to the new realities. Here I explore cultural and historical reasons for this Sino-German convergence.

I. Introduction

The environmental crisis confronts civilization with an unfamiliar difficulty. The long-term but inexorable consequence of climate change is an overall loss of biospherical fertility. The loss of fertility is measurable in the declining biological productivity of land surfaces and the seas. On the land, rising heat speeds up the rate of evaporation. It also speeds up the rate of precipitation. But beyond a certain temperature the additional rainfall does not keep pace with the quicker evaporation. So the land dries out, precipitation drops, and plants wilt. Harvests will shrink. In the sea, the rising heat warms surface waters. As the water warms, fish need more oxygen, but warm water retains less of it. Colder oceans teem with fish while warmer seas are rather empty. The exception is coral reefs, the marine equivalent of oases in the warm aquatic deserts, but they die off when it gets too hot, too. So there will be less fish. On the land and in the seas, climate change makes for a barren world that is tough on life.

This sketch is a simplification, but the details left out—marine acidification and the dissolving of sea shells, permafrost thaw and the

---

MARTIN SCHÖNFELD, Professor, Department of Philosophy and School of Global Sustainability, University of South Florida. Specialties: climate philosophy, sustainability, civil evolution. E-mail: mschonfe@usf.edu

outgassing of methane, continental deglaciation and the running dry of rivers—do not change the picture in any way. On the contrary, the more climatological details are filled in, the darker and starker the picture becomes. The causal cascades triggered by the crisis all feed into the same consequence. The consequence of climate change is the *reduction of planetary carrying capacity*.

Fertility reductions happened before. But this new change is not unfolding in the cycle of ice ages and interglacials, or because of random volcanism. It is happening because of us, and here a differentiation is in order: climate change is entirely anthropogenic (humans are at fault), but it is primarily made in the United States (the major culprits are Americans). The U.S. population is only five percent of the world population but is responsible for a third of total greenhouse gas (GHG) emissions. Since GHGs linger for decades, and climate change is cumulative, emissions add up, and this is how a mere five percent of the species have been changing life on Earth for everyone. Anthropogenic climate change is *Amerigenic* climate change.[1]

There is a clear normative, analytic dimension to global warming, which has spawned climate ethics as a new line of inquiry. But what is truly intriguing, I think, is the larger existential aspect.[2] We know that climate change is the result of a design flaw of contemporary civilization. Nobody desires climate change, but it is perpetrated anyway, because doing so is dictated by economic rationality together with the pursuit of the oil-based, prosperity-driven American Dream. Thus a climatic reduction of carrying capacity is occurring because of arbitrary cultural causes.

II. Reaching the Limit

Heating up the climate signals that the Earth system is being overwhelmed. This marks the limit of viable expansion. Since environmental stability is now incompatible with growth, but economic stability continues to need growth, civilization finds itself unprepared for the present realities. This maladaptation is understandable because the situation is unprecedented. There are historical precedents for encounters of cultures with environmental limits, but it never happened before that the entire human society is hitting a universal environmental limit simultaneously.

This collision is occurring sooner than expected. As the biotic resource base shrinks and global warming speeds up, a limit once assumed to be a problem for future generations comes back from the future to the present. In our biospherical *Oikos* or house, the walls are now closing in from all sides. There is no technological fix. The limit cannot be engineered away. There is no conceptual fix either. We cannot debate or interpret the limit away either. Human society faces an absolute material limit.[3]

Especially in the Far West—the cultural hemisphere encompassing the United States, Canada, and Australia—we are not used to such situations, not the least because of the frontier experience. The frontier has created a mentality of bold exploration and boundless expansion. Sustainability was not an issue. In the Eurasian societies, by contrast, such as in China or Germany, which lacked a frontier, landscapes have been cultivated for millennia. This has created a mentality of intergenerational sustainability. Unless they wanted their children to emigrate, parent generations had to take care in managing the land, so as to be able to hand it down to their offspring. When a century ago the technical know-how of refining crude oil into an energy source had matured to the point of switching from coal to oil as the primary fuel of civilization, another contrast between the Far West and Eurasia emerged. North America had plenty of oil (Australia is blessed with ample oil deposits and gas reserves), while Europe and China had next to none. Whatever oil was used in Europe and China had to be imported from abroad. A highly efficient urban and transit infrastructure was the consequence of this energy austerity. In the Far West, the superabundance of oil had the opposite result, spawning an inefficient infrastructure of interstates and suburbs. Intergenerational land use and urban density in Europe and China already reflect long-standing cultural adaptations to invariant material limitations. For geographical reasons alone, the encounter with the limit does not come as much of a shock to Central European and East Asian cultures as it does to societies in the Far West.[4]

Intellectual conventions in the Far West are accordingly ill-equipped of conceptualizing this new reality. Human existence, conceived as being-in-the-world, is shifting into a wholly new order. In the conventional Western reasoning, this new order seems utterly improbable. A limit is considered there to be either material or absolute. But it is never both. If it is material, it will be contingent and relative; there are always exceptions or possible ways around it. If it is absolute, it will be formal or transcendent, but in any case it will not be of this world. So the collective encounter with an omnipresent limit constitutes an improbable oxymoron, a *material absolute* or an *existential universal*—neither of which should even exist according to normal reasoning in the Far West.

The unfamiliarity with material constraints and the inability to conceptualize secular limits in absolute terms are joined by a third cognitive maladaptation, namely that the conventional Western thinking is disproportionately steeped in skepticism. The skeptical bent of the Far Western mentality has all sorts of reasons, ranging from the empiricism of the Scottish Enlightenment to the liberalism of American democracy, and it finds expression in all sorts of traits, ranging from climate denial to the declining public trust in science, especially among conservatives.[5]

The weight given to skepticism in the Far West can be illustrated by the comparison to *critical* reasoning, a centerpiece of which is the conclusion of the *Critique of Pure Reason*. In the final paragraph of the *Critique*, Kant maps out the terrain of Philosophy as being bounded by the extremes of dogma and doubt, with Wolff at the one pole and Hume at the other. The critical path runs along the fertile middle ground in between.[6] Kant's last word, as it were, is that philosophical progress hinges on balancing skepticism and dogmatism. In Kant's day, David Hume and Christian Wolff were emblematic of these two extreme cognitive stances, and both names were equally known to the educated public. Wolff's secular, pro-scientific, and communitarian influence turned out to be seminal in the shaping of Europe, especially as regards the fiscal rules and regulations on private wealth so characteristic of the social democracies. In the Far West, however, Wolff is known only to historians, while Hume enjoys perfect name recognition to virtually all and any American philosopher. What is more, today Hume is not considered a radical in the Far West. Conventional Western philosophy has mainstreamed skepticism. Thus an adequate rational inquiry into the climate crisis and the environmental limit pose difficulties to conventional thought. Philosophy in the Far West cultivates open questions. The problem with the environmental limit, however, is that it confronts us with a conclusive answer.

The conventional thinking has mainstreamed skepticism, but the rational dimension of climatological information points to a new dogmatism. Before climate change got under way, science and ethics had been separate; there was no overlap between the sphere of scientific findings and that of moral values. But through climate change, the two spheres have begun to merge. Unlike any other scientific enterprise, climatology in the twenty-first-century grounds moral imperatives. In late 2012, for example, it had become clear that "observed emission trends are in line with ... the highest temperature projections in the scenarios, with a mean temperature increase of 4.2–5 C in 2100."[7] In the report *Turn down the Heat*, commissioned by the World Bank, and released at the 2012 United Nations Climate Change Conference in Doha, H. J. Schnellnhuber et al. write that for U.S. corn, soybean, and cotton production in 2100, "yields are projected to decrease by 63 to 82 percent."[8] The projected yield decrease would be catastrophic by any measure. The likelihood of destructive nonlinear effects of a 4 C mean temperature increase on major crops is well known—too much heat causes harvest failures. So: we know how, and why, a 4 C warmer world would threaten stability, safety, and survival. Consequently we know that this particular future must be avoided. There is no arguing with the desirability of survival, and neither is there with the existential threat posed by elevated global mean temperatures. The subtitle of this report is *Why a 4 C Warmer World Must Be Avoided*. By way of the trivial desirability of survival and the plain magnitude of the threat, climatological projections involve practical imperatives considerably more forceful than the normative exhortations of old. Avoiding a 4 C warmer world is not something that ought to be done. It *must* be done. This new imperative is nonnegotiable. As was evident at the Doha conference, global civilization is not yet capable of recognizing this.

III. The Cognitive GAP Between the Far West and Eurasia

A consequence of this cognitive failure of grasping secular absolutes such as universal existential boundaries is a topical distortion. Philosophy in the Far West puts topics at center stage that are the *opposite* of topics with existential significance. If anything, the limit discloses that being human means nothing in Cartesian isolation, and only means something when conceived as *being-in-the-world*. And yet, in the Far West, due to historical factors such as Protestant individualism, Cartesian dualism, and British liberalism, all of which shape conventional reasoning to this day, we pretend that the real topics are aspects of humanity considered in isolation. Hence conventional thinking is about self-centered topics such as mind, personhood, freedom, rights, and culture. The limit reveals the significance of the antitheses: *matter* instead of mind; *environment* instead of personhood; *adaptation* instead of freedom; *obligations* instead of rights, and *nature* instead of culture. In the perspective of the limit, conventional thinking is narcissistic and autistic.

On the level of practice, the answer of the limit is a perfectly trivial categorical imperative: *act so that you stay under the limit!* If one asked why, the answer would be formal, as it should: because if we do not stay under the limit, we will eventually not be able to act. Acting-under-the-limit is the only type of action that can serve as a principle of legislation. Solitary agents can transgress the limit and get away with it as parasitic free riders on others. But if everyone transgressed the limit (or to say it in Kantian jargon, if a maxim of transgression was universalized), such agency would spawn collapse, precluding further transgression. Acting-above-the-limit is collectively self-reducing.

Both theory and practice point to the revolutionary implications of the limit. Environmental ethics is an example. In present day the Far Western thought, environmental ethics is a familiar but marginal field. It is now slightly more important than it was a generation ago, but not by much; compared to the greening of the academy, with all the new research and teaching on climate and sustainability across virtually all disciplines, philosophy is lagging behind. Environmental ethics continues to be treated as an elective, not as a core requirement. The reasons are easy to see: environmental ethics is applied and not very rigorous; it is not purely ethics but also involves metaphysics; its ideas and information constitute a strange bundle of facts and values; it raises questions but also defends answers; and the answers it suggests are a mix of earthy commonsense and native wisdom alien to the skeptical bent of the Far Western convention. Compared to impeccably conventional inquiries such as philosophy of mind, environmental ethics is a misfit. But as soon as we take the limit seriously, as a watershed moment in civil history and conceptual inquiry, we will have little choice but to turn priorities upside down and inside out—to shift pursuits such as philosophy of mind from the center to the periphery, and to make environmental ethics the heuristic core of philosophical inquiry.

This gesture of turning philosophy inside out and upside down, this act of *Umstülpen*, delineates the boundary between conventional reasoning in the Far West and its Asian and European counterparts. Chinese and German philosophies serve as examples to illustrate this alternative to the dominant convention, but other approaches elsewhere in the geography of thought would do just as well: Russian and Japanese thought, African sagacity, and indigenous wisdom around the planet, including in the Far West before the Catholics arrived from Spain and France, and the Puritans sailed from England.

The long-standing hegemony of the Far Western approaches in the so-called American Century that began with Pearl Harbor and ended with 9–11 should not distract us from recognizing how much the *exception* Far Western reasoning has been. This may well be due to the demarcation being not only a spatial boundary, in the geography of thought, but also a boundary in time, in the progression of history. The Far West has come into its own by obliterating the indigenous perspectives that had come before it. The culture of the United States of America, influenced in equal measure by the Bible, David Hume, Adam Smith, and Ayn Rand, never managed nor wanted to integrate the cultures it crushed. Native ways of thinking were isolated as ultimate form of cognitive alterity. The Far Western reasoning emerged through a violent historical rupture, as a murderous disavowal of earlier traditions.

This cognitive rupture in the Far West is quite unique. China has suffered a rupture during Maoism, when the state-led anti-Confucian campaigns—in concert with the persecution of exponents of Daoism and Buddhism—sought to modernize the country by means of a violent break with its past. But the break was mitigated by subsequent attempts at normalizing the relationships to the oppressed groups and their suppressed perspectives, not only by accepting them as a legitimate alterity, as native Americans exist in the United States today, but by reintegrating them into the postrupture fold. Daoism and Buddhism could return to a semblance of traditional normalcy, and a new type of Confucianism began to emerge in post-Maoist China.[9] And while the Maoist spasm was comparatively short-lived, it was also limited inside China's cultural space—outside the mainland, in offshore Taiwan, China's spiritual and ethical traditions were able to thrive in a context of nonideological and pluralistic modernization. Elsewhere in the Chinese diaspora, for example, in the city-state of Singapore, Confucian and Daoist traditions were successfully integrated in the pursuit of modernity as well.

In Europe, a similarly successful integration of ancient perspectives in the pursuit of modernity occurred in Germany. The spasms of superlative aggression and repeatedly self-destructive violence of German history should not distract us from the outcome: compared to other European societies, especially to those of Western and Southern Europe, modern Germany managed to integrate its ancient identity rather well. The cultural force that helped to shape Europe more than any other was the Roman Empire, whose provinces connected the Mediterranean region to the Western and Northwestern parts of Europe. When Christianity became state religion in Rome, all the provinces had to follow suit, from Portugal to Spain, from France to Ireland, and from England to Wales and parts of Scotland. Only the Germans did not. With the exception of the imperial provinces of Austria and Bavaria south of the Danube, and the Western bank of the Rhine along France and Holland, Germany was out of Rome's reach, and remained so well after the fall of the Roman Empire to Rome's Frankish successors. France and England, the feeder cultures of the Far West, had been docile sheep in the Christian flock since Constantine, but German Vandals and Visigoths remained utterly out of control. Seven centuries would pass before priests from Western and Southern Europe managed to cross the rivers to *Mitteleuropa* and begin converting German pagans whose faith was similar to Daoism and Shinto. The gradual missionary success came with a price. Time and again the Great Commission had to engage in religious horse-trading to allow the Gospel to spread—results of which are now ubiquitous in the Global Village, with Germanic tree worship at

Christmas and Teutonic fertility rites involving rabbits and eggs at Easter.

In the history of Christianity, Germany was far more trouble than it was worth. Soon after the lands were subdued, along came Luther and triggered a schism splitting the Church into two. When the two rivaling churches went to war a century later, wiping out a third of the German population in doing so, the ultimate result was that Christianity was discredited, that a groundswell of secularization proved unstoppable, and that, in stark contrast to the split of church and state elsewhere in Europe, secularization made room for a renewal of ancient ideas, now in the guise of uniquely German metaphysical aspirations. This renewal was begun by the Leibniz–Wolffian School Philosophy with its Spinozist leanings, radicalized by the young Kant, sustained by Schelling and Hölderlin, mainstreamed by Schopenhauer and Goethe, and pushed into the present by Hegel and Engels, Nietzsche and Heidegger.

The uneven success of the Great Commission in the West discloses a pattern over the preservation of ancient identity. The more successful the missionaries were, the fewer pagan perspectives survived. At the same time, missionary success was not necessarily long lasting. England and France had been in complete Christian control, with a tightly woven network of bishoprics, monasteries, and chapels since the fourth century, and yet succeeded to develop into some of the world's most secular societies after the Age of Reason. Germany is just as secular, but differs from France and England by its comparative integrity of pre-Christian perspectives. Little of the indigenous wisdom survived in the European West, with the result that secularization opened up a void filled with skepticism. When the power of the churches broke, the English and the French had nothing to go back to. The Germans did.

The indigenous wisdom that did survive in *Mitteleuropa* concerns sustainable world outlooks and holistic ways of reasoning. Its visible expression today, compared to Europeans in the West and South, is that Germans are earthy. German customs include a love of the natural that is quite unique in Europe. It expresses itself in customs as diverse as the traditional Sunday walk in the forest or in the park, the *Sonntagsspaziergang*, so that even if you are a good Christian and go to church on Sunday morning, you would head to the woods and be close to the trees in the afternoon. It also expresses itself in an exceptionally sane relation to embodiment. The modern concept of athletic fitness, for instance, originated in the German *Turnverein* of "sports father" (*Turnvater*) Friedrich Ludwig Jahn (1778–1852). The postwar sexual revolution was spearheaded by German feminists who asserted sexual freedom as a woman right, such as by the pioneering pornographer Beate Uhse (1919–2001). The nonsexual but idyllic concept of nudism-in-nature originated in the German "free body culture" or *Freikörperkultur* or *FKK*, the carefree nudity in summer months on the beaches of the North Sea and the Baltic, along river banks and around lakes, and even in regular city parks such as Munich's English Garden. German tourism exported naked flesh to Mediterranean beaches, to the great surprise of their less pagan and more pious European neighbors. Yet the Germans succeeded: today all European beaches tolerate at least partial, bare-breasted nudity.

Next to earthiness and celebration of embodiment, another visible expression is that German culture is the center of environmentalism in the West. The Western pioneers of environmental philosophy were German (such as Arthur Schopenhauer and Albert Schweitzer) or Norwegian (such as Arne Naess) or sons of German immigrants (such as Aldo Leopold). The Western pioneers of political environmentalism were the Greens or *die Grünen* founded in Germany in 1979. The German Greens were the first environmental party of any democratic nation to join the legislative by making it into the federal parliament in 1983. They were also the first in any democracy to join the executive, by sharing in the government coalition from 1998 to 2005. Finally, the Western pioneers of technological environmentalism have been German engineers. Germany continues to spearhead the global effort at a postcarbon transformation of the energy and transit infrastructure; it relies more than any other highly developed nation on solar, wind, and geothermal energy, and the current post-Green government made headlines in 2011 with its declaration to phase out not only fossil fuels but also nuclear technology.

The connection between a modern integration of pagan wisdom and a social, critical, and political cultivation of environmentalism is not coincidental. For our purposes it serves as a marker to delineate the perspectival distinction between the Far West and the Sino-German way. Symptomatic of this difference of the Far Western normalcy to the German and Chinese variants of world philosophy is environmental ethics. Like the philosophical discipline of environmental ethics, Chinese and German ways of reasoning are already turned upside down and inside out; compared to the perspectives in the Far West, they are *umgestülpt*. The ontological quintessence of this difference hinges on the relation of facts and values. In *Mitteleuropa* and the Middle Kingdom facts and values are connected by way of function and form; the flow of "being" aspires to the emergence of the Good, and whoever splits the "is" from the "ought" lacked a realistic understanding of Nature, and is guilty of the Fallacy of Bifurcating Nature.[10] The Far Western stance, by contrast, is captured evidently in Hume's Guillotine that sliced values off from facts, a cut made permanent by G. E. Moore with the dire warning that all those who beg to differ are logically challenged, unsophisticated, and guilty of the Naturalistic Fallacy.

IV. Perspectival Convergences of German and Chinese Culture

Understanding the difference leads to ontology. The two "fallacies" are the key. Although there are different senses of naturalism, and (scientistic) "naturalism" is a prevalent model in American philosophy, conventional reasoning in the Far West considers naturalism, normatively understood, as an approach somehow wanting in rigor and at least in need of further study. Conventional wisdom in Germany and China, however, places facts and values in a continuum, and rates dualism as the crude fiction of monotheistic fanatics, who once spoke Latin and now preach with American accents. The famous dictum about the history of European philosophy being only a series of footnotes to Plato is therefore just not true.[11] German philosophy is central to Western philosophy and yet different. Here, Plato is problematic, and his Dialogues have not been all that seminal. To the extent German thinkers have engaged with the Greeks, they have done so more often and more typically by way of an exegesis of Aristotle and the Presocratics.

Platonic dualism is the stance of the Far West. The divine and the secular inhabit spheres as opposite as that of creator and creation. The divine is the sphere of the mind, value, and freedom. The secular is the sphere of matter, fact, and fate. The bifurcation opens a gap no logical argument can bridge. This spawns problems unique to the Far West, such as the problem of free will and determinism, which is puzzling only in a Platonic outlook. For the Aristotelian alternative, this problem deflates to the issue of power-in-networks; in a holistic ontology informed by dynamic structures, the event of free agency in a determinate field is intelligible. The Far Western inability to solve its pseudo-problems is, paradoxically, the incentive to keep such problems alive. There are degrees of problematization, and the individual stances of conventional American philosophers vary. Nonetheless, in a Socratic spirit that reduces philosophy to questions, it is not the solutions, but the *problems* that sustain Far Western philosophical identity.

In the Platonic gap, the divine and creative cannot be anything but supernatural; it is impossible that a creative power is part of the creation itself. Just as artists are not paintings and authors are not books, the creative or divine dwells outside the created or natural. The fact-value distinction expresses itself accordingly as a rejection of

Spinozism. Spinoza's ontological continuum, with its poles of dynamic agency and lawful structure, matters for understanding the Far Western need to appropriate German philosophy and to make it truly its own.

The Far Western appropriation of German philosophy highlights the complex status of German perspectives in Europe. On the one hand they are authentically Western, on the other they are akin to world-philosophical views, and the best that one can conclude from this uneasy outcome is that the West itself is split; that its own geography of thought falls apart, as it were, into a Christian–Platonic culture spatially coextensive with the former provinces of Rome and its later colonial dependencies, and a Spinozist–Aristotelian culture in *Mitteleuropa* and points east. German philosophy is accordingly rather odd—while it is certainly influenced by a Christian, Platonic mindset, it is not *dominated* by it. The result is a characteristic ambiguity, a tension between Plato and Aristotle, or the Bible and Spinoza, whereby the tension itself is constitutive of the peculiar dynamism of German thought from Eckhart to now.

German contemporaries of Spinoza felt uneasy about the fact-value continuum, for although the continuum suggests the fundamental insight sought, its frank articulation would incur the wrath of the authorities. A philosopher like Kant, who articulated Spinozist–Aristotelian positions in an audacious and quasi-pagan way in early books such as *Living Forces*,[12] *Universal Natural History*,[13] and *Physical Monadology*,[14] would marginalize himself, no matter how much else he wrote, until he composed something as circumspect as *Inaugural Dissertation*,[15] which could comfortably be read as a recanting of Spinoza. Only by this gesture of pretending to reinstate the Platonic gap could he deal himself back into the academic game and find a university appointment. Kant was not alone in this. From Leibniz to Hegel, and from Schopenhauer to Nietzsche, German philosophy is characterized by a Spinozist ambiguity, and it is this very ambiguity that makes German philosophy sound difficult and obscure to the Far Western readers. The Far Western appropriations of German philosophy are readings in a Platonic lens designed to extirpate whatever does not fit. Such appropriations are accordingly recognizable by their exegetical attempts to *de-Spinozise* German philosophy, so as to purge it of its holistic taint.

The holistic taint is a subtle but essential trait of German thought, and it intensifies to a not-so-subtle uniform feature of world philosophy in general and Chinese wisdom in particular. Only the Far West slices reality into halves. Outside the Platonic enclave, the cosmic egg of being remains intact. The energetic, normative, and rational aspects are distinct from their structured, factual, and material counterparts, but their distinctness places them on a spectrum, as discrete degrees of one and the same being along a shared continuum. An Aristotelian polarity, no Platonic gap, reigns in between. Values, in this holistic spectrum, are pragmatic algorithms reflective of facts in the natural flow.

That values, in holism, are reflections of facts makes them a priori ecologically relevant. Environmentally and existentially speaking, values linked to facts are safer values. Dangerous in the contemporary American Disenlightenment is its blind insistence on jingoistic, religious, and consumerist values, in defiant disdain of the facts spelled out by scientific information. Freely contrived values, spawned by reality-disconnect, fuel the behavior patterns that worsen the crisis. It is no coincidence that the Platonic enclave to bifurcate reality is also the culture that perpetrates most of anthropogenic climate change. And it is no surprise that the societies that managed to maintain some social relevance of traditional values attuned to material reality, have been making the greatest strides toward a postcarbon future. Coordinating values and facts in a continuum, and thereby *grounding* values in facts as well as *valuing* facts for what they are, is the first cognitive step of civil evolution toward staying within the limit.

In Chinese philosophy, Daoism and Confucianism are evidently guilty of the naturalistic "fallacy"; each philosophy illustrates what it means to stay within the limit. In the *Dao De Jing* 《道德經》 virtue (*de* 德) as embodied in the sage (*shengren* 聖人) is in accordance with the Way, the pulse of being that spawns nature. One of Laozi's points is that the "ought" better follow the "is," and that doing so is in the self-interest of any norm wanting to stay a norm, for if values ever went against the Way, they would come to an early end.[16]

Just as Laozi 老子 grounds Daoist ethics in the factual flow of nature, Mencius (Mengzi 孟子) grounds Confucian political philosophy in the factual characteristics of the masses. The *Mencius* (*Meng Zi* 《孟子》) begins with a sharpening of value: the essence of the good is not merely sympathetic humanity or graceful benevolence (*ren* 仁), but also infused by principled and ethical righteousness (*yi* 義). But just as virtue in Laozi needs to be a mirror of the Way, value in Mencius, whether benevolence or righteousness, is reflective of the universal needs of rational beings. And while the liberal bourgeoisie in its self-complacent relativism would hasten to deconstruct an absolutist concept such as universal needs, Mencius is adamant about the earthy constancy of mortal limits, public vulnerabilities, and economic wants. Thus his advice to the ones in positions of power comes down to a single admonition, with singular authority: strengthen the people so as to strengthen the empire.[17]

Values such as Daoist virtue (*de*) and Confucian righteousness (*yi*) are distinct but based on the same foundation: there is a certain way the world works and how one may flourish in it; just as there is a certain way to how humans are and what they need, what upsets them, and what befriends them. These ways are fluid and yet regular; they are dynamic and yet structured, similar to steady currents and constant eddies in the flowing river of reality. Following the ways of nature and of the people is how one can make things work out, how one prevails, and how, ultimately, agents retain power (*li* 力). It is possible to declare and enact values floating free from factual reality, but doing so tends to be a losing proposition. Epistemic stances in denial of reality have a way of spiraling into cataclysmic failure.

In German philosophy, a more subtle example of the same kind of fact-value-attunement is Kantian ethics. As I have tried to show elsewhere, this affinity to Chinese wisdom is not coincidental.[18] What remains to be done is to elucidate the way Kant grounds value, while differentiating his approach from its Far Western appropriation.

The Platonic appropriation of Kant makes the distinction between the sensible and the intelligible look as if the former housed facts and the latter housed values—as if the sensible and the intelligible are both houses of being, as it were. But one should not forget that the differentiation between sensible appearance and intelligible thing in itself is first and foremost an *epistemic* distinction. The appropriation, however, invests the epistemic upshot of the Copernican turn with ontological substance, as if Kant were a Platonist. The problem is that this reading tries to eliminate an intrinsic ambiguity (or critical balance, if you wish) to a flat, one-sided account. While it is true, for Kant, that the material ineffability and pure intelligibility is what makes values of moral relevance categorically imperative, it is nonetheless also true that the information comprised in values stems from factual structures accessible to the senses.[19]

The grounding of value is clearly disclosed in the second version of the Categorical Imperative: *act so as to treat humanity, whether in your person or in that of another, always as an end and never as a means only*. Kant explains:

> Beings the existence of which rests not on our will but on nature, if they are beings without reason, still have only a relative worth, as means, and are therefore called *things*, whereas rational beings are called *persons* because *their nature already marks them out as an end in itself*, that is, as something that may not be used merely as a means, and hence so far limits all choice (and is an object of respect). These, therefore, are not merely subjective ends, the existence of which as an effect of our action has a worth *for us*, but rather *objective ends*, that is, beings the existence of which is in itself an end, and indeed one such that no other end, to which they would serve *merely* as means,

can be put in its place, since without it nothing of *absolute worth* would be found anywhere; but if all worth were conditional and therefore contingent, then no supreme practical principle for reason could be found anywhere.[20] (Emphases added)

Persons, for Kant, are what they are since "their nature already marks them out as an end in itself." A person is not merely a normative artifact but also a factual entity. Autonomy is a moral desideratum as well as a material given. What bridges the Platonic gap, fusing it into an Aristotelian continuum, is that humans, who are autonomous agents, enlightened persons, and ends in themselves, are not born but are made. All humans are heteronomous at the outset, but all can grow into autonomous personhood. That they *can* be made that way implies that they *should* be made so, for the autonomy humans lack in infancy is nonetheless their intrinsic and inalienable character, if only as a potential.

The factual grounding of value accordingly hinges on the realization of potentials—humans are potentially persons, they can be ends in themselves, and out of sheer respect for the facticity of this potential, any being bestowed with such a talent should actualize their personhood. The way to do so in moral practice is to treat oneself and others, regardless of how far along a given individual is on the path to autonomy, *as if* we all are ends and never means only. A revealing corollary of "categorical imperative" is that slavery, the archetype of treating humanity as mere means, not only amounts to a moral wrong but also involves a cognitive error, for the practice of slavery means to treat the humanity of others as if they lacked the potential for autonomy—which is factually wrong. In this precise sense, and in Kant, too, values are *limited* by facts.

The quintessential convergence of Chinese wisdom, as illustrated by Laozi and Mencius, and German philosophy, as exemplified by Kant, concerns a shared embrace of normative naturalism. In the Middle Kingdom as well as in *Mitteleuropa*, values are grounded in facts. One could accordingly say that the insight that normative pulses are channeled by factual structures binds China and Germany together into a Sino-German perspective.

V. The Evolution of Sustainability

Having argued that key figures of Chinese and German thought embrace what in the Far West is called a fallacy, namely that factual constraints inform normative substance, it needs to be clarified in closing how this staying-under-the-limit amounts to the quintessence of sustainability.

The principle of sustainability has enjoyed a remarkable career. Originally conceived as a policy principle in the context of resource exploitation, it has grown into one of the most central concerns of transnational policy—and with good reason. Just as environmental problems were originally many and varied, without much of a common cause or shared center, policy responses had been correspondingly diverse. But in the past two decades, a great simplification has occurred. As deeper humankind is edging into crisis, and as closer civilization pushes the world to the brink, the simpler the issues become. In the roster of ecological problems, climate change has grown into the mother of all issues, to the extent that it serves now as the frame of reference for virtually any of the older problems, whether this is preservation of wilderness, or biological diversity, or integrity of the land. Likewise, among the old list of policy responses, sustainability has transformed from one specific target to the universal objective everything else is subject to. So climate change is on the level of facts what sustainability is now on the level of values.

This transformation of sustainability to the center of environmental policy has also altered the interpretation of this concept. Its first label, coined about forty years ago, right before the historic crossing of sustainable yield thresholds of the resources we depend on, was "sustainable development." This concept was a reflection of the hope that economic growth would remain compatible with staying under the biospherical limits. After this hope was dashed, around the turn of the millennium, "sustainable development" was shortened to "sustainability." The encounters with freak weather and climate events, such as the Australian drought, the inundation of New Orleans, the fires in Siberia, and the floods in Pakistan, spawned new characterizations of sustainability, updating it in terms of *durability* and *resilience*.

These semantic variations and definitional updates orbit around a lexical core. Sustainability, the noun, stems from the verb, to sustain. What is to be sustained can be explicated in two ways, in a reflexive, self-referential fashion, and in a transitive, relational manner. The reflexive variant of sustainability is captured in a thoughtful definition by J. Baird Callicott: "sustainability is the property of an activity or complex system of activities capable of going on and on indefinitely, if not forever."[21] The transitive variant, which refers to the interaction between humankind and the biosphere, is expressed in the classical definition by H. Brundtland: "Sustainable development is development that meets the needs of the present without compromising the ability of future generations to meet their own needs."

The German for "sustainability" or "sustainable development," once more nicely ambiguous, lending itself to either the intransitive or the relational reading, is *Nachhaltigkeit* or *nachhaltig zukunftsorien-*

tierte Entwicklung: a development (*Entwicklung*) attuned to the future (*zukunftsorientiert*) such that it can keep going (*nachhaltig*). Sustainability or *Nachhaltigkeit* is the "keep-going" style of a process in principle.

Evidently this is captured in Laozi's admonition that practices better stay within the constraints of the Way, and in Mencius' warning that empires can stay together and make history only if the needs of the people are heeded. It is also captured in Kant's critical ethics, namely in the first formulation of the categorical imperative: act so that the maxim of your action can always serve as a principle of legislation. The well-known universalizability-test to determine whether maxims can serve as the sought-for legislative principles and qualify as categorical imperatives captures the form of sustainability in perfect precision. An action that everyone can do, in the strong sense of "can-do," namely such that everyone can repeat the action and keep repeating it, without such infinite replication of the action across all agents ever leading to a self-reducing outcome, is the hallmark of morality. Moral actions are consequently only those that remain indefinitely sustainable under the condition of universal implementation.

This, then, is the outcome of our inquiry. Civilization is sliding into an unprecedented crisis whose overall guise and pervasive symptom is climate change. Climate change spells the end of growth and translates into a looming bottleneck of scarcities, the risk of which is not only biodiversity collapse but also a dieback of our kind. For the first time in history, the totality of humankind encounters an omnipresent environmental limit. This encounter necessitates civil evolution—a radical transformation toward a postcarbon, postconsumerist, and postcapitalistic world order, whose overarching objective is to ensure that the increasingly chaotic "earth system" will not destabilize any further. Put in positive terms, this means to manage social needs while staying within biospherical limits. We can expect civil evolution to be a heterogeneous progression—some societies will catch on faster than others. Those that will catch on—and this is the contention of the article and the bet of the author—are Germany and China. For conceptual reasons alone, their perspectival convergence will allow their children to weather the coming storm.

UNIVERSITY OF SOUTH FLORIDA
Tampa, Florida

Endnotes

This article was originally written for my presentation at a panel coordinated by Professor Robin R. Wang and organized by Professor Eric S. Nelson for the 2012 meeting of the Pacific Division of the American Philosophical Association. The article has not appeared in print anywhere else. Any errors in the ideas advanced here are the full responsibility of the author. The author is grateful to the co-editor of this special issue, Eric S. Nelson, Managing Editor, Dr. Linyu Gu, and Editor-in-Chief, Professor Chung-Ying Cheng, for their valuable and thoughtful comments to this article.

1. As this article is a synthesis of ideas substantiated in greater detail elsewhere, I will have to refer the reader repeatedly to other articles for documentation so as not to overburden the synthetic argument. I apologize for the inconvenience. For a quantitative analysis of GHG emissions by national average, per capita, and by cumulative totals, and for how the United States is coming out as the worst perpetrator by any fair measurement, cf. Martin Schönfeld, "Amerigenic climate change: an indictment of U.S. normalcy," in *Environmental Ethics for Canadians*, ed. Byron Williston (Oxford and Toronto: Oxford University Press, 2012), 283–90. For the details of how China's GHG emissions compare favorably in international comparison despite negative U.S. media coverage, cf. ibid, 286.
2. For what was probably the first systematic inquiry in analytic climate ethics, cf. Stephen M. Gardiner, "Ethics and Global Climate Change," *Ethics* 114, no. 3 (2004): 555–600. For a survey of analytic climate ethics, cf. James Garvey, *The Ethics of Climate Change: Right and Wrong in a Warming World* (London: Continuum, 2008). For current works in analytic climate ethics, cf. Simon Caney and Derek Bell, eds., *Morality and Climate Change*, special issue of *The Monist* 94, no. 3 (2011): 305–452. For a different and synthetic approach to climate ethics, cf. the papers collected in Martin Schönfeld, ed., *Climate Ethics*, special issue of *Journal of Global Ethics* 7, no. 2 (2011): 129–218.
3. A recurrent and correct theme in Bill McKibben's work is that while we can negotiate in culture and politics, the laws of physics and chemistry are what they are; for example, cf. "Everything Is Negotiable, Except with Nature: You Can't Bargain about Global Warming with Chemistry and Physics," *Huffington Post*, December 16, 2010; "Earth to Obama: You Can't Negotiate with the Planet," *The New Republic*, October 1, 2009, both retrieved April 1, 2012.
4. For an analysis of the climate shock on American cognition, cf. Martin Schönfeld, "Climate Philosophy and Cognitive Evolution," in *Climate Change and Philosophy: Transformational Possibilities*, ed. Ruth Irwin (London: Continuum, 2010), 21–31.
5. Gordon Gauchat, "Politicization of Science in the Public Sphere: A Study of Public Trust in the United States, 1974 to 2010," *American Sociological Review* 77, no. 2 (2012): 167–87, esp. 177–8.
6. A855/B883: "Now as far as the observers of the *scientific* method are concerned, they have here the choice of proceeding either *dogmatically* or *skeptically*, but in either case they have the obligation of proceeding *systematically*. If I here name with regard to the former the famous Wolff, and with regard to the latter David Hume, then for my present purposes I can leave the others unnamed. The *critical* path alone is still open. If the reader has had the pleasure and the patience in traveling along in my company, then he can now judge, if it pleases him to contribute his part to making this footpath into a highway, whether or not that which many centuries could not accomplish might not be attained . . . namely, to bring human reason to full satisfaction in that which has always, but until now vainly, occupied its lust for knowledge." Immanuel Kant, *Critique of Pure Reason*, trans. Paul Guyer and Allen W. Wood, *Cambridge Edition of the Works of Immanuel Kant* (Cambridge and New York: Cambridge University Press, 1998), 704.
7. Glen P. Peters, Robbie M. Andrew, et al., "The Challenge to Keep Global Warming Below 2 C," *Nature Climate Change* (2012), doi: 10.1038/nclimate1783, online December 2, 2012, retrieved December 14, 2012.
8. Hans Joachim Schnellnhuber, William Hare, et al., *Turn Down the Heat: Why a 4 C Warmer World Must Be Avoided*, a report for the World Bank by the Potsdam Institute for Climate Impact Research and Climate Analytics (Washington, DC: World Bank, 2012), 61.
9. Daniel A. Bell, "From Communism to Confucianism: Changing Discourses on China's Political Future," in Daniel A. Bell, *China's New Confucianism* (Princeton and Oxford: Princeton University Press, 2008), 3–18.

10. Shi-chuan Chen, "How to Form a Hexagram and Consult the *I-Ching*," *Journal of the American Oriental Society* 92, no. 2 (1972): 237–48, esp. 248: "The Principle of the Three Participants (三才之道) is demonstrated in a trigram or a hexagram and is repeatedly referred to in the 'Ten Wings.' Because of this principle the ancient Chinese avoided becoming victims of the *fallacy of the bifurcation of nature*. The derivatives from this bifurcation, namely: the *separation of the subjective from the objective; the distinction of the primary and secondary qualities*; and the *confrontation of the ego and non-ego*, have not tortured the Chinese mind." (Emphases added)
11. Alfred North Whitehead, *Process and Reality: An Essay in Cosmology* (New York: Humanities Press, 1929), 63: "The Safest General Characterization of the European Philosophical Tradition is that it Consists of a Series of Footnotes to Plato."
12. Immanuel Kant, *Thoughts on the True Estimation of Living Forces* (1747), trans. Jeffrey B. Edwards and Martin Schönfeld, in Kant, *Natural Science*, The Cambridge Edition of the Works of Immanuel Kant, ed. Eric Watkins (New York/Cambridge: Cambridge University Press, 2012), 1–155.
13. Immanuel Kant, *Universal Natural History and Theory of the Heavens* (1755), trans. Olaf Reinhardt, in Kant, *Natural Science*, loc. cit., 182–308.
14. Immanuel Kant, *The Employment in Natural Philosophy of Metaphysics Combined with Geometry, of which Sample I Contains the Physical Monadology* (1756), trans. David Walford and Ralf Meerbote, in Kant, *Theoretical Philosophy 1755–1770*, The Cambridge Edition of the Works of Immanuel Kant, ed. David Walford (New York/ Cambridge: Cambridge University Press, 1992), 47–66.
15. Immanuel Kant, *On the Forms and Principles of the Sensible and Intelligible World* [Inaugural Dissertation] (1770), trans. David Walford and Ralf Meerbote, in Kant, *Theoretical Philosophy 1755–1770*, loc. cit., 373–416.
16. Laozi, *Dao De Jing* 《道德經》 Chapter 30, "*Bu dao zao yi*" (不道早已).
17. Mencius, *Meng Zi* 《孟子》, 4A: 9, "*De qi min si de tian xia yi* 得其民, 斯得天下矣."
18. Martin Schönfeld, "From Confucius to Kant—The Question of Information Transfer," *Journal of Chinese Philosophy* 33, no. 1 (2006): 67–82.
19. This also applies to the relation of Kant in ethics to Confucianism; cf. Chung-ying Cheng, "Theoretical Links between Kant and Confucianism: Preliminary Remarks," *Journal of Chinese Philosophy* 33, no. 1 (2006): 3–15; Chung-ying Cheng, "Incorporating Kantian Good Will: On Confucian *ren* 仁 as perfect duty," in *Cultivating Personhood: Kant and Asian Philosophy*, ed. Stephen R. Palmquist (Berlin/New York: De Gruyter, 2010), 74–96.
20. *Groundwork of the Metaphysics of Morals*, in Immanuel Kant, *Practical Philosophy*, trans. Mary J. Gregor (Cambridge and New York: Cambridge University Press, 1996), 79 (4): 428.
21. J. Baird Callicott, "Sustainability," in *Sustainability and the Quality of Life*, ed. Jack Lee (Stanford: Ria University Press, 2010), 19–34, esp. 22.

LIN MA

LEVINAS AND THE *DAODEJING* ON THE FEMININE: INTERCULTURAL REFLECTIONS

Abstract

This article revisits the theme of the feminine in Levinas's writings and the *Daodejing*. First it addresses the question why the feminine as thematized through eros (and habitation) in Levinas's early work loses her centrality in his later texts. Second it explores the feminine water metaphor and the *Dao* of *ci* 雌 in the *Daodejing*. On the basis of these interpretations, it attempts at an analysis of relevant ambiguities and problematics concealed in Levinas's philosophical enterprise, and urges for the exigency of an intercultural perspective, instead of remaining within a singular intellectual tradition.

I. Introduction

From the twentieth century onward, Western philosophy has hardly been able to take further steps without recourse to what is now customarily called non-Western philosophy.[1] Even if Levinas's own writings contain no references to Chinese philosophical texts, their presence still emerges occasionally. In a text of 1964, Levinas writes:

> For a Frenchman there does exist the possibility of learning Chinese and passing from one culture into another, without the intermediary of an *Esperanto* that would falsify both tongues which it mediated. Yet what has not been taken into consideration in this case is that an *orientation/sense* [*sens*] is needed to have the Frenchman take up learning Chinese instead of declaring it to be barbarian (that is, bereft of the real virtues of language) and to prefer speech to war.[2]

If one reads this passage out of its context, it seems that Levinas rightly points out that ideal languages such as *Esperanto* cannot serve as the medium of intercultural understanding, and that choosing to learn Chinese is bound up with a necessary precondition, or sense. However, if one situates this passage in Levinas's article, it becomes

---

LIN MA, Associate Professor, Renmin University of China; Researcher, Higher Institute of Philosophy, University of Leuven. Specialties: Continental European philosophy, comparative philosophy, Wittgenstein. E-mail: lin.ma.2007@gmail.com

clear that the Levinasian sense is not something neutral, but is embedded within the Judaeo-Greek tradition. Only Western civilization can provide an orientation to understanding and evaluating other cultures, which "never understood themselves."[3] Levinas acknowledges the possibility and necessity for a European to pass into another culture; nevertheless, this is set within a vision that assumes the priority of Western civilization.

Even if Levinas begrudges, without justification, *ancient* people from non-Western cultures an adequate understanding of their own legacy, it seems that, in the current globalized world, where various intellectual traditions are playing increasingly more important roles, he can hardly deny that *contemporary* "non-Western" mind is making sense of ideas inside and outside of their inherited world. For example, in an interview of 1983, such a question was raised to Levinas: "How could one explain to a contemporary Chinese person what it means to be Jewish?" Levinas does not hint at the possibility that a Chinese can never be able to understand his ideas. Instead, he explains that being a Jew after Auschwitz is not a particularity but a modality; therefore, "everyone is a little Jewish, and if there are men on Mars, one would find some Jews there."[4]

Apart from a sense of superiority of the Jewish/Western tradition in Levinas's answer, it is noteworthy that "a contemporary Chinese person" was put forward as a possible respondent to his thinking. The formulation of the question is also thought-provoking: In what ways can Levinas's writings become accessible to a Chinese philosopher? What would a contemporary interpretation of the *Daodejing* 《道德經》 have to say about Levinas's philosophical claims? If Levinas could have been aware of how a Chinese philosopher would have read, responded to, and even forcefully challenged his ideas, how could this have helped him to pursue and fully develop some of the potentialities dormant in his philosophical meditations.

The other side of the question is: In what ways can Chinese philosophy be intelligible to a Western mind such as Levinas's? In introducing Chinese Daoist thinking to the Western world, should not a contemporary Chinese philosopher have in mind the jointures where a Daoist discourse could be initiated into current discussions? Should not he/she be able to bring contemporary concerns to bear upon his/her researches in Chinese philosophy, and channel ancient resources into current terrain?

These questions that incorporate intercultural considerations are particularly significant when it comes to the theme of the feminine, which is perplexing both in Levinas's thinking and in the *Daodejing*. In a previous work, I have discussed Levinas's idea, as reflected in his early work, that the feminine is the absolute alterity that cannot be subsumed into the totality of the same, and shown how this resonates with the Daoist principle of abiding by the feminine.[5] In this article, I examine Levinas's other writings on the feminine with such a question as the lead: why does the feminine as thematized through eros (and habitation) lose her centrality in Levinas's later texts?

Daoist philosophy has often been characterized as "feminine" in terms of its orientation. In the earlier article, I have analyzed the inadequacy of three readings of the role of femininity in the *Daodejing*, namely, a quasi-feminist historical reading, a correlative reading, and a political reading, and argued that the feminine occupies a central place in this scripture. In this article, I explore the feminine water metaphor and what I call the *Dao* 道 of *ci* 雌. On the basis of such a *contemporary* interpretation of the *Daodejing*, I develop an analysis of some relevant problematics that remain concealed in Levinas's philosophical enterprise.

II. Levinas's Equivocation on the Feminine in "Phenomenology of Eros"

In an interview of 1989, Levinas admits,

> At the time of my little book entitled *Time and the Other*, I thought that femininity was this modality of alterity—this "other genus"—and that sexuality and eroticism were this non-in-difference to the other, irreducible to the formal alterity of terms in an ensemble. Today I think that it is necessary to go back even further and that the exposition, the nudity, and the "imperative demand" of the face of the other constitute this modality that the feminine already presupposes: the proximity of the neighbor is the non-formal alterity.[6]

In referring to *Time and the Other* as "my little book," Levinas disclaims his early idea that the feminine is the Other *par excellence* and that the erotic relation is the event of the ethical relation. He pronounces that it is the face and proximity of the neighbor that provides the locus for the concretization of the pre-original relation to alterity. In spite of an ostensible attempt at keeping her under the rubric of his philosophy of the Other, Levinas clearly re-assigns the feminine a secondary and derivative role.

The transmutation of the role of the feminine is undeniably manifest in the "Phenomenology of Eros" in *Totality and Infinity*, despite the re-occurrence of similar expressions from *Time and the Other* in an all too confounding and complex discourse. When referring again to the myth Aristophanes narrates in Plato's *Symposium*, where love is a matter of re-unification of the two halves of a former whole being, Levinas does not resolutely oppose this kind of love that aims at overcoming a lack and satisfying a need. Instead, he articulates a double-sidedness of love as need in that this need "presuppose the total, transcendent exteriority of the other, of the beloved."[7]

Just as the event of love is situated at the limit of immanence and transcendence, the epiphany of the feminine shows a structure of equivocation. Levinas combines his philosophical insight with observations of social reality: on the one hand, woman can be an interlocutor, collaborator, and even a "superiorly intelligent" master, "so often dominating men in the masculine civilization [she] has entered."[8] Regarding this aspect, one is put in mind of the fact that it is a woman scholar, Gabrielle Peiffer, who first introduced Husserl's work to Levinas at Strasbourg, and who later on translated together with Levinas Husserl's *Cartesian Meditations* into French. From this experience, Levinas must have no doubt of woman's intellectual capacity.

On the other hand, woman "[has] to be treated as a woman, in accordance with rules imprescriptible by civil society."[9] This aspect consists in a negation of traditional rules that have confined woman's sphere of behavior and social activities. *Woman as such* points to the dimension of unruliness and wantonness beyond the reins of civil codes. This characterization receives a hint in *Time and the Other* as the "brutal materiality."[10] In juxtaposing these two aspects, Levinas seems to have felt acutely the discordance between the height which woman's intellectual capacity can attain, and the roles to which she has been confined, and against which certain forms of rebellion have been recognized.

Nowadays feminists are keen to seek for social positions that once were man's prerogative; but this was not common in the early twentieth century. At that time, the forms in which woman protests against the seemingly inviolable "rules" entrenched in man's mentality, including hers, which restrict woman to the domestic sphere, were more often indirectly reflected in a resort to "the *manner* of the tender" that "consists in an extreme fragility, a vulnerability."[11] As Levinas explicates, the manner of the tender is dis-individualizing; it dissolves the weight of being by a retreat to non-signifying ultra-materiality. The sheer ultra-materiality refers to an exorbitant and wanton presence of the nudity of a female body, which profanes and is profaned. The beloved that presents herself as "an irresponsible animality" has quitted her status as a person, as an existent. "The face fades, ... The relations with the Other is enacted in play; one plays with the Other as with a young animal."[12]

Levinas's account of profanation precisely catches phenomena where woman is not treated as a person and neither does she treat herself as a person, and hence is degraded and degrades herself to become an animal-like object. Ironically, precisely this retreating to the status of animal constitutes an implicit protest against the civil society. Profanation is also double-sided. After contrasting the signifyingness of the face through which the ethical principle "Thou shall not kill" shines with the equivocation that is produced in the femininity of the tender, which at most approaches a language of silence, Levinas claims, "The frailty of femininity invites pity for what, in a sense, is not yet, disrespect for what exhibits itself in immodesty and is not discovered despite the exhibition, that is, profanation."[13]

The hither side of wantonness meanwhile hints at the thither side of profanation and the feminine. This is because "disrespect presupposes the face."[14] In one sense, erotic nudity provides innuendos of obscenity; but in another sense, precisely in its exorbitant exhibitionism, it opens moral perspectives that prescribe what is socially inappropriate. What are at play in profanation are *both* the exposed and the clandestine. "*The essentially hidden throws itself toward the light, without becoming signification.*"[15] This equivocation between hiddenness and light, between vulnerability and wantonness constitutes the essence of femininity [*féminité*]. The feminine harbors "future in the present," embraces what "is *no longer*" but also "what is not yet."[16] "What is not yet" is explained in the section following "Phenomenology of Eros" in terms of fecundity.

What concerns us is that the sense of transcendence Levinas attempts to convey is manifestly different from that in *Time and the Other*. Instead of resisting the Platonic account of love that treats the feminine as something like material to feed a need, and providing in the meantime a contrasting philosophy of love that presents the feminine as irreducible alterity, he appears to be attempting at articulating a sense of transcendence of the feminine from within the Platonic account of love as need. Restricted to an erotic relation, woman always verges upon closing herself up in immanence, which nevertheless presupposes and points toward transcendence. This transcendence is possible insofar as a child can be born, which can intervene the non-sociality of the two that are closed up in ultra-materiality.

Authors such as Irigaray have criticized Levinas for the reason that he restricts the feminine within the realm of phenomenology of eros and excludes her from his ethical metaphysics.[17] Whether this criticism is justified turns upon the question whether and to what extent the sense of possible transcendence ascribed to the feminine is authentic. This question is imbued with equivocity and does not allow a straightforward answer. What is clear is that the feminine is not presented as alterity as such. Nor is she deliberately assigned a subordinate place. There are profound ambiguities in Levinas's phenomenology of eros.

Irigaray has also taken issue with Levinas's statements where such phrases as "irresponsible animality" on account of their derogatory meaning regarding woman. However, one need to be aware that they are reflective of only *one* aspect of the feminine that could go profaning and being profaned, that is, the hither side, and that they are meant as *descriptions*, rather than *justifications* of such possibilities. On the other hand, it remains perplexing why Levinas fails to connect the thither side of the feminine with the first aspect that occurs only fleetingly, that is, woman as an interlocutor, collaborator, and "superiorly intelligent" master.[18] The only possibility of transcendence finds concretization only in fecundity. However, the realm of human erotic love leading to fecundity need not be the only locus where woman can achieve transcendence.

III. Habitation: Appropriating Sources from Judaism

In times when woman cannot be treated as a proper Other in the sense of *vous* of interlocution despite her intelligence, she often approaches becoming an other in the sense of *tu* of familiarity in habitation.[19] The theme of habitation draws heavily upon Judaistic sources. In the late 1940s Levinas made intensive studies of the Talmud under the tutorship of Chouchani. Starting from 1957, Levinas continued to deliver Talmudic readings at a Jewish colloquium. The 1969 article "Judaism and the Feminine" shows clearly the Judaistic influences in Levinas's reflection on the feminine.

Using the Talmudic saying "The house is woman" as a cue, Levinas not only affirms its psychological and sociological significance, but also describes it as a primordial truth and a moral paradigm, and thus ascribes to it ontological significance.[20] The scripture states: Man brings home corn and flax; woman grounds corn and spin flax. Levinas stresses that one cannot read these descriptions as merely a justification of the ancillary status of woman. Both corn and flax come from nature by the work of man; they are the products of the conquering masculine civilization. Such a civilization is cold, hard, and impersonal. It can neither clothe nor feed humans. It "lives outdoors" and is inhabitable.[21] It is woman who turns corn into bread and flax into clothing, and thus makes habitation possible. Levinas thus highlights the ontological significance of woman:

> To light eyes that are blind, to restore to equilibrium, and so overcome an alienation which ultimately results from the very virility of the universal and all-conquering logos that stalks the very shadows that could have sheltered it, should be the *ontological function* of the feminine, the vocation of the one "who does not conquer."[22]

Levinas tries to adjust traditional prejudice against woman by ascribing more importance to usual roles she plays at home. Nonetheless, no matter how much ontological significance is ascribed to woman in this connection, it is clear that in "Judaism and the Feminine" the feminine is not the absolute alterity who initiates ethical transcendence. Rather, her significance is construed as an ontological principle alongside a masculine one. Levinas writes, "if woman completes man, she does not complete him as a part completes another into a whole but, as it were, as two totalities complete one another—which is, after all, the miracle of social relations."[23] In the following, we will see the consequence brought about by the reduction of the feminine to ontology within Levinas's own paradigm wherein ethics is most fundamental.

IV. "And God Created Woman"

The 1972 article "And God Created Woman" is a complicated article that defies a straightforward treatment. Levinas's text proceeds from two different interpretations Rabbi Rab and Rabbi Samuel, respectively, provide for the Talmud statement: "And the Lord God fashioned into a woman 'the rib which he had taken from man.'"[24] Rab reads "rib" as face; Samuel reads it as tail. In Levinas's eyes, these two saints share the same opinion that one should not regard woman as merely the opposite sex of man and thus not define her in relation to man. Instead, because woman is created from the rib, something that belongs to the human, she is a proper human being in the fullest essence.

Their disagreement is: for Rab, who interprets the rib as face, woman comes into being together with man. Although she takes shape later, woman enjoys the same degree of dignity as man does, and so is perfectly equal with man. The creation of man is the creation of two beings in a single human being. Thus, sexual difference is a fundamental content of human essence. For Samuel, who interprets the rib as tail, the appearance of woman is an event of genuine creation, not of evolution. The relation between the two beings that appear out of the two events of creation is personal. Therefore, ontological relevance is absent in their relation, and the particularity of woman is secondary. This does not mean that woman herself is secondary, but that the relation with woman is secondary. Samuel concludes that, rather than sexual difference, it is the tasks that man and woman each accomplish that are fundamental.

Another exegetical problem concerns two statements from the *Genesis*: "Male and female he made them simultaneously (5:2)";

"Man was made in the image of God (9:6)."[25] A hypothesis is implied in the first statement that man and woman enjoy the same degree of humanity; whereas on the basis of the second statement that suggests a masculine spirituality, one could draw a corollary that feminine specificity is not on the same plane as spirituality as such. How to reconcile such a scriptural inconsistency? Is it possible to derive sexual equality from the apparent priority of the masculine?

According to Rabbi Abbahu, another exegete, God *wanted* to create two beings, male and female, but in the end he created in his own image a single being. Levinas takes on this lead and explains: God has willed beyond his own image. God *wanted* that equality be in place from the beginning; therefore, he *wanted* to create two beings at the same time. However, this is in fact not possible, because "these two initial independence of two equal beings would no doubt have meant war."[26] "Humanity is not thinkable on the basis of two entirely different principles;" therefore, "[t]here had to be a difference which did not affect equity . . . a certain preeminence of man, a woman coming later, and as woman, an appendage of the human;" God "had to subordinate them one to the other."[27] For this reason, Levinas favors the interpretation that takes the rib to be tail, since it pays more attention to the subordination of sexual difference.

Levinas may not have intended to use the word "subordinate" in the derogatory sense. For him, "man" in the phrase "God created man" refers to universal humanity to which sexual differentiation has not yet occurred. Since sexual difference originates in humanity as such, it does not harm equity. Furthermore, that woman comes out of the flesh of man implies a natural correlation of harmony and collaboration between the two sexes. Nonetheless, the speeches in which woman is said to be "an appendage of the human" are shocking. In "Judaism and the Feminine," Levinas tends toward a reduction of the feminine to the realm of ontology; here the reduction leads to a justification of subordination of woman, to such an extent that Levinas declares: "*The very femininity of woman is in this initial 'after the event.'* "[28]

Levinas enlists another reason why he refuses to incorporate sexual difference into human nature. Some theorists presuppose a primary role of sexual difference in human nature and argue that only at the level of libido can one achieve genuine liberation of humanity.[29] In opposition to this view, Levinas stresses that sexual difference is derivative and contingent, and culture is not determined by libido.

In *Time and the Other*, Levinas attempts to carry out an internal critique of Freudian libido in presenting eros as the locus where ethical radiance shines through. In "Phenomenology of Eros," Levinas shows profound ambiguities in his depictions of erotic relation. In "And God Created Woman," Levinas seems to finally subscribe to the Freudian conception of eros as the simple and blind libido. This somehow explains why he subjugates sexual difference to a derivative position.

The eclipse of the role of eros goes in tandem with the eclipse of the significance of the feminine. In his notes from the captivity period, Levinas criticizes Plato for not having included woman into his account of eros.[30] Starting from *Totality and Infinity*, while eros no longer functions as the locus of true ethical relation, the feminine no longer figures as the absolute alterity. Both themes evaporate from Levinas's second magnum opus *Otherwise than Being or Beyond Essence*, apart from maternity without any erotic sensibility.[31]

In connection with a book by his former student Catherine Chalier, Levinas comments,

> This book shares a lot of commonality with the efforts of contemporary feminists: it is opposed to the practice of excluding woman from the most superior mission of mankind, no matter how respectable the outside places are. In addition, the protests against the descriptions of woman as housewives are also present in the current book, which are similar to the criticisms against novelists and poets's practice of restricting the realization of woman within the whirlpool of love.[32]

The first half of Levinas's remark reminds one of the first aspect of woman as an interlocutor, collaborator, and "superiorly intelligent" master, as sketched in *Totality and Infinity*. In the second half, Levinas articulates disagreement with restraining woman to eros or love, and with respectfully confining woman to the kitchen.

It seems that a major reason why Levinas finally disclaims the account of the feminine as the absolute alterity is related to failing to find a proper ontological grounding, or locus, for this account (here the ontological cannot be not taken in a Levinasian sense in which ontology is opposed to ethics), with the consequence that when eros quits its place of centrality, the importance of the feminine also diminishes. This is absolutely not the case with the *Daodejing*. From analyses in the following sections, we can see how the primordiality of the feminine receives an ontological grounding in which the ways of the feminine resonate with the ways of the natural world.

V. The Pervasiveness of the Water Metaphor in the *Daodejing*

Researchers from the generation of Joseph Needham to that of Hans-Georg Moeller cannot but marvel at the prominent role of the water metaphor in the *Daodejing*, and are unanimous in acknowledging a necessary connection between it and the feminine.³³ The pervasiveness of the water metaphor constitutes the milieu wherein the primordiality of the feminine finds its articulation.

First, water is frequently invoked in delineating *Dao*. Chapter 4 states: "*Dao* constantly flushes and sprays (*chong* 沖), and yet use will never drain it. As deep as a spring (*yuan* 淵), it seems to be the origin of the ten thousand things (*wanwu* 萬物).... so clear and yet profound (*zhan* 湛), it only seems to persist."³⁴ *Dao* comports itself as water does. It flows ceaselessly like a persistent and profound stream that brings forth the ten thousand things without trying to possess them.³⁵ For this reason, it is forever nourishing and can never be exhausted. In chapter 32, the way of *Dao* is compared to small creeks flowing into rivers and seas. Chapter 34 exclaims, "How *Dao* flows! Left and right it takes its course at ease.... Ten thousand things are allegiant to it, and yet it does not make a proprietary claim." Water does not have any determinate form, so it can easily fit itself to whatever channel available in order to make its way in all directions. That is how it can be constant and embrace all the sources without aiming to be their master. The way of *Dao* remains the same as the way of water. As chapter 62 reiterates, "*Dao* is the flowing together (*zhu* 注) of ten thousand things."

Second, despite its important beneficiary role, water always modestly lies in a lower position and does not enter into contention with other things. Chapter 8 states: "The highest good is like water. Water is good in that it benefits ten thousand things but yet vies to dwell in places loathed by people. Therefore it comes closest to *Dao*.... Just because it does not enter into contention, it incurs no misfortune." In chapter 61, taking a lower position is connected with both water and *pin* 牝, a crucial word for the female: "A large state is the lower reaches of a river—The place where all the streams of the world unite. In the union of the world, the female always gets the better of the male by stillness. Being still, she takes the lower position. Hence the large state, by taking the lower position, annexes the small state." The way in which a large state annexes other states is here described as tolerant and submissive, instead of aggressive and militant.

Third, although water is soft and weak and thus seems powerless, it always prevails over what is strong. This finds expression in chapter 78: "Nothing under the heaven is more soft and weak than water, and yet none can surpass it in overcoming what is hard and strong. That the soft prevails over the hard, and the weak prevails the strong, no one under the heaven has no idea about it. However, no one is capable of doing accordingly." Chapter 43 explicates: "What is softest under the heaven rides roughshod over what is the hardest. What is almost nothing can penetrate what looks seamless. This is how I know taking no coercive action (*wuwei* 無為) is beneficial." It can be recognized that "what is almost nothing" bears reference to water. In the natural world, only water can seep through invisible crevices.

In "*Taiyi Shengshui*" 《太一生水》(The Great One Gives Birth to Water), a text that has been considered to be part of an original edition of the *Daodejing*, water plays a most important role in cosmological formation: "The Great One gives birth to water. Water returns to persistently assist the Great One; In this way the sky is formed. . . . Therefore the Great One remains concealed in water and moves according to appropriate time. Completing a cycle, (the Great One) starts over again, making herself the mother of the ten thousand things."[36] Water is where the Great One conceals itself; thus, water is almost co-originary with the Great One. If one takes the Great One to be a synonym of *Dao*, which is the mother of the ten thousand things, then this passage seems to provide a cosmological background for the prevalent presence of the water metaphor in the *Daodejing*.

From our discussion of Levinas, we see an attempt to reduce the role of the feminine as the absolute Other in his early work to what he calls "ontological function."[37] Nevertheless, there is an equivocation in the discourse of "ontological function" with respect to habitation, which equivocation is similar to that in "Phenomenology of Eros." Under Levinas's pen, the natural world is hard, hostile, untamed, and inhabitable. Man conquers nature in wrenching corn and flax from it. This form of life retains the rawness of nature and is "buried in the immediacy of nature as given."[38] It is woman that turns corn into bread and flax into clothing, and that can "feed those who are hungry," and can "clothe those who are naked," and thus makes habitation possible.[39] The feminine is "the origin of all gentleness on earth."[40] In spite of Levinas's efforts to restrict woman's roles at home to the ontological level, one can discern from his text an opposition between the natural and the ethical/human, and in analogy between the masculine and the feminine. The word "gentleness" has a strong ethical overtone that is absent in the unruly nature. The feminine is situated at the line of demarcation between ontology and ethics.

In contrast, we find no such oppositions in the *Daodejing*. The ways of nature as manifest in the ways of water do not contradict the ways of the human world. Rather, it serves as the ethical paradigm which is a reminder for human conduct: staying in the lower position, not entering into contention, and acting non-coercively. This becomes more important in view of the fact that actually it is the human world that tends to be violent and coercive when humans are negligent of the ways of nature. In the vision of the *Daodejing*, the natural world manifests feminine ways of being, other than masculine ones or a monstrosity as the Levinasian *il y a* conveys. The feminine is not only the source of such human values as "gentleness," but the origin of ten thousand things. This mode of ontology extends beyond Levinas's vision, in which a presumably masculine ontology remains harsh and aggressive.

VI. The *Dao* of *Ci* versus the *Dao* of Sex

In the Daoist thinking there is not a strict differentiation between the human and the natural world. However, one cannot go to another extreme, as Hans-Georg Moeller does, in declaring that relevant philosophical considerations, as delineated in what he calls the "*Dao* of sex," bear solely upon the cosmic.

Moeller does not provide a clear definition of sex; it is vaguely presented as an interaction between two cosmic elements that are seen as a pair, such as clouds and rains. He claims that the "*Dao* of sex" is not "a *Dao* of human sexuality," but a "*Dao* of the cosmos."[41] The sexes are "not *socially* but *cosmically* defined" in that the cosmos is "a continuous process of fecundation and birth."[42] Moeller cites the word *yunyu* 雲雨 as an evidence for the fact that sexuality is non-anthropomorphic. This is disputable. Literally meaning a play between clouds and rains, *yunyu* is a classical metaphor for human sexuality. It conveys a resemblance between human sexuality and cosmic interaction. Both human and natural factors are involved in it. In disallowing human factors, Moeller's suggestion implies that the original meaning of sexuality is defined by a play between clouds and rains. But what could *cosmic sexuality* be, if human sexuality is not invoked in establishing *yunyu* as a *human* metaphor? Moeller's idea tilted toward a rigid boundary between the human and the natural.

Moeller's other readings of some chapters from the *Daodejing* remind one of the Freudian method of projecting human sexuality onto natural phenomena. Their difference is, while Freud utilizes the theory that human sexuality can be symbolized in natural images for the purpose of reducing the latter to an interpretation and possible cure of the former, Moeller employs this method to produce a "sexual" interpretation of the cosmos in identifying the natural with the sexual. His interpretation conforms to an anthropologist's description of a superstitious primal society where people believe that thunderstorm and whirlwind are *actually* "the premature ejaculation of the weather."[43] This mode of explanation may help one understand the beliefs of primitive tribes in anthropological studies; however, it possesses little philosophical import, the reverse of which Moeller tries to convince us.

It seems that the most fundamental problem with Moeller's explication of the *Dao* of sex resides in a dualism of the social and the cosmic sphere. However, one cannot find passages in the *Daodejing* where cosmic observations are distinctively set in opposition to the social and human affairs. The natural world shows a rhythm of generation and movement produced by the interaction among myriad elements. The ups and downs in the human sphere somehow resemble this rhythm. On the other hand, human beings also extend designations of their forms of life to the cosmos. For example, the word *mu* 母 in the *Daodejing* is commonly understood as a human mother: "The named was the mother of the ten thousand things;" "It is capable of being the mother of the world."[44] In these places, the human figure of mother is invoked in speaking of the origin of the world, which includes both the human and the natural world. What is at issue is that the human is not the origin and center of the ten thousand things. In other words, the central spirit of the *Daodejing* is better described as *non-anthropocentric*, rather than non-anthropomorphic, as Moeller avows. There is not an exclusion of the human from the cosmic.

This point can be better appreciated when one considers the subtlety with which the words *ci* 雌 and *pin* 牝, which originally denote a female animal, are employed in the Daoist reflections upon the *dao* of the feminine. One passage from the *Mozi* 《墨子》, a text composed around the times of the *Daodejing*, runs,

> The Sages have such teachings: concerning Heaven and earth, [the terms] upper and lower are used; concerning the four seasons, *yin* 陰 and *yang* 陽 are used; concerning human beings, *nan* 男 and *nü* 女 are used; concerning birds and animals, *mu* 牡 and *pin* 牝, *ci* 雌 and *xiong* 雄 are used.[45]

The word *nü* 女 may restrict philosophical considerations to the human sphere; while *yin* 阴 bears predominantly upon cosmological vicissitudes. In comparison, *ci* and *pin* point to an intersection between the cosmic and the human.[46] In this light, the "*Dao* of *ci*," rather than Moeller's "*Dao* of sex," is a suitable encapsulation of the Daoist consideration of the feminine.

A further problem with Moeller's "*Dao* of sex" is: For him, sex is related to the interactions between two parties leading to fecundation. However, there is an irreducible asymmetry of the feminine-denoting words versus the masculine-denoting words.[47] The *Dao* of *ci* does not focus so much upon interaction or mutuality between two parties than upon a primordial principle of abiding by the feminine, or by the soft or weak.[48] This is indisputable in view of the text, for example, chapter 10: "When the gates of heaven open and shut, are you capable of keeping to the role of the female (*ci*)?" The idea of the asymmetry of the *Dao* of *ci* is consonant with Levinas's insistence that the feminine is to be defined in herself, instead of in terms of complementarity or reciprocity. The *Dao* of *ci* has to be considered in its own right. In the following section, I accentuate this point by way of a contrast between divergent comportments regarding femininity and masculinity.

VII. *Zhi* and *Shou*: Differing Comportments Concerning *Xiong* and *Ci*

Chapter 28 famously claims, "Know (*zhi* 知) the male/masculine (*xiong* 雄), yet abide by (*shou* 守) the female/feminine (*ci*), and be a river gorge to the world." It cannot be taken for granted that the masculine and the feminine receive the same degree of importance. The meaning of *zhi* stands on a completely different plane from that of *shou*, such that an idea of complementarity cannot be ascribed to them.

It is well known that, in the *Daodejing*, *zhi* as rational knowledge is thoroughly resisted. Chapter 19 admonishes, "Cut off sagacity and abandon knowledge, and this would benefit the people a hundredfold." Chapter 3 describes the administration by the sage as "keeping people innocent of knowledge and free from desire." Chapter 10 states, "Loving people and breathing life into the state, are you able to achieve this without recourse to *zhi*? When the gates of heaven open and shut, are you capable of keeping (*wei* 為) to the role of the female (*ci*)?" Notice here that the admonishment of keeping to the role of the female parallels a critique of a recourse to *zhi*. That *zhi* has negative associations finds confirmation in etymology. The composition of 知 is an arrow on the left side and a mouth on the right side. Thus, it has a sense of something coming straightforward out of the mouth as speedy as an arrow.[49] What can be quickly committed to words, obviously, is susceptible of superficiality, rashness, and even crudity.

Quite a number of central ideas from the *Daodejing* are unanimously phrased in terms of *shou*. For instance, chapter 5: "Much speech leads inevitably to silence. Better hold fast (*shou*) to the void;" chapter 16: "I do my utmost to attain emptiness; I hold firmly (*shou*) to stillness." What is still is the female, and is what should be adhered to. What merits particular attention is chapter 52, which is another place where *zhi* appears in contrast to *shou*:

> The world has a beginning, which is considered to be the mother of the world. When you have the mother, you can know [*zhi*] her progeny [*zi* 子]. When you have known her progeny, you return to abide by [*shou*] the mother. Then to the end of your days you will not be visited by danger.... To see the small is called discernment; To hold fast [*shou*] to the soft is called strength.

The privilege is evidently ascribed to *shou*, and *zhi* evidently belongs to another order. The significance of the mother resonates with that of the soft. The uniqueness of *shou* can also be confirmed by etymology. The composition of 守 is a house at top and a measure below. Thus, it has a sense of duty, post, principle, and "to preserve, to safeguard." An extended meaning of *shou* is moral integrity, as reflected in such words as *caoshou* 操守 and *chishou* 持守.

The message of chapter 52 can be better appreciated in connection with the famous verse "Reversing is how *Dao* moves; Weakening is how *Dao* functions" from chapter 40. One can acquire all varieties of knowledge about the world, as symbolized by *zi* in chapter 52; but one should be aware that what makes knowledge possible in the very first place is the feminine, or the mother. Therefore, when one acquires knowledge, one cannot stay complacent with it, but needs to take a reversal to abide by the feminine, or the soft and weak, that is to say, to remain in a lower position, to conduct non-coercively, and not to enter into contention, in order to be receptive of the ten thousand things.

In chapter 52, the progeny (*zi*) is juxtaposed with the mother (*mu*) in terms of a contrast between *zhi* and *shou*. This juxtaposition gives a hint how one should take the connection between seemingly paired *xiong* and *ci* in chapter 28. Just as there is no suggestion of considering *zi* and *mu* as a complementary pair, there is tenuous ground for regarding *xiong* and *ci* as a pair of complementarity. *Xiong* originally refers to a male animal. Here the emphasis falls upon such characteristics as restlessness and strength of a male animal, as contrasted with stillness and softness of a female animal (*ci*).[50] *Ci* is the ultimate condition of *xiong*, just as the river gorge can embrace all the things in the world, and just as the mother is the source of the progeny.

To "know the male" means that one should not remain content with and abide by *xiong*, since that is doomed to failure.[51] When one obtains the masculine knowledge, one needs to return to and abide by the feminine way of comportment that is decisive and that shows how *Dao* functions. Being a "river gorge" is consonant with the idea of remaining in the lower position. The verses that follow up in chapter 28 run: "Being a river gorge, then the constant efficacious power (*de* 德) will not desert you; And you will return to being a babe." Here the way of the unsexed babe resonates with the similarly unsexed way of the feminine. This resonance is also suggested in chapter 10: "In concentrating your breath, can you become as soft as a babe? . . . "When the gates of heaven open and shut, are you capable of keeping to the role of the female (*ci*)?"

VIII. Conclusion

Levinas's idea that the feminine is the "*of itself other*" and the "origin of the very concept of alterity" has been illuminating for our appreciation of the *Dao* of *ci* in its own terms.[52] *Ci* unambiguously receives privilege, which cannot be rendered as a symmetrical correlate to *xiong*. *Shou ci* 守雌 is situated at a completely different level than *zhi xiong* 知雄. These two can never be seen as complementary principles. The *Dao* of *ci* assumes an asymmetrical importance, such that it is not at all coincidental that Needham discerns from chapter 28 "analogies with Goethe's *ewig weibliche*."[53] We cannot obscure the significance of the *Dao* of *ci* by reading *shou ci* as a filling up of a lack of *zhi xiong*.

On the other hand, Levinas ultimately disavows the centrality of the feminine as alterity itself. This is somehow related to his restriction of the feminine to eros or habitation as set in opposition to the context of being as non-ethical, which implies a dualism that later can hardly sustain true ethical relation. Alternatively speaking, there has always been an essential ambiguity in Levinas's thinking with respect to the locus of the feminine: the ethical or the ontological. According to Levinas, "[e]very civilization that accepts being—with the tragic despair it contains and the crimes it justifies—merits the name 'barbarian.' "[54] With this extremely disparaging opinion, he cannot possibly envision an alternative ontology that is not opposed to ethics, but nevertheless grounds and sustains ethics.

In reading "rib" as side, Levinas has tried to attribute a same origin (as man has) and thus equality to woman.[55] However, the idea of asymmetry is suppressed and even made impossible by the scriptural text. Besides, when the feminine can only be given an account at the level of ontology in Levinas's surface discourse, the final fate of her subjugation is already in place.

Furthermore, it has been difficult for Levinas, being entrenched within the framework of Judaism, to ascribe a role to the feminine, which is more than helping initiating man into an ethical life. Even Levinas himself has to admit the existence of "masculine domination" in the Jewish tradition,[56] and that the idea of "Eternal Feminine" as Goethe advocated is lacking in Judaism, wherein the feminine "will never take on the aspect of the Divine."[57]

Levinas's failure to sustain an account of the feminine as alterity *propre* warns us of the danger of imprisoning oneself to a *singular* intellectual tradition in philosophical refection, and thus makes an intercultural perspective most crucial and exigent. In contrast to Levinas, Daoist thinking on the feminine is grounded in an ontology wherein the true ways of being *are* feminine. This does not mean that there are no "masculine" traits or that there is no distinction between feminine and masculine values, only that the latter is subject to the *feminine* paradigm of non-contention. It is only against the general picture of the *Dao* of *ci* that the masculine can have any import.

Chapter 36 of the *Daodejing* states, "The soft and weak is superior than the hard and strong. Fish cannot survive when it goes outside water. The sharpest instruments of a state cannot be shown to others." What is masculine cannot survive without relying on feminine milieu of being, just as a fish would soon expire when it leaves water. Feminine ways of being are most fundamental and therefore always take precedence. In addition, just as a fish can flourish only by modestly dwelling in deep water, a state can attain peaceful existence only by adhering to the *Dao* of *ci*, instead of readily resorting to sharp instruments. Such labels as equality, mutuality, or androgyny have to be defined against a prior confirmation of an ontology in which the superiority and asymmetry of the *Dao* of *ci*, which consist in softness and non-contention, is recognized not as an artificial construction, but as an articulation of the way of the ten thousand things.

RENMIN UNIVERSITY OF CHINA
Beijing, China

Endnotes

Professor Chung-ying Cheng has carefully read this article and raised two substantial questions, which could not be adequately addressed in the space of one paper. I shall keep these questions in mind in my further study. I am also grateful for the earnest editorial work by Dr. Linyu Gu.

1. For a relevant argument, see Lin Ma, *Heidegger on East-West Dialogue* (New York/London: Routledge, 2008), 1–9. In this article I shall refer solely to Chinese philosophy; but my analysis applies *mutatis mutandis* to other branches of non-Western philosophy.
2. Emmanuel Levinas, "Meaning and Sense," in *Basic Philosophical Writings*, eds. Adrian Theodoor Peperzak et al. (Bloomington and Indianapolis: Indiana University Press, 1996), 33–64, 46; emphasis original. The French word *sens* means both sense and direction/orientation.
3. Ibid., 58. Levinas's biased statements regarding non-Western traditions have been discussed and criticized. Cf. Lin Ma, "All the Rest Must Be Translated: Levinas's Notion of Sense," *Journal of Chinese Philosophy* 35, no. 4 (2008): 599–612.
4. Emmanuel Levinas, *Entretiens avec le Monde* (Paris: Editions la Découverte, 1984), 147.
5. Lin Ma, "Character of the Feminine in Levinas and the *Daodejing*," *Journal of Chinese Philosophy* 36, no. 2 (2009): 261–76.
6. Emmanuel Levinas, *Is It Righteous to Be?* ed. Jill Robbins (Stanford: Stanford University Press, 2001), 115.
7. Emmanuel Levinas, *Totality and Infinity*, trans. Alphonso Lingis (Pittsburgh: Duquesne University Press, 1969), 254.
8. Ibid., 264.
9. Ibid., 264.
10. Emmanuel Levinas, *Time and the Other*, trans. Richard A. Cohen (Pittsburgh: Duquesne University Press, 1987), 86.

11. Ibid., 256; translation modified; emphasis original.
12. Ibid., 263.
13. Ibid., 262; translation modified.
14. Ibid., 262.
15. Ibid., 256; emphasis original.
16. Ibid., 258; emphasis original.
17. Luce Irigaray, "The Fecundity of the Caress: A Reading of Lévinas, *Totality and Infinity*, 'Phenomenology of Eros,' " in *An Ethics of Sexual Difference*, trans. Carolyn Burke and Gillian C. Gill (London/New York: Continuum, 2004), 154–79.
18. Levinas, *Totality and Infinity*, 264.
19. Cf. ibid., 155: "The Other who welcomes in intimacy is not the *vous* of the face that reveals itself in a dimension of height, but precisely the *tu* of familiarity." Because of limit of space, habitation in *Totality and Infinity* is not treated in this article.
20. Emmanuel Levinas, "Judaism and the Feminine," in *Difficult Freedom*, trans. Seán Hand (London: The Athlone Press, 1990), 31.
21. Ibid., 32.
22. Ibid., 33; emphasis added.
23. Ibid., 35.
24. Emmanuel Levinas, "And God Created Woman," in *Nine Talmudic Readings by Emmanuel Levinas*, trans. Annette Aronowicz (Bloomington and Indianapolis: Indiana University Press, 1990, 161–77), 167.
25. Ibid., 173.
26. Ibid., 173.
27. Ibid., 173.
28. Ibid., 173; emphasis original.
29. Cf. ibid., 170.
30. Emmanuel Levinas, *Carnets de captivité et autres inédits* (IMEC: Bernard Grasset, 2009), 76.
31. Because of limit of space, in this article I shall not discuss maternity.
32. Emmanuel Levinas, "Préface pour Catherine Chalier, *Les Matriarches: Sarah, Rebecca, Rachel et Léa*" (Paris: Les Éditions du Cerf, 1991), 8.
33. Joseph Needham, *Science and Civilization in China*, Vol. 2 (Cambridge: Cambridge University Press, 1956), 57–61; Hans-Georg Moeller, *Daoism Explained* (Chicago and La Salle: Open Court, 2004), 36–40.
34. For the English translation, I have consulted various renditions, including Roger T. Ames and David L. Hall, *Daodejing "Making This Life Significant"* (New York: Ballantine Books, 2003) and Din Cheuk Lau, *Tao Te Ching* (Hong Kong: The Chinese University Press, 1982). Some versions have the word *chong* from chapter 4 as 盅, which thus was translated as "empty." The *Mawangdui B* version has 沖, which shares with the other two characters *yuan* and *zhan* the same root 氵 that denotes water. *Shuowen Jiezi* 《說文解字》 thus explains *chong*: "to flush and to spray (*yongyaoye* 涌搖也)." Cf. http://ctext.org/etymology?searchu=沖.
35. Cf. chapter 34 of the *Daodejing* below.
36. Robert G. Henricks, *Lao Tzu's Tao Te Ching* (New York: Columbia University Press, 2000), 123; translation modified.
37. Levinas, "Judaism and the Feminine," 33.
38. Ibid., 32.
39. Ibid., 32.
40. Ibid., 32.
41. Hans-Georg Moeller, *The Philosophy of the Daodejing* (New York: Columbia University Press, 2006), 26.
42. Ibid., 26; emphasis original.
43. Ibid., 27.
44. Chapters 1 and 25.
45. *Mozi*, Vol.1, Chapter 6.
46. In ancient poetry, *ci* is often invoked to refer to the human female. For example, the last verses from the *Mulanci* 《木蘭辭》 run: "When two hares are running together,

how could you tell whether I am *ci* or *xiong*?" http://www.stnn.cc:82/culture/poetry/t20060414_193465.html (my translation).

47. This has been argued in my early work. Cf. Ma, "Character of the Feminine in Levinas and the *Daodejing*," 269–71.
48. Various commentators point out that *ci* is synonymous with the soft or weak (cf. Gu Li 古棣 and Guan Tong 關桐): *Laozi Shijiang* 《老子十講》 (Shanghai: Shanghai Renmin Publisher, 2009), 225. There is a similar remark in the *Huainanzi*《淮南子》: "Therefore the sage abides by the *Dao* of stillness and embraces the principle of *ci*" (my translation).
49. This is pointed out by Duan Yucai 段玉裁. Cf. http://www.zidiantong.com/zd/zhi/zhi17908.htm
50. Cf. He Rongyi 賀榮一, *Daodejing Zhuyi yu Xijie* 《道德經注譯與析解》(Tianjin: Baihua Wenyi Chubanshe, 1994), 211–2.
51. As He Rongyi elucidates, to "abide by the female" suggests that one should not abide by the male, and that one should abandon restlessness and hold fast to stillness. Ibid., 211.
52. Emmanuel Levinas, *Ethics and Infinity*, trans. Richard A. Cohen (Pittsburgh: Duquesne University Press, 1985), 66; emphasis original.
53. Joseph Needham, *Science and Civilization in China*, vol. 2 (Cambridge: Cambridge University Press, 1956), 59. Even Heidegger's appropriation of "Know the white, yet abide by the dark" from chapter 28 rightly gets the univocal emphasis placed upon the dark. Cf. Lin Ma, "Deciphering Heidegger's Connection with the *Daodejing*," *Asian Philosophy* 16, no. 3 (2006): 154–6.
54. Emmanuel Levinas, *On Escape*, trans. Bettina Bergo (Stanford: Stanford University Press, 2003), 73.
55. Levinas stresses this again later. Levinas, *Is It Righteous to Be?* 162.
56. Ibid., 162.
57. Levinas, "Judaism and the Feminine," 37.

LINYU GU

"WAITING FOR GODOT"?
CONTEMPORANEITY, FEMINISM, AND CREATIVITY[1]

Abstract

This article speaks to contemporary women *and* men, who both suffer from gender issues such as disconnection, separation, oppression . . . and who *forever* wait for a so-called "tomorrow." Through comparing process thought and Chinese philosophy, my study analyzes how process feminism synthesizes *our* demands for interconnection and how it alerts *our* narrow desires in seeking "a way out." I further challenge a fundamental weakness in this genre of Whitehead's organic multiplicity by contributing "creative harmony" of *yin* 陰 and *yang* 陽 in the *Yijing* 《易經》 cosmology. This contribution offers process feminism a humanistic "creative creativity," which avoids the oversight in Whiteheadian philosophy of organism and therefore prospects that the mutual connectivity in Chinese cosmology is "a way through" the actual practicability of both men and women, who share a common goal.

Overture

"We men and women are all in the same boat, upon a stormy sea. We owe to each other a terrible and tragic loyalty."[2]

Women *or* men in modern life often stand hesitating among diverse alternatives. However, this study is femininity and feminism thematized and it concretizes, analyzes and focuses on contemporary women and *our*[3] new perplexities. Today, on the one hand, *we* women anxiously celebrate *our* triumphs of feminist movements and *our* professionally grown powers; on the other, *we* remain undeniably troubled by endless confusion arisen from a "new self."[4] In other words, while *we* are ecstasized by *our* abundant privileges, *we* again find ourselves in fighting rather abundant, delicate dilemmas and doubts in a novel fashion. However reluctant *we* are, *we* end up a classical option: wait for a better "tomorrow."[5]

LINYU GU, Ph.D., Managing Editor, *Journal of Chinese Philosophy*, University of Hawaii at Manoa. Specialties: process philosophy/theology/feminism, classical Chinese philosophy, modern Japanese thought. E-mail: linyu@hawaii.edu

I call such predicament in our new age "waiting for tomorrow." To be vivid and specific, now I share two dilemmas of such "waiting" in personal experience, which more or less mirror a general façade. One of them is associated to a collective occasion and the other an individual encounter. Both intend to explain what background this study is from and to whom I speak to.

The first story traces back to an international conference site, whereas festive air was overflowing and the opening ceremony was solemnizing. To our surprise, among woman scholars who were more than 1/3 of the total size, not a single figure was invited to the main speeches at the ceremony. We held a secret faith for the closing ceremony. Again, no woman was there! The tolerance had finally reached to its end . . . until a firm promise arrived: this embarrassment will not happen in the next conference! Thereafter, we wait . . .

My second dilemma may sound rather annoying, because *we* are often convinced by such quick confirmation: "Here the gender issue is not relevant!" or "There the gender issue is the case!" This dilemma tears *us* apart: no matter how disdainfully we try to pass by "our annoyance," there doesn't seem to be a graciously middle way out; as *we* strive not to sniff a political aroma, *we* are nevertheless troubled by the consequence. Henceforth a respect may not be paid or a right may not be given, because *we* appear *irrelevantly* "irritating," "offensive," "overreacting". . . . Frustrated as such, *we* then cannot help but continue to "wait," till a tomorrow to come.

Suppose that *we* are guaranteed by a promise from "tomorrow," shall *we* wait? The question automatically leads my eyes to the play *Waiting for Godot*: the characters wait, wait, wait . . . for someone named Godot who never arrives.[6] Godot's absence implies the future presence to an endless waiting, in spite of that no one knows when and whether it will take place. What does "tomorrow" mean to *us*? Why are *we* drawn to waiting? Whether there is a hopeful connection between "today" and "tomorrow"?

I set my task in the following journey of an intercultural dialogue between process feminism and Chinese cosmology, through which I should prospect a harmonious finale in the worthiness of "waiting." My goal is to search for a door which leads a botanic garden: "waiting women" and "waiting men" embrace and rejoice one another. Such enthusiasm foresees a gender-friendly landscape, in which we are free from sufferance of disconnection, separation, and oppression.

Three chapters are choreographed for the above task. Chapter I, Contemporary Predicament, anchors two feminist intellectuals as models of *our* new predicaments, in order to discern what *we* "wait" for and the nature of *our* "waiting," namely, the "savage" patriarchs of God and Confucian *Tian* 天. Chapter II, Breaking the One, anticipates into Whiteheadian God and the process inseparability through an analysis of how process feminism metaphysically both synthesizes *our* demands for connection and alerts *our* narrow desires for replacing One God with a female singularity, One Goddess. Chapter III, Harmonizing the Many, offers Chinese cosmology on creative *Tian*[7] (cosmic heaven)[8] and creative harmony in the dipolar relation of *yin-yang* 陰陽.[9] Particularly, such creative cosmology contributes a broadened and deepened interconnection in the level of human practicality, to avoid the Whiteheadian philosophy of organic multiplicity. I conclude that both process feminism and Chinese cosmology are illuminating, for that both lead interconnection to replace disconnection, togetherness to replace differentiation, in a shared destination. Doing so, the arrival of "Godot" shall not be afar.

I do not offer a way out but a way through, among many; *our* voice is not only for being heard but for being echoed. [10]

I. Contemporary Predicament

By "contemporary," I allow it to focus on a concrete group: woman intellectuals. Within such a sphere, my vision may come more naturally and knowledgably to a certain degree. Meanwhile, being an academic Asian woman may also privilege my thinking, in a sense, particular, diverse, and far-reaching. Nonetheless, my claim ensures no generalization of other conditional circumstances.

In this chapter, I shall question the nature of *our* "waiting" in order to unfold what blocks *our* way out emotionally, socially or historically. My individual confession may rather be a situational concreteness, which might not suffice a diagnosis of *our* "root" symptom of a habitually mentality. To invoke a deeper sophistication in *our* physically distanced from and yet spiritually yarned for "tomorrow," I believe my personal sensibility nevertheless can be empathized by a universal recognition. With this wish, I shall start with two woman intellectuals who may symbolize the stereotypical genre of "waiting women." Through them, I wish my own experience may be hopefully put forward a particular struggle into a wide landscape of women's shared perplexity.

The two women I shall bring to the scene are considerably recognized as modern feminist icons: Sylvia Plath (1932–1963)[11] and Hong Ying 虹影 (1962–). Although they strikingly astound us in a bold, throaty and electrifying voice, they, however, have not discarded a classical dilemma: "waiting for tomorrow." At this point, *my* confession may become *our* confession: What "tomorrow" really is? What *we* are waiting for after all? The answer is: it seems a twin of "Godot."

"His" presence lives in the absence, and "he" never comes... Why? Because our waiting is toward a one-way and leaner direction, and to be more precise: we reach out to "Godot," whilst this imaginary visitor does not return the same!

In both Plath and Hong Ying, this "Godot" no double hides in the back of an abstract form. By all means such an absent fantasy is attractive, for it in the same old charm all over again draws us towards the time-honored reliance and androcentric complexity about the masculine savior. Such complexity[12] is a re-occurring "ghost," who has haunted *us* from the dawn of time, in God or in *Tian*. *We* have long lost in the haunting, to our male ancestries, fathers, husbands, male leaders, dreamed knights...

Sarcastically, however, particularly since the last century, to seek breathing room, to detach from bondages, and to thrive in an affirmative subjectivity, *our* independent awareness, desires, voices... have been through ceaseless ages of battles and at long last, indeed won dramatically remarkable victories.[13] *We* have taught ourselves: a genuinely respectful relation is presumably a team work on the common goals of two partners, a man and a woman. Both are leading authors of life, equal at professional advances and social privileges, and both have legitimate fields of their own, for which each must respect the other. Like any other human relations, the connection between men and women cannot be otherwise but mutually respectful, genuinely free and independently autonomous.

We have eventually infused into an established role of self-strength. But ironically, the "contemporary" perplexity emerges: *She* seems to devote *her* independency to a novel form of *his* increased possession: *She* continues to dissolve *herself* in *himself*.[14] Meanwhile, as *she* is fulfilled with self-affirmation and self-realization, after a "successful" working day, after a legacy of marriage, after a disappointed relation... *she* finds *herself*, again, alone—waiting, for a new "hero."[15] History repeats itself, in an entirely unexpected outcome: *she* is split apart by both the classical dependency *and* the contemporary independency, because neither an ancient "hero" nor a modern partner wants *her* independence more than "obedience, devotion, loyalty, and, if ideally, beauty."[16]

Sylvia Plath and Hong Ying renewed the drama of "waiting." Intellectually, both have created undeniable and significant and glowing self-identity, and both strike us as exceptionally challenging writers. They incidentally have a comparable style: direct, rebellious, and truthful. The strong colors of their prolific works similarly appear shockingly creative, beautifully melancholy, and lively opinionated. They are uniquely illuminating simply by being themselves: honest and uncompromising.

No doubt that Plath enlightened her time and has been continually admired by this date, and her journal illustrates: a woman's marital life should be conditioned in a husband's recognition and respect of her own independent value and equal competence.[17] However, in both Plath and Hong Ying's biographical literature, unavoidably they share a similar childhood, a childhood which has formed their adult years of timeless doubts, searches and struggles for a fathering icon and a male hero.

This inner continuum shapes the initial resemblance in them, behind the enormous body of their successes, in which we are unfortunately sometime tickled by currents of sorrow. That is, the sensitivity of the threatening patriarchal as if it sheds the light on two women's life journey. At the age of eight, Plath swore to the death of her father: "I'll never speak to God again!"[18] For a desperate way out, when Plath thought that a father figure or a man idol betrayed and then abandoned her, she autonomously had opted to mark a stop to her life at the age of thirty and in her extraordinary creative period of a frozen February morning of 1963.

The death that Plath finally succeeded in achieving is a rather serious, deliberate and meaningful expression of her disappointment towards God, a masculine savior to whom she had fantasized to be near for too long.[19] Once it is broken, her rage turns to God as she did at a young age, when the separation from her father had inflicted her feeling injured and betrayed. The tremendous upset-ness and wounds, which her diseased father brought to her, had remained in a profound torment throughout the years of both her childhood and adulthood. Without God's help, it became a plain and natural and logical end to leave God and His[20] created world, as life is a creation of God, to reject it is to reject Him, to abandon it is to abandon Him, and to destruct it is to destruct Him.

While I find that annihilating patriarchalism motivates Sylvia Plath's final act, there is a roughly paralleled case in the Chinese contemporary woman writer Hong Ying.[21] Her many versions of the "waiting women" always endure a different ending, by comparing with Plath, namely a rather victorious and ceremonial picture. Nevertheless still it remains not too far away from the classic: seeking a patriarchal guidance or approval for *her* self-assurance and self-realization. *Her* value, *her* goal, and *her* social triumphs somehow are hungry for to be discovered and defined by fathers, male masters, heroes . . .

In comparing with Plath's predicament in God, Hong Ying's heroine *personae* are no doubt associated to the Chinese belief in *Tian*, the cosmic heaven, the *yang* force, the masculine creativity. The poignancy of *Tian* in both intellectual cannons or common belief is immanently connected to *ming* 命 (pre-determined life or unchangeable fate) of human existence. Thus in classical Confucianism *Tian* implicates a symbolic patriarch: it is the dominating power of the universe at the same time it is the natural threat and challenge to our fate. The inseparable relation between *Tian* and the world affirms Hong Ying's understanding of the internal and tangling connection between her leading woman characters and their masculine surroundings those women are set in.

Strikingly similar, Hong Ying's female characters share a delicate confusion and a vulnerable struggle with those deliberations in Sylvia Plath. Throughout Hong Ying's life, she constantly quests of a father, to whom she feels both painfully separated from and desperately attached to. This process returns to a classical habit: her achievement stereotypically succumbs to a masculine vision. In her biographical novel *Jier de Nüer* 《飢餓的女兒》 (the Hungary Daughter)[22] (Title in English version: *Daughter of the River*[23]), the heroine, Liuliu's 六六 spends her lifetime to search for the real identity of her father and what it means to her. Such complexity lingers in all of her subsequent works.

Being a provocative and controversial writer, Hong Ying characteristically challenges the conventional *genre* of Chinese woman writers. She exhibits herself in two two epic characterizations. On the one had, she faithfully adulates the cosmic *Tian* which gifted a grandiose creativity of her womanhood, and secondly, she proclaims this same *Tian* which importunes her with threatening *ming*. *Ming*, an inaudible request, submits her subjectivity and liberty to a pre-determined unchangeableness which leads to her future misfortune.

Given these two faces of one portrait of *Tian*, Hong Ying's women nevertheless are torn by two destinies: they are themselves unbound, rebellious and revolt against *ming*. At the same time, they remain wont to wait and stuck in the same old entrapment. They long for masculine discovery from their fathers, husbands, or lovers, to grant them a "pseudo-selfhood," which is to please the eyes of their man sponsors, authorities, savior, or judges. In another word, the women of Hong Ying have not autonomously renewed: they continue to wait and pray for the mercy of a paternal salvation.

No matter how anxiously Sylvia Plath and Hong Ying compose a creative self, they after all are eager to compete with the recognition of "post-patriarchs."[24] The achievements of the two writers have eventually turn women against themselves in order to appear acceptable to their own the classical attachment. In Plath, God and "daddy" (and later her husband) are always part of her hungry and passionate goal of life; while *Tian*, *ming*, and fathers are always braided in the main thread of Hong Ying's writings.

Here and now, such struggles plunge into the following depth and therefore a metaphysical question comes to the fore: how shall we free from *our* perplex attachment to the "savage"[25] God and the "fatal" *Tian/ming* and is there a possible "tomorrow" liberating *us* from all of the above forms of stubbornly "waiting"?

II. Breaking the One

W. B. Yeats remarks: ". . . after all our subtle colour and nervous rhythm, after the faint mixed tints . . . what more is possible? After us the Savage God."[26] This God is the most ineffable deity in the monotheism of Judaism, Christianity and Islam; beyond time and change. He is the sole reality and infinite perfection among us, regardless of that He is abstract, shadowy, distant, and physically unseen. Without this absolute sense, the world would seem to lose the eternal truth and our life would be led without purposes. Most remarkably, this singular and pompous and arrogant image seems particularly androcentric and traumatic towards womanhood, for that He from the first day was already personified into the male divine to "[l]et a woman learn quietly with complete submission" of him.[27] Hence, after *us* the Savage God; after *her* the Savage Him.[28]

Inasmuch *we* cling to the masculine masks of God or *Tian*, my next question shall call for itself: can such patriarchal captivity be re-understood, reinterpreted and thus re-construed by a reformed theory and a new vision of God? My voluntary answer is: "Yes." No doubt that neither the above patriarchal sacralization of God in the traditional orthodox texts nor the heavenly sage-hood of *Tian* in the Confucian hierarchal advocate suffices a restorative transformation. A brand new project that discovers interrelated, reconnected and mutually-integrated with God and *Tian* should be called upon our anticipation without further delay, since it has been prolonged for ages, centuries. This is a relation to be understood as a two-way, equal and harmonious affinity between divinity and the world, between external power and internal humanity, and between masculine-complexity and women's self-assurance. It may have to be a harsh, challenging and unrewarding process, however, many pioneers have nevertheless paved the path for us in their long battles. They have led us to a prosperous and promising hope: they have offered their alternative worldviews on God or Heaven, and in their endeavor an achievement of alleviate the controlling monopoly that creates the inharmonious boundaries.

But since the current chapter focuses on process feminism, my valuation shall essentially distribute to process feminist Catherine

Keller and her most stimulating insights on separation and reconnection. For her, God is not to be abandoned but rediscovered in an open and dynamic approach.

Whilst I assess the renaissances in her, there is a need to acknowledge a clear number of other Christian philosophers and theologians, whose competing views have also flourished in the open understanding of God. To mention the least, they are: John B. Cobb and the Center for Process Studies, William Hasker and Open Theism, Robert C. Neville and the Boston Confucianism, Joseph Grange and his new "pragmatism"[29] on Cosmology and Soul, and beyond . . .

William Hasker, one of the major "open theist" philosophers, synthesizes these five theories as open theological views, though there is no absolute consensus among them: Calvinism's "free will," Molinism's "middle knowledge," "simple foreknowledge," process theology, and the openness of God theory ("free will theism").[30]

Hasker believes that, although the emphasis of process theology on God's persuasive power has its impressive strength, yet it is as much vulnerable to the criticism of excessive deference to philosophy as the classical theism is; the former is singularly and heavily subjected to Greek philosophy and the latter to Whitehead. As a free will theist as he titles himself, Hasker presumes that the result of this Whiteheadian "synthesis" could be damaging to the biblical conception of God. To set a more appealing affirmation, Hasker prospects that the openness of God in "free will theism" puts forward a portrait of God "as majestic yet intimate, as powerful yet gentle and responsive, as holy and loving and caring, as desiring for humans to decide freely for or against his will for them, yet endlessly resourceful in achieving his ultimate purposes."[31] In spite of all of the disagreements that Hasker has presented to process divinity, by and large I adulate the lens of free will theism which offers a break-through illumination, particularly for anyone who pursues a satisfying understanding of God.

However, I worry that open theism remains vulnerable to its own quest for Calvinism: why should we think that God would prefer a world like that in free will theism? Or, is God, as open theism conceives, able to create a world in which there are "genuinely" free creatures? Therefore, such "free will" has not strictly or ultimately overcome the Calvinist separation between an omnipotent God and His creatures. Open theism indeed has improved our relationship with God into a rather modest and equal and friendly way, nevertheless, it remains to allow God staying afar to project His plan and action and love towards us. It is also to be pointed out that there is an oversight in Hasker's collection of five theories. Robert C. Neville has outstood himself as a remarkably open-minded theologian and philosopher, who accepts as much of Whitehead but comes to be independent of him.³² Meanwhile, together with his distinctive contribution to philosophical theology, Neville grasps a comprehensive perspective of non-Western traditions, which was inadequate in the early process studies of the Center for Process Studies in Claremont.

As an ecstatic change that process philosophers have made, Whiteheadian philosophy and theology are to be read as such: the world and God are interdependent, and the relation of the two is not to be viewed as one-sided dependence—the world relies on God; but rather, He is one of us:

> God is primordially one, namely, he is the primordial unity of relevance of the many potential forms ... The World is primordially many, namely, the many actual occasions with their physical finitude ... Thus God is to be conceived as one and as many in the converse sense in which the World is to be conceived as many and as one.³³

Open theism *does* show the logically evident strength on a resourceful God who responses to human actions and who takes risks of his providential governance of the world.

However, we cannot help asking: how does this Whiteheadian openness of God respond to such a query—whether there should be both masculine and feminine pronouns associating to Him? Open theism has not yet answered this, to my current knowledge. The leading process thinkers, John B. Cobb, Jr. and David Ray Griffin remind us of that Carl G. Jung was one of those who first realized that the psychological impoverishment is the result of lacking female images of God, and Jung's view has become especially valid, challenging and valuable today.³⁴

In the process views, God's power is to be understood as persuasive and never oppressive: "... God transcends the World, as that the World transcends God. ... God creates the World, as that the World creates God."³⁵ It is a harmonious affiliation: God intends to persuade humans and all creatures, but he does not control or compel savagely "His" created beings to depend on his will. To be careful though, it is not that Whitehead has formed a feminist theory on God, but that Whitehead's metaphysical interpretation of God rejects the traditional stereotypical masculine image. Whitehead portrays God as one of men *and* women, and He is a persuasive love, tender feeling and compassionate sharing.

And these are recognized as the foremost reinterpretation of the orthodox divinity, and they have shaped the fundamental grounds of Whiteheadian metaphysics on empathy and balance. Because of this emphasis on the mutual manifestation of God and the world, God and man, a shift from the masculine attributes to the feminine attributes. As charming and dazzling and flowing as Leibniz's world of monads,

Whitehead prospects, "actual entity," the micro being, reflects the wholeness of macro beings, and *vice versa*. In his fascinating and revelatory analysis of Whiteheadian cosmology, Joseph Grange presents such stimulating relationship of one and many:

> There are only modes of wholeness that shine forth for a time and then recede before the onrush of process in its physical, living, and cultural forms. Such is the consequence of the harmony of the One and the Many. The many which become one are always increased by another one. Imbalance follows on the heels of balance. Disjunction succeeds conjunction. No matter how pleasing, wholeness is always but for a moment.[36]

Equally, if not specifically, relevant and important and crucial to my on-going deliberation, here is to single out one of the frontier process feminists, Catherine Keller. She nevertheless seriously warns by a clarification: while process feminism attributes their appeal to connection instead of separation, distance and difference, their vision is not to be mistaken in the sheer emotions.[37] A radical switch merely directs to an opposite dead extreme: as long as any doctrines that identify a portrait of God in male gender or fixed ethnic *personae* or sole heterosexual ..., He should immediately be abandoned or destroyed. Keller affirms that such visions are not capable to resolve the problem, if it turns around to be that One God exclusively becomes One Goddess. Keller keenly proclaims, the feminist contemplation on interrelating and reconnecting must not idolize a fashionable banner which binds itself with another particular mode of simplistic authority. Rather, the process feminism ought to be built in a consciousness of mutual achievement of the common goal, that is, an independent and autonomous self-assertiveness cannot satisfy itself if it is not a mutual-reaching, pluralistic-becoming and inter-weaving network. This is not an annihilating process but an endless and multiplying endeavor in merging "one" to "many" and "many" to "one," again, again, again ...

When weaving into the Whiteheadian web, Keller questions the common sense of selfhood which identifies oneself with a separate world away from its surroundings.[38] This turns out a result in which freedom is expected somehow a name that is clearly estranged from a relational realm. It is true that a complex relation that we are enmeshed in does generate the boundaries, among a self and others. However, for Keller and process feminism, our sensibility of being a true self does not necessarily mean to choose arriving at separation against connection. Keller then continues to put eyes on a fundamentally problematical issue of modern culture which not only assumes a single view of separation but heads to an extreme vision: sexism. Neither "separation" or "sexism" functions as a help to the world of men, *or*, that of women. Hence Keller does not believe seeking an empowered center, either in a man or in a woman. For her, such genre of consciousness and mentality in repudiating connectedness ultimately fertilizes an opposite direction to women's freedom.

What alternative can there be to liberate a separated individuality? Keller's own anticipation recommends: "Something new is needed."[39] In moving into Whiteheadian metaphysics, Keller requires her alternative thinking to go beyond a limited array such as selfhood or gender identity or relational community... in order to obtain a farther reach to ideas, feelings, souls, lives... Meanwhile, for her, this is not a step to escape from our concerns with the classical confusion on masculine or feminine selfhood, but to think collectively and feel intrinsically in a deeper affinity that is found in "connective and fluid selves."[40] This is what Keller calls an unlimited array of four non-polar conceptual motifs: being one / being many, being public / being private, being body / being soul, being here / being now.[41] She illustrates, the highlight of these stimulating pairs have staged the Whitehead's metaphysical sense of individuality: "Unlike James, or almost any professional philosopher before him, Whitehead attributes feeling by analogy to every actual individual being in the universe,... A new theory of one and many, of subject and object, is here taking shape."[42]

In Keller's "something new," through the above reflection, we have realized that, God as The One is broken into The Many. This is what Charles Hartshorne would sympathize: only if a God is a related one, who is thus capable of self-enriching and feeling the experience of the world; this God is more perfect, only if he is capable to surpass himself and depend on the world he created.[43] Keller interprets these words in a furthermore affectionate tone: the world has a heart, if we embrace the world; God/Goddess lives in us, if we meet Him/Her in the core of our hearts. However, does "something new" unconditionally supposes a mutual dialogue between I and Thee, or does it simultaneously and automatically promise a relational connectivity and give its birth to both *her* and *him*? It is clearly not. The central characteristic of a process connection can only be illustrated by a metaphor of multidimensional reaching and growing and connecting among one another. That is what Whitehead has in mind for the cosmological process of "concrescence":

> The novel entity is at once the togetherness of the "many" which it finds, and also it is one among the disjunctive "many" which it leaves; ... The many become one, and are increased by one.... the "production of novel togetherness" is the ultimate notion embodied in the term "concrescence."[44]

A particular individual man or woman is only one rhythm of the pulses of the stream, and each such single effort can only be activated in a complex synthesis of massive feelings. To feel, to understand, to relate one another takes two or numerous partners and participants and "dancers." As mentioning this, why I myself know such "laws" personally well, as far as that I once happened to have the training of a theatre dancer. For a duet performance, my knowledge and experience told me that there was never a partner could be omitted in a dance of two and there was no audience could visualize such partner performing in a shadow!

To connect means to merge into other feelings, and a feeler to feel is choreographed in the feeling to be felt, namely, it is a multi-way street. In this "concrescence," a subjective selfhood can occur only because diverse objectivities have made a new oneness. Such metaphysical connection between the masculinity and the femininity, between a waiting man and a waiting woman, calls for us to give each other our hands, to help each other rising up, and to respond to each other's feelings, voice and predicament. In order to make a collective self[45] out of a plural world and to take down the mask of God or Goddess, we are to take off our own "masks." These efforts lie in the loyalty, duty and love which both men and women own each others, as they are sailing together on an adventurous and a life-risky sea.

III. Harmonizing the Many

Joseph Grange has a crystal line portraying the balanced and friendly relation between God (the One) and the world (the Many), Chung-ying Cheng has given a thorough, piercing and deepened vision through a hermeneutic reconstruction of the Chinese cosmology on the generative mutual creation of *yin* and *yang*. What Granges says precisely can be applauding for what Cheng has to say about harmony and disharmony:

> The world ... is a process of change and development.... there may appear variation, difference, divergence, tension, opposition, and antagonism in the world ... the overall tendency of cosmic and social processes as well as individual life conduces to unity and harmony. ... Reality ... which encompasses Haven, Earth, humans and the myriad things, in both a process of change and an ordered structure.[46]

In Chinese cosmology, *Tian*, as we discern above, namely the cosmic heaven or the *yang* 陽 force of the nature, is identified with the paternal symbol of *qian* 乾 (the creative originativity). Whilst opposed and yet connected to *Tian*, *Di* 地, the cosmic earth or the *yin* 陰 force of the nature, is embodied in the maternal image of *kun* 坤 (the creative productivity). The whole philosophical metaphor of the *Yijing* 《易經》 (or the *Zhouyi* 《周易》 or the *Book of Changes*) philosophy focuses the succinct characterization of harmony between *Tian* and *Di*.

However, interestingly but ironically, as God is a portrayal of masculine lord in classical Christianity, in the politicized application of Confucian cannons (excessively referring to those after Han Period), the cosmic relations of *Tian* and *Di*, *qian* and *kun*, and *yin* and *yang* are defined as well as enhanced into a set of patriarchal morale. Both rationally and emotionally, Confucian women are taught and expected and honored by a highest virtue, that is, the virtue of swallowing, enduring and subordinating their life to the "fate (*ming* 命)," namely, a "pre-determined (by *Tian*)" journey. In the Confucian *fude* 婦德 (the essential virtues of a woman), *her* moral perfection is beatified by a valuable world under a husband's (as well as a dominant male group's) leadership, for that this man is an exemplary icon who bears cosmic heaven's will (*tianzhi* 天志) and intention (*tianyi* 天意), and consequentially they represent four principal excellences of a gentleman:

> The Confucian age begins with Confucius's explicit recognition that the external *t'ien* (*tian*, my addition here and hence forth) (heaven) has an essential link with the internal *te* (*de*) (virtue, power) of man ... The rationality of man is to be realized in the practice and perfection of virtues such as *jên* (*ren*) (love and benevolence), *yi* (or *i*) (righteousness), *li* (propriety) and *chih* (*zhi*) (wisdom in distinguishing good from bad).[47]

A man who owns these four virtues is recognized as *shengren* 聖人 (a man of sage-hood) and *junzi* 君子 (a gentleman of goodness). Confucian-masculine personality of these Confucian gentlemen is fulfilled by great missions on behalf of *Tian* and thus they are named as *tianzi* 天子 (male descendants of cosmic heaven), and they are also the ones who forward reigns and inherit thrones. And they determine the rise and fall of dynasties and they are the ones who are considered as the actual exemplifications among the mass of people.[48]

No one is not familiar with this well-cited solemn belief of Meng Zi[49]: "It is *tian* that has honored this man with the glorified mission; to accomplish it, *tian* as well honors him the strength and courage to overcome the unbearable and intolerable hardship."[50] Men Zi has also nuanced it with a supplementary: "This man practices Dao 道 in himself, so that he may guide his wife; he practices Dao with others, so that he may cultivate his own wife."[51] Such masculine severity particularly separates women from experiencing and possessing the equal excellence and autonomy.

We now have a vivid vocabulary to read the case: men are by destiny emerged from *Tian* at the same time merged into *Tian*; and it is *Tian*, namely, the metaphorical symbol of men, which provides *us* women lordship, guardianship and educator-ship. Moreover, aside from the above social and political and intellectual qualities of the Confucian masculinity, Kam Louie explores one neglected but important dimension of it: *wu* 武 (martial valor). For him, Chinese masculinity is a model of combining *wen* 文 (cultural attainment) that is what we discussed above, and *wu*.[52] I appreciate this study as it clearly holds against extreme feminist positions such as biological reductionism which can be in a danger of turning into a cultural determinism.

However, I also find that such a cultural-physical advantage entitled by Chinese masculinity, both literally and intriguingly, implies a disadvantaged model of Chinese femininity which seems neither culturally (*wen*) or martially ideal (*wu*). This is untrue, but as for how in history Chinese women are competitive both culturally and martially is not my task here to debate in length. By and large, together with Confucianism, Louie's own model eventually and helplessly falls into the same tragedy: after *us* the Savage *Tian*; after *her* and the Savage Him. Whether it's a Christian woman or a Confucian one, *our* "painful confusions"[53] are identical. Such "savage" whimsy has been not going away and it is continually hunting around today's men *and* women, like a dead metaphor which resurrects from time to time.

We often are overjoyed with "victorious" modern fellow women and wowed by such transformation: the traditional roles are now switched around... *We* may therefore have forgotten *our* fellow men's own impartment: reaching out for the fellow women comrades. "Something new is needed" for our contemporary predicament. I have earlier asked: How do *we*, men *and* women, both make effort for an interconnection? Is there a running stream in which "tomorrow" lives within every drop of "today"? My response is continually prosperous. And now I shall defend it in re-contemplating *Tian*, namely, the cosmic heaven and the "creative creativity" as featured in the *Yijing* cosmology.

My argument is theorized by the idea of *shengsheng rixin zhi hexie* 生生日新之和諧 (harmony of creative and re-creative creativity), which consists the metaphysical structure of the *Yijing*. I shall foresee: when men and women spin together in a new collaboration of mutually caring, equally connecting, and constantly reconnecting to one another, a creative harmony may end the "waiting." Upon stressing so, I shall also try to avoid a quick response: "Sure, please reach me and I have waited long enough, and I am totally ready for the harmony!" A collaboration requires a two-way jump, and this is a price paid by one's genuine attentiveness and actual recognition and practical action. "Tomorrow" will not come on its own if we do not make it "today."

If God can be a changeable and improvable deity in Whitehead: He is divine and creative but also personal and emotional, *Tian* in Chinese cosmology primordially is not a "savage" metaphor of masculinity either. Unlike that in the later canonic elaborations, in the *Yijing Tian* in the paternal form of *qian*, spurs the *yang* energy of creativity; *Di*, in the maternal form of *kun*, nurtures the *yin* energy of productivity. *Tian* and *Di* as well as *qian* and *kun* are to be observed as a co-creating and co-productive process in production and reproduction, and they together constitute one totality of polarities and multiplicities. I am a little surprised at Kam Louie's out-dated and limited information: "Within the common superficial appreciation of *yin-yang* theory, femininity and masculinity are placed in a dichotomous relationship whereby *yin* is female and *yang* is male."[54] Today whether a Western or a Chinese scholar would hardly regard *yin* and *yang* as binary dichotomies other than a harmonious unification of opposites. Nor it is the current situation that *yin* and *yang* have been understood simply as female and male persons or such terms which are merely operated for the references of sexual etiquette.[55]

However, I am pleased by that Louie does come to this genuine and correct interpretation: *yin* and *yang* are to be seen as two essences co-existing in a constant interaction whereby *yin* is generated and re-created in *yang* whilst *yang* is emerged and renewed in *yin*, and *yin* and *yang* are in each other throughout a perpetual dynamism.[56] This is what the magnum opus, the *Yijing*, advocates: *dayi* 大易 (the great change) and *shengsheng*. Chung-ying Cheng affirms:

> ... change is nothing but the continuous production and generation of life (*sheng-sheng*). The process of continuous generation of life is conceived in terms of the *yin-yang* metaphysics, *yin* and *yang* are universally observed and experienced as qualities of things and forces of happenings. They stand for two aspects, two sides, and two polarities of reality.... they are dynamically one ... The totality of things forms the context in which such change will take place.[57]

"The continuous production and generation of life (*shengsheng* 生生)" can be also interpreted as "creative creation" or "creatively creative" or "creative creativity." *The Yizhuan* 《易傳》 (The Commentary of the *Yijing*) writes: "*Shengsheng zhiwei yi* 生生之謂易 (Creatively creating is what means by *yi*)."[58] This creativity, which is contributed by and indebted to the dynamic harmony of *yin* and *yang*, satisfies the mutual changes and multiple interchanges in the universe and human life. *Tian* subjects to restless change and it is aroused and stimulated by *yin* and *yang*: "... the whole world of things is conceived of as resulting from the same source of life, which is Heaven.... The original Confucian concept of Heaven gives place to the idea of change."⁵⁹

However, to be noticed, the later Confucian interpretations from Han onward, have gone far to a credible power of *Tian* and promotes it as if it bursts a controlling creativity in the level of governmental, social and moral oppression. In the Confucian virtue theories, *Tian*, though being conceived to attach internally to and inseparable from *Di*, it nevertheless becomes enlarged as an independent source to surpass *Di*. The natural law and order of the cosmic heaven are thereafter conceptualized as moral principles such as *tianli* 天理. Such Confucian ideas of *Tian* reflect almost a "savage" image of God, which is the sole creator and dominant oneness of the world. In a monumentally long history of the Confucian domination, the heavenly creativity has substituted a breathless bondage of the Chinese femininity.

In order to rediscover the original cosmological nature of *Tian* in the *Yijing*, *Tian* ought to foremost be recognized as a harmonious being. As a potential creativity, *Tian* should respond to the productivity of *Di*. To accomplish a creative creation, the *yang* energy of *Tian* cannot stand and act alone, if there is no *Di* to compliment and equally supply the *yin* creativity. The *Yizhuan* says, "*Yi yin yi yang zhiwei dao* 一陰一陽之謂道 (The natural way or cosmic law is composed by one *yin* and one *yang*.)⁶⁰

Harmony does not equate with singularity or oneness, just as what Whitehead proposes that the pre-established harmony in God is potentially made possible by God's dipolar natures/poles. As much as what God should be given with both masculine divinity and feminine divinity, *Tian* or *qian*, as the source of the created world, is to be enriched and multi-folded by *Di* or *kun*. The *Yijing* seems rather telling aloud in this regard:

> *Da zai qian yuan! Wanwu zishi* ... 大哉乾元！萬物資始。。。。。。(The great *qian* and the great beginning! Ten thousands of things are richly created and originated from here ...)"⁶¹ and "*Zhi zai kun yuan, wanwu zisheng* ... 至哉坤元，萬物資生。。。。。。(The ultimate *kun* and the ultimate beginning, ten thousands of things were produced and flourished and manifested ...)"⁶²

Tian or *qian* is the origin of all things and life and forms in the world, however, without *Di* or *kun* as the productive and nurturing co-creator, we may find nothing can be brought to existence at all! If God's creation is the co-creative and co-productive process of "emotional (physical) feeling" and "conceptual (mental) feeling," *Tian* and *Di* each imparts a harmonious activity.⁶³ I can't help questioning the Confucian "gentlemen": if we root our contemplation deeply into the

Chinese cosmology and its metaphysical metaphors, what on earth the cosmic heaven can alone be a male tribute to the privilege of this planet?

At long last, to be mentioned, there seems a problem of incoherence and inconsistency with process connectivity. In the process theory, tensions, contradictions, disjunctions . . . , The Many are connected by "becoming" actually occasions. Here we cannot but notice that the world of Whiteheadian creativity ultimately implies a realization of organic growing. It takes place through a cosmic evolution of organism rather than an autonomous practicality of humanism that signifies Chinese philosophy. In Whitehead, the whole point of weaving a creative web of interrelatedness has very much less to do with how an oneness is susceptible to deconstructing monolithic divinity of God and how an androcentrical ego is dissolved in connecting to other humans in a practical society and actual humanism. A cosmology like such has not expanded the life of organic "occasions" and cells and plants or other creatures further to the humanistic extent of our life, and it has not answered how interconnection replaces disconnection and how togetherness displaces differentiation, in our rational or social or emotional anticipation. This frail characteristic ultimately and fundamentally distinguishes Whiteheadian cosmology from Chinese cosmology, and the latter reveals an interconnection in a concrete level of human cultural, social and virtuous practicality.

Furthermore, one claim is: by embracing a metaphysical togetherness, do we risk for taking prevalent positions such as "universal humanism"? Anyhow, like Keller, I do not believe universal humanism can skip over the question of gender identity which is rooted in all of our painful contemplations and traumatic struggles. Our bodies are gifted in diverse gender and our histories are glorified by glowing thrives. The promise of universal humanism seems to offer a void affinity to human particularities. I hold: there is no God without dipolar natures of physical and mental poles in Whitehead, and there is no *Tian* without binary natures of *yin* and *yang* in Chinese cosmology; thus there is no human being but a man or a woman.[64] The attempt or the illusion of abolishing *our* identity serves no self-affirmation, just as killing our feminine form cannot declare that *we* are liberated from bondages. Humanism is universal, only if we do not transcend beyond and away from our female bodies and identity and personae. Men *or* women do not ask for respected and connected in *abstract forms*, and we long for being together but being whom we are. We do seek our shared humanism, but we want more: a harmonization of colorful differentiations, in which we connect separated selves and broken hearts.

To do so, let's not to wait—we had done that since long time ago, long enough.[65]

JOURNAL OF CHINESE PHILOSOPHY, UNIVERSITY OF HAWAII
Honolulu, Hawaii

Endnotes

The present article is a revised version of my previous publication which appeared in the *Journal of Chinese Philosophy* 36, no. 2 (2009): 211–22. A short variation of the above article was published in the *APA Newsletter on Asian and Asian-American Philosophers and Philosophies* 9, no. 1 (2009) and I thank Amy Olberding's warm invitation and outstanding work. The mentioned full publication was selected by Wiley-Blackwell for 2013's International Women's Day Campaign on feminist philosophy. My special acknowledgment belongs to the leading editor of this Supplement Issue Professor Chung-ying Cheng and the co-editor of it Professor Eric Nelson, for the opportunity of republishing. And I am obliged to have Eric's scholarly faith in this and other publications of mine, and meanwhile I greatly appreciate his brilliant article in this collection as well as his generous professionalism throughout our collaboration. To renew my previous acknowledgment in Note 1 below, I would like to deliver the following tributes. My deepest thanks and warmest prayers are sent to Professor Yang Hongsheng in this particular moment. Once again, my profound gratitude and endless admiration are given to Professor Joseph Grange. The following individuals exist in the precious source of genuine care and inspiration solidary inspirations: Friederike Assandri, Xiaoyang Wei, Qianfan Zhang, Timothy Connolly, Mathew Foust, Morny Joy, Lin Ma, Eric Piper, Renee Kojima, Jinmei Yuan, Shirley Chan, Xiaomei Yang, Xiyi Huang, Robert Neville, Yong Huang, Xinzhong Yao, Qingping Liu, Daniel Bell, Ping Zhang, Song Pan, William Day, and many more. My particular thanks go to Michelle, Joyce, and all editors at Wiley Blackwell for their extremely supportive patience. Finally, I dedicate this republication to my former teacher Professor Zai Tingjin of Shanghai Academy of Social Sciences, in honoring his noble integrity and exemplary virtue, and there are no words can convey my enormous debts.

To highlight a timely expression and to celebrate the world-humanity, I would like to pay a special tribute to Lingzi Lu, a young woman of a sparkling soul, who vanished in the latest tragedy of Boston.

1. In the previous publication, I had written the following acknowledgment under "Endnotes" and herewith it has been slightly modified: "I dedicate this work to both women and men. Particularly this is a tribute to two dear people, Professor Liu Youlan of Beijing Dance Academy and Dr. Jesse Fleming of the *Journal of Chinese Philosophy*, who both unexpectedly passed away during the time of my writing. My former teacher and friend Professor Liu represented a remarkable scholar and my role model of femininity. Dr. Fleming, one of the Associate Editors of this journal, was a devoted colleague and a bright scholar of the *Yijing*, Daoism, European philosophy, and much more. My fondest memory of him and my regrets of not knowing enough of his sickness are endless. For my work on Whitehead, without Professor Steve Odin's guidance in this creative and glittering world, it is not impossible. I owe Catherine Keller so much: her immense inspiration and beautiful mind. In myriad ways these individuals are also precious to my research: Jing T. Gussin, Hong Ying, Friederike Assandri, Joseph Grange, William Hasker, Yang Hongsheng, Xinyan Jiang, Morny Joy, Philip J. Ivanhoe, Franklin Perkins, On-cho Ng, Lauren F. Pfister, Sandra A. Wawrytko, and Amy Olberding. Finally, I am in debt to the firm support, synthetic remarks, and critical discussions of Professor Chung-ying Cheng, Editor-in-Chief, during preparing this special volume and my article.
2. I am grateful to Mathew A. Foust for introducing this quote from G.K. Chesterton, "Christmas," in *All Things Considered* (Methuen: Methuen, 1910), http://www.cse.dmu.ac.uk/~mward/gkc/books/11505-h.htm.

3. I italicize such pronouns to specify the groups rather than certain individuals.
4. I do not intend to label myself a "feminist" or a "non-feminist."
5. Catherine Keller calls such mentality "women in waiting" or "waiting women" in *From a Broken Web: Separation, Sexism, and Self* (Boston: Beacon Press, 1986), 11 and beyond. I have adopted this name throughout.
6. A play by Samuel Barclay Beckett (see Wang Zuoliang and Zhou Jueliang, eds., *Yingguo 20 Shiji Wenxueshi* 《英國20世紀文學史》 [History of English Literature of the 20th Century] [Beijing: Waiyu Jiaoxue yu Yanjiu Press, 2006]), 435.
7. In contrast to this journal's house-style, I use the title case for "*tian*," in order to serve the particular purpose of the discussion.
8. The common translation of *tian* as "Heaven" or "heaven" can be confused with that in Christianity. My translation "cosmic heaven" bears more accurately what is intended in Chinese philosophy. Upon the present article was completed, Mathew A. Foust (see Endnote 37 in his article, "Grief and Mourning in Confucius's *Analects*," published in this journal of Vol. 36, no. 2 [2009]) brought my attention to Roger T. Ames and Henry Rosemont, Jr., who similarly suggest to avoid translating *tian* as "Heaven" for it causes the confusion I mentioned above. Meanwhile, I would not agree with their own translation. According to Foust, Ames and Rosemont define *tian* as "both *what* our world is and *how* it is." This definition may in turn fall into another confusion: can *di* (cosmic earth, my translation) and other cosmological elements be defined the same, namely, "*what* our world is and *how* it is?" The translations in this manner seem to appear rather general and abstract, and it may not serve a sufficient or concrete purpose of translating.
9. Hereafter all English translations of Chinese terminologies are mine and in the cases of overlapping with any individuals merely coincidental.
10. Instead of "waiting," in order to come forward and speak out for my rights, I was both obliged and obligated to have published a correction of a misleading reference produced by the following author, Professor Liu Xiaogan, and the original version of my correction should be found in this journal of Vol. 36, no. 2 (2009). With legal assistance, I continually request Professor Liu to publish his own correction in the next availability, as he had responded to my initial contacting. Herewith I shall single out the main text of my correction.

In Liu Xiaogan's "An Inquiry into the Core Value of Laozi's Philosophy" (see Mark Csikszentmihalyi and Philip J. Ivanhoe, eds., *Religious and Philosophical Aspects of the Laozi*, SUNY Series in Chinese Philosophy and Culture [Albany: State University of New York, 1999], 236–237), Note 22 states:

> It is the opinion of the author that the abstract concept of "the Way" (*Dao*) provides the value of naturalness and the principle of *wuwei* with a metaphysical basis, while the interdependence of thesis and antithesis of dialectic theory provides naturalness and *wuwei* with a concrete proof. The author has discussed this subject in other works. Additionally, near the beginning of 1987, Ms. Gu Linyu (Linyu Gu, my addition) 顧林玉, who was then working on an M.A. at the Shanghai Institute of Social Science, expressed a desire to write on the subject of naturalness as a value in Laozi's thought, and came to Beijing to discuss her ideas with me. I helped her to define a project that looked at Laozi's reverence for naturalness from the perspective of value theory. Her work discusses the issue from the perspective of epistemological value, moral value, and aesthetic value. It is not clear where or when this paper will be published. The opinions expressed in this article may have been influenced by the insights of Ms. Gu.

I wish that Professor Liu may have intended to acknowledge the intellectual credit he owed to the influence from reading the manuscript of my M. A. thesis, although the effect of his expression turned out falling into the opposite direction: it has ended up harming my scholarly name in the means of presenting a false credit for himself. To point out more exactly, here Professor Liu has misaddressed the actual event.

The true history was: with the arrangement of my M. A. thesis's advisor and the Committee of Shanghai Academy of Social Sciences, at the beginning of 1988, I went to Peking University to consult one of the specialists, Professor Chen Guying 陳鼓應, to pursue his review of my completed draft of the thesis, and during the time Professor Chen introduced Professor Liu Xiaogan 劉笑敢 to read my manuscript in full completion, titled "*Lao Zi Chongshang Ziran de Jiazhi Quxiang* 《老子》崇尚自然的價值取向" (Literally, *Lao Zi*'s Value Approach [or perspective or orientation] in Honoring *Ziran* [naturalness or naturality]). The above date clearly showed: before I met Professor Liu Xiaogan I had already accomplished my manuscript which was supervised by my advisor Professor Zai Tingjin 翟廷瑨. To clarify this history and confirm his recommendation, Professor Zai Tingjin has provided me a written statement.

Therefore, Professor Liu Xiaogan had not participated in any supervision or any process of the project related to my thesis. Instead, nearly ten years later, in 1997 upon Professor Liu's visitation of University of Hawaii at Manoa, personally he assured me that my M. A. thesis impressed him deeply at our meeting in early 1988 and thus influenced his later works on Laozi. He commented that my approach was an original exploration of the ontological importance of *ziran* 自然 in associating to the value orientation in Lao Zi. He also informed me that he planned to acknowledge my influence to him in certain publication of him. But I had not received such acknowledgment until I otherwise happened to notice his inaccurate description in the above Note 22 of his article.

For bibliographical references, please find my M. A. thesis in *Shanghai Academy of Social Sciences M. A. Theses Collection*, June 1988, and for a published version of this thesis under the same title, see *Xueshu Yuekan* 《學術月刊》 (Academic Monthly), January 1989.

11. Although died in early 60s, Sylvia Plath always is viewed as a contemporary for her characterizing a direct edge connecting to today. See the similar view of Frances McCullough's Foreword in *The Bell Jar* (New York / London / Toronto / Sydney: Harper Perennial, 2005), xvi.
12. Here it is not my task to associate a certain psychological anamnesis of Sigmund Freud or Carl G. Jung.
13. In the West, there are George Sand, the Brontë sisters, Jane Austen, Simone de Beauvoir, A. S. Byatt . . . ; in China, especially after the May 4th Movement in 1919, educational and economic self-sufficiency have become opportunities, and these women are prophesied in the earliest Chinese feminism: Xiao Hong 蕭紅, Zhang Ailing 張愛玲, Lin Huiyin 林徽因, Xie Bingxin 謝冰心. . . .
14. *We* habitually remain hesitated to announce *our* female names, from George Sand (born as Aurore Dupin [1804–1876]) to A. S. Byatt (1936–) and till today . . .
15. WowOwow.com was created for discussing these concerns among professional women: Charlie Rose's interview with the editors of <wowOwow.com> in PBS on April 8, 2008.
16. "Not My Life," a television drama broadcasted in Channel of Lifetime, 3:00 p.m., November 16, 2008. However, can this standard be a "*vice versa*"? That is the question.
17. Ted Hughes and Frances McCullough, eds., *The Journals of Sylvia Plath* (New York: Anchor Books, 1998), 29–43.
18. Sylvia Plath, *Letters Home: Correspondence 1950–1963*, selected and edited with commentary by Aurelia Schober Plath (New York: Harper Perennial, 1992), 25.
19. Scholarly, after Sylvia Plath's death, a study on suicide has been engaged by, for example, A. Alvarez. For him, the act of Plath, like for many other exceptions, explains what an art is about: A. Alvarez, *The Savage God: A Study of Suicide* (New York: W. W. Norton & Company, 1990), 17. Alvarez intends to counterbalance two prejudices: the high religious theory which places suicide as one of the moral crimes and the current scientific treatment which dismisses every serious meaning of the act.
20. I choose to use the conventional masculine pronoun in capital to serve the purpose of this particular discussion.

21. Hong Ying has proclaimed in various occasions that her writings are largely based on her life events, but all of my discussions are drawn from her published works but not her personal life which is unknown to my documentation.
22. Hong Ying 虹影, *Jie de Nuer*《飢餓的女兒》(Beijing: Wenhua Yishu Press, 2006).
23. Ibid.
24. Keller, *From a Broken Web: Separation, Sexism, and Self*, 220.
25. Alvarez, *The Savage God: A Study of Suicide*, 245.
26. Ibid.
27. Timothy, 3: 11.
28. "Him" is not to be confused with any individual male person.
29. My own definition for Grange.
30. William Hasker, "A Philosophical Perspective," in *The Openness of God: a Biblical Challenge to the Traditional Understanding of God* (Downers Grove: InterVarsity Press, 1994 and Carlisle: The Paternoster Press, 1994), 134.
31. Ibid., 154.
32. Robert Cummings Neville, *Eternity and Time's Flow* (Albany: State University of New Year Press, 1993), xiii.
33. Alfred North Whitehead, *Process and Reality*, eds. David Ray Griffin and Donald W. Sherburne, corrected edition (London / New York: The Free Press, 1978), 349.
34. John B. Cobb, Jr. and David Ray Griffin, *Process Theology: An Introductory Exposition* (Philadelphia: The Westminster Press, 1976), 134.
35. Whitehead, *Process and Reality*, 348.
36. Joseph Grang, *Nature: An Environmental Cosmology* (Albany: State University of New York Press, 1997), 242–243.
37. Refer to Keller, *From a Broken Web: Separation, Sexism, and Self* (Boston: Beacon Press, 1986).
38. Ibid., 2.
39. Ibid., 4.
40. Ibid., 6.
41. Ibid., 5.
42. Ibid., 183.
43. Ibid., 214.
44. Whitehead, *Process and Reality*, 21.
45. Carl G. Jung describes such a collective individuality through discussing "collective unconsciousness" in *The Essential Jung: Selected Writings*, selected and introduced by Anthony Storr (Princeton: Princeton University Press, 1983).
46. Chung-ying Cheng, "Toward Constructing a Dialectics of Harmonization: Harmony and Conflict in Chinese Philosophy," Journal Supplement Series to *Journal of Chinese Philosophy* (Oxford / Boston: Blackwell Publishing, 2006), 28.
47. Chung-ying Cheng, *New Dimensions of Confucian and Neo-Confucian Philosophy* (Albany: State University of New York Press, 1991), 69.
48. There were few exceptional woman sovereigns such as Wu Zetian 武則天 and Ci Xi 慈禧, who had ruled out the long dynasties. However, both are, on the other hand, the counter-evident illustrations of that such woman rulers are intimately linked to and constituted by namable male power.
49. It can be an unintended misunderstanding as to that the prevailed Western translations impart "*Zi*" (an honorific title to address a teacher character: Master) in the surname. I appreciate and confer that other scholars such as Tongdong Bai and myself nevertheless continue to differentiate the surname from the honorific title, regardless of the commonly accepted misuse.
50. 〈告子下〉(*Gaozi Xia*), 12: 15 in《孟子》(*Meng Zi*): "*Gu tian jiang jiang daren yu shiren ye, bi xian ku qi xinzhi, lao qi jingu, e qi tifu, kongfa qi shen, xing fuluan qi suowei*. 故天.將降大任於是人也，必先苦其心志，勞其筋骨，餓其體膚，空乏其身，行拂亂其所為。"
51. 〈盡心下〉(*Jinxin Xia*), 14: 9, ibid. Some scholars have a tendency to "re-interpret" the Confucian terms such as *nu* 女 (female people) or *nuzi* 女子 (girls and women)...in a neutral meaning, in order to avoid the significant oppression toward women in Confucianism. Therefore I selected this passage which refers to *qi* 妻 (a

wife), to exclude other possible "re-interpretations" which seemingly would otherwise have to claim that "wife" is not female related!
52. Kam Louie, *Theorizing Chinese Masculinity: Society and Gender in China* (Cambridge: Cambridge University Press, 2002), 5–6.
53. Keller, *From a Broken Web: Separation, Sexism, and Self*, 4.
54. Louie, *Theorizing Chinese Masculinity: Society and Gender in China*, 9.
55. Ibid.
56. Ibid.
57. Cheng, *New Dimensions of Confucian and Neo-Confucian Philosophy*, 95.
58. Huang Shouqi and Zhang Shanwen, interpretation and commentary, *Zhouyi Yizhu* 《周易譯註》 (The Interpretation and Commentary of the *Zhouyi*) (Shanghai: Shanghai Guji Press), 538.
59. Cheng, *New Dimensions of Confucian and Neo-Confucian Philosophy*, 95.
60. Huang and Zhang, *Zhouyi Yizhu*, 588.
61. Ibid., 5.
62. Ibid., 25.
63. Nonetheless, *Tian* in Chinese cosmology has no divine implications, but in Whitehead God is continuously carried forward in a divine image. I agree with Julia Ching as to that China never produced a personal deity as God in the Jewish-Christianity, whilst I do not simply agree with her notion of the cult of Heaven or her implication of a transpersonal deity in Chinese religions. Specifically refer to her *Chinese Religions* (Maryknoll: Orbis Books, 1993), 2.
64. The usage of "human being" here refers to a narrow sense in order to concrete this study in a focus on feminism.
65. Editor-in-Chief of this journal, Chung-ying Cheng, had again given his review comments to this revision. He pointed out: "Concerning the content and theme, it is a fact that there is 'waiting for Godot' in both Western and Chinese forms of feminism. The author's criticism is basically sharp and rich: instead of waiting, women or men could come to a common or shared awakening for a metaphysical reconfiguration of the man-woman or woman-man relationship in the spirit of process philosophy and onto-cosmology of the *Yijing*. Once this awakening is achieved, then hopefully those problems for social and sexist tensions would disperse and no residue of male ruler or super-ruler would has to exist. However, one still wonders whether there remains the problem of practice, namely the problem of how psychological interdependency and social needs for mutual dependency could not be answered by metaphysical thinking."

To respond to this intriguing and perplex question, first of all, I would like to hope it shall be taken into a more lengthy size of deliberation in another time of writing. Nonetheless, I should affirm that the whole endeavor of my present article is meaning to inquire into the dimension of actual practice *vs.* a mere metaphysical meditation. Such inquiry demands, like any theoretical thinking must, a philosophical wake-up call which is necessary before the practice follows up. This is because the central concern of this study is disclosing that the psychological awakening regarding the mutual participation of men and women in inter-reaching, inter-connectivity, and inter-dependence in fact is unfortunately and largely absent and missing in our contemporary life. I have given two approximately stereotypical models of such cases at the beginning of the paper. A practice (*xing* 行) is to practice a *zhi* 知 (learning), and without a philosophical contemplation, "to practice what" may be another bigger question. Accordingly and consequentially, social needs for mutual dependence should not necessarily have conflicts with psychological independence, if a metaphysical analysis, as I have substantially elaborated in the paper, is perceived as a two-way awareness and in the form of mutual respect, in which each party has own social role, independent profession, respective achievement, and so on so forth.